The Virtue of Faith and Other Essays in Philosophical Theology

The Virtue of Faith

and Other Essays in Philosophical Theology

Robert Merrihew Adams

New York   Oxford
OXFORD UNIVERSITY PRESS
1987

Oxford University Press

Oxford   New York   Toronto
Delhi   Bombay   Calcutta   Madras   Karachi
Petaling Jaya   Singapore   Hong Kong   Tokyo
Nairobi   Dar es Salaam   Cape Town
Melbourne   Auckland

and associated companies in
Beirut   Berlin   Ibadan   Nicosia

Published by Oxford University Press, Inc.,
200 Madison Avenue, New York, New York 10016

Library of Congress Cataloging-in-Publication Data

Adams, Robert Merrihew.
The virtue of faith and other essays in philosophical
theology.

1. Religion—Philosophy.   2. Ethics.   I. Title.
BL51.A42   1987   200'.1   86-8776
ISBN 0-19-504145-3
ISBN 0-19-504146-1 (pbk.)

2 4 6 8 10 9 7 5 3 1

Printed in the United States of America
on acid-free paper

"The Virtue of Faith." From *Faith and Philosophy*, vol. 1, no. 1 (January 1984). Reprinted by permission of *Faith and Philosophy*.

"Kierkegaard's Arguments Against Objective Reasoning in Religion." *The Monist*, 60 (1976). Reprinted by permission of the publisher.

"Must God Create the Best?" *Philosophical Review*, 81 (1972). Reprinted by permission of the publisher.

"Existence, Self-interest, and the Problem of Evil." *Nous*, 13 (1979). Reprinted by permission of the publisher.

"Middle Knowledge and the Problem of Evil." *American Philosophical Quarterly*, 14 (1977). Reprinted by permission of the publisher.

"A Modified Divine Command Theory of Ethical Wrongness." From *Religion and Morality: A Collection of Essays*, edited by Gene Outka and John P. Reeder, Jr. Reprinted by permission of Doubleday & Company, Inc.

"Autonomy and Theological Ethics." *Religious Studies*, 15 (1979). Published by Cambridge University Press. Reprinted by permission of the publisher.

"Divine Command Metaethics Modified Again." *The Journal of Religious Ethics*, vol. 7, no. 1 (Spring 1979), 66–79. Reprinted by permission of the publisher.

"Moral Arguments for Theistic Belief." Reprinted with permission from C. F. Delaney, ed., *Rationality and Religious Belief*. Notre Dame: University of Notre Dame Press, 1979, pp. 116–40.

"Saints." *The Journal of Philosophy*, 81 (1984). Reprinted by permission of the publisher.

"Pure Love." *The Journal of Religious Ethics*, vol. 8, no. 1 (Spring 1980), 83–99. Reprinted by permission of the publisher.

"Has It Been Proved That All Real Existence Is Contingent?" *American Philosophical Quarterly*, 8 (1971). Reprinted by permission of the publisher.

"Divine Necessity." *The Journal of Philosophy*, 80 (1983). Reprinted by permission of the publisher.

"The Logical Structure of Anselm's Arguments." *The Philosophical Review*, 80 (1971). Reprinted by permission of the publisher.

For Marilyn

Acknowledgments

My teachers in the philosophy of religion, John Marsh and John Hick, and my *Doktorvater,* Nelson Pike, will recognize in some of the papers ideas on which I was working under their tutelage. I am grateful to them for their guidance and encouragement, and to Professor Hick in particular for the suggestion that led me to assemble this collection.

It is also a pleasure to acknowledge the generous opportunities for research provided to me as a faculty member by the University of Michigan, Ann Arbor, and the University of California, Los Angeles. Fellowships from the National Endowment for the Humanities and the Center of Theological Inquiry in Princeton, New Jersey, provided much-appreciated support during periods of leave, when some of the papers were written or reworked. Detailed acknowledgments are also contained in notes to the individual papers.

I am grateful to Cynthia Read and Henry Krawitz of Oxford University Press for their editorial work on this volume, and to my research assistant, Marleen Rozemond, for much help in the final stages of its preparation.

Contents

The Virtue of Faith and Other Essays in Philosophical Theology

Introduction

This volume includes most of the work in the philosophy of religion that I have published in the last fifteen years, with two additional papers (chapters 3 and 16) that are published here for the first time. The previously published papers are reprinted with little change. A few notes (indicated by an asterisk) have been added, and misprints (including a major dislocation of six paragraphs in the original publication of chapter 5) have been corrected. Chapter 15 presupposes some knowledge of symbolic logic, otherwise I have tried either to avoid or to explain technical language. I hope that the present collection may be of interest to a wider audience interested in questions about religion, as well as to the analytical philosophers to whom the largest part of it was originally addressed. In that hope I here offer some brief explanations concerning the approach I have taken.

The philosophy of religion is not divided by rigid boundaries from the rest of philosophy. Aspects of it also belong to metaphysics, to epistemology (the theory of knowledge), and to ethics. Religion affects a person's view of the whole of life and reality; and a main theme of some of the papers gathered here (notably chapters 10, 11, 14, and 16) is that theistic belief makes possible certain attractive positions in such fields as ethics, epistemology, and the philosophy of mind. Conversely, I believe that all of the major philosophical disciplines are important for religious thought. The fourth part of this volume is primarily concerned with metaphysical aspects of religious belief, and the third deals with the relation of religion and ethics, while the first involves both epistemology and ethics and the second involves both metaphysics and ethics.

The title of the book identifies its subject matter as "philosophical theology." Philosophical theology is the part of philosophy of religion that is primarily about God. Other parts of philosophy of religion are primarily about religion as a human phenomenon, or about issues that arise in relation to nontheistic religions, such as Buddhism. Philosophical theology constitutes a natural focus for study because the concept of God involves a set of metaphysical, epistemological, and ethical issues that will not necessarily arise in connection with the rest of the philosophy of religion. By 'philosophical theology' in this context I do not mean a discipline that can be practiced only by those who believe, as I do, that God exists. Atheists as well as theists can and do contribute to it. Indeed, it is a subject in which atheism is one of the competing positions. It is about God in the sense that it is about whether God exists or not; what God is like (if God exists, or would be like if God did exist); how we ought to relate ourselves to such a being (if one exists); and so forth.[1]

Contemporary American analytical philosophy of religion is largely devoted to philosophical theology in this sense, to the puzzlement or dismay of some students of religion. In part these objections to our focus arise from the eminently reasonable wish that Eastern as well as Western religions should receive analytical attention. Another factor, however, is that the whole philosophical debate about the existence and nature of God has come to seem naively old-fashioned to some who believe that there is no objective fact of the matter about it, and that human religious phenomena are therefore the only religious subject matter available for a study that is to be "scientific" in the broad sense, or academically respectable. To this latter ground of objection I am not disposed to concede anything.

In saying this I am affirming the *realism* that characterizes my approach to philosophical theology. By 'realism' here I mean the belief that there is a truth about the subject matter that is independent of our opinions, and even of our best evidence. Whether we believe it or not—indeed, whether we have good reason to believe it or not—God exists or does not, is omnipotent or is not, will raise us from the dead or not, and so forth. This conviction is presupposed in all the essays in this volume.

This realism is combined, in my approach, with a *moderate skepticism*. On the matters discussed here, as on most other characteristically philosophical issues, I do not believe that conclusive proof is possible. (It does *not* follow that I think firm convictions are inappropriate, or that beliefs on these topics cannot be more and less reasonable.) There are no "knockdown" proofs or disproofs of the existence of God. This does not mean that the classical arguments are to be despised. In them, and elsewhere as well, are to be found considerations that have, and deserve to have, some persuasive force. It will not be reasonable to rest the whole weight of conviction on any one of them; their force is cumulative. But even cumulatively they do not amount to a rationally coercive demonstration, and cannot be expected to lead to unanimity on the issues.

In parts of this collection (most obviously in chapters 10, 14, and 16) I may be viewed as attempting to contribute to a cumulative case for the existence of God, adducing theoretical advantages (though certainly not conclusive proofs) of theistic belief. Most of the essays are meant to contribute at least indirectly to such a case, rebutting some objection, or setting some aspect or form of theistic belief in a more favorable light. However, you will not find in this book any summation of the case. That is partly because it is a collection of essays and not a comprehensive treatise; and I will not promise never to publish such a summation. But I also confess to having a certain suspicion of that sort of crowning of the argument. In the best books presenting a cumulative case for either theism or atheism,[2] it seems to me that the toting up of pros and cons is much less impressive than the detailed discussion of particular arguments. I suspect that is because cumulative cases in these matters do and should work on us in a way that resists reduction to any sort of balance sheet, as we live with and savor the various considerations and test them against our experience of life.

My approach to philosophical theology, then, is a *skeptical realism*. To some these terms may seem a strange combination. Should not skepticism lead to subjectivism, that is, to antirealism? I will argue (briefly here) that, on the contrary, realism goes naturally with at least a moderate skepticism. Kant provides a good starting point for reflections on this subject. In his *Critique of Pure Reason* (A368ff.) he says that with regard to the existence of physical objects, it is the "transcendental realist" (the realist, in my sense) who becomes an "empirical idealist" (a skeptic). That is, a philosopher who begins with the assumption that physical objects exist, if at all, and have whatever properties they have, independently of our perceiving them and thinking about them, will find that this independence introduces a gap between our experience and the supposed physical objects, so that "we can never, by way of any possible experience, be completely certain of their reality." With regard to physical objects Kant himself opts for "transcendental idealism," that is, for the view that they are not things in themselves but appearances, constructed by our minds, that we know them, and even conceive of them, only as they appear to us. As a transcendental idealist he thinks he can be an "empirical realist," that is, that he can have certain knowledge of many facts about physical objects (as appearances constructed by the mind).

Kant does not take this line about God, however. The *idea* of God is given to us, necessarily, by our reason as a regulative idea. But God himself is not an idea and not an object of our experience. God is, if anything is, a "noumenon," a thing in itself, existing and having its properties independently of our thought. As such, God is beyond the reach of our theoretical knowledge; we cannot prove his existence or even his more than formal possibility (though Kant thinks morality can give us a sort of reason for believing in God's existence nonetheless). Thus, it is precisely as a transcendental realist about God that Kant is a sort of skeptic about God.[3]

Without wishing to endorse everything in Kant's position as I have sketched it, I believe there is a deep truth here about religion and, more broadly, about metaphysics. The objective or "transcendental" reality of the objects of our beliefs—be they God or other human minds, or even our own past and future—is an independence from our own present thought and experience which is bought at the cost of an ontological gap between subject and object. This gap inevitably introduces a greater or smaller degree of unprovability into our beliefs about the objectively real. Realism thus goes naturally with some kind of skepticism, and with a need for faith.

Notes

1. In this use of 'philosophical theology' I am influenced, of course, by the example of Antony Flew and Alasdair MacIntyre, *New Essays in Philosophical Theology* (New York: Macmillan, 1966), p. viii.

2. For instance, in Richard Swinburne's *The Existence of God* (Oxford: Clarendon Press, 1979) and J. L. Mackie's *The Miracle of Theism* (Oxford: Clarendon Press, 1982).

3. My reading of Kant on this point differs from that of Gordon Kaufman, *An Essay on Theological Method* (Missoula, Mont.: Scholars Press, 1975), pp. 22–25. Kaufman seems to interpret Kant as holding that because we cannot experience God, God must be regarded as an imaginative construct. I think it is much more consonant with Kant's whole philosophy to take him as concluding that because God, if he exists, is transcendentally real, he therefore cannot be experienced and we cannot have certain knowledge of his existence.

PART ONE
FAITH

1

The Virtue of Faith

It is a prominent and very well-known feature of the Christian tradition that faith is regarded as a virtue, and unbelief (at least in many cases) as a sin. This seemed puzzling to me as long ago as I can remember thinking about it all, for two reasons: (1) Belief and unbelief seem to be mainly involuntary states, and it is thought that the involuntary cannot be ethically praised or blamed. (2) If belief is to be praised at all, we are accustomed to think that its praiseworthiness depends on its rationality, but the virtuousness of faith for Christians seems to be based on its correctness and independent of the strength of the evidence for it. I shall try to deal with these issues in the first two sections of this paper, arguing in the first section that many cognitive failures, though not voluntary, are ethically blameworthy and in the second section that there are many cases in which it is rightness rather than rationality that ought to be praised in beliefs.

I approach this topic with some hesitancy because in addition to being puzzling, for the reasons I have mentioned, it might be felt to be offensive. Fears may be raised that the stigmatization of unbelief as sin will feed the flames of persecution. We may reply, correctly, that persecution does not spring from the virtue of faith, but from a deceptively faithless

Versions of this paper have been presented to several groups, and many people have helped me clarify my thoughts. I am grateful for some discussion with Gregory Kavka that led to an improvement in the paper, and for thoughtful written comments from James Muyskens and Allen Wood. I am indebted to Marilyn McCord Adams for much discussion of these topics, and especially for her insistence on the centrality of trust in the midst of uncertainties and trials, as a part of God's goal for human life, in the Bible. I owe a debt of another kind to A. Orley Swartzentruber. I enjoyed a sabbatical leave from UCLA, and the hospitality of Princeton Theological Seminary and Princeton University, during the period when this paper was written.

fear of other people and their opinions. But it cannot be denied that the Christian Church, as a concrete community of sinners, has much to be embarrassed about in this regard. I think it will be best to concentrate our attention, as far as possible, on *our own* sins of unbelief.

This essay is addressed therefore to Christians. It is intended as a rather rough-and-ready sketch for family discussion.[1] And it is not my aim here to justify Christian belief, either to those who are in it or to those who are out of it. The question we shall be concerned with is "What is virtuous about faith, *given that it is true*?"

I see two motives that Christians have for studying the idea of faith as a virtue. The first, which will concern us especially in the third section of the paper, is that we are conscious of unbelief as a sin in ourselves— indeed as one of the most fundamental sins in ourselves. The second motive is that the Bible presents God as prizing faith so highly as to make it one of the principal goals of his dealings with the human race. This motive will be central to the fourth and final section of the paper.

I. Cognitive Sins

There are many cognitive failures that we regard as morally reprehensible. Some examples are: believing that certain people don't have rights that they do in fact have; perceiving members of some social group as less capable than they actually are; failing to notice indications of other people's feelings; and holding too high an opinion of one's own attainments. These failures are not in general voluntary. *Trying* to pay attention to other people's feelings will not necessarily be successful, if I am insensitive or afraid of emotions. And *trying* to assess my own abilities and accomplishments accurately may not keep me from thinking too highly of myself, if I am vain. We do give people credit for trying in these matters, but we still regard the failure to notice other people's feelings or one's own deficiencies as a fault—and in some sense an ethical or moral fault.

To be sure, not all cognitive failures are moral faults. A false mathematical belief, for example, would not normally be regarded as an ethical fault, though in a professional mathematician it might be evidence of a morally culpable negligence. How, then, are we to draw the line between those cognitive failings that are ethical faults and those that are not? I confess that I do not have a complete or general answer to this question. I will mention three types of cognitive error that seem to me to be morally culpable. But the classification is not intended to be exhaustive; there may well be additional types of cognitive sin.

(1) False *ethical* beliefs are apt to be culpable, even if they are not acted on. If someone thinks there is nothing wrong with shoplifting, for example, I think that would be morally blameworthy in most cases—even if the person never shoplifted, for fear of getting caught. I do not know whether *all* false ethical beliefs are sins. Some opinions seem heinous; belief in the principles of Nazism would be an extreme example. But errors of judgment on some difficult, disputed ethical issues do not seem particularly dishonorable. Perhaps the best argument for blaming *all* errors about ethical principles is this: Suppose I have done something that is materially wrong, believing it to be right. Now that I recognize the action to be wrong, I should not blame myself for it if I did it out of ignorance of a nonethical fact that I could not be expected to have known (for instance, if I did not know that my light switch was wired to set off a bomb in a neighboring apartment). But if my relevant nonmoral beliefs were correct, and I did the materially wrong action because of what I now see to be an error about ethical principles, I think I should blame myself in every case. And it is plausible to say that an error that is or could be the root of a blameworthy action in this way must itself be ethically blameworthy in some degree.

(2) Harmful false beliefs about any subject are culpable if they are due to *negligence*. That is, they are blameworthy if we hold them because we have neglected to perform *voluntary actions* that we ought to have performed, and that would have cured or prevented the error in us. Many maintain, indeed, that this is the *only* case in which cognitive errors are culpable. In a very interesting recent discussion of the issue, Alan Donagan maintains this position: "Ignorance, whether of the principles of morality, or of precepts derived from them by means of specificatory premises, is culpable or inculpable according as it proceeds from negligence—from want of due consideration."[2] Donagan points out that false beliefs about moral principles may be due to bad education rather than to negligence, and concludes, "A graduate of Sandhurst or West Point who does not understand his duty to noncombatants as human beings is certainly culpable for his ignorance; an officer bred up from childhood in the Hitler *Jugend* might not be."[3]

I disagree with Donagan on this point. I think the cruel graduate of the Hitler *Jugend* is in terrible sin, even if he is also a victim of his education, and even if he has no opportunity to act on his corrupt beliefs. Bad moral beliefs can make a bad man or woman, no matter how we came by the beliefs. There are at least two ways of being a sinner: one is to have done a bad thing; the other is to be, in some respect and in some degree, a bad person. The second way is no less dreadful and no less fundamental than the first. Badness of character need not be explained by a previous bad deed of one's own. We may be corrupted by our own wrongdoing, but that is not the only way in which we can be corrupted.

This is not at all to deny that someone who has been corrupted by an evil education is also a victim, and has a claim on our sympathy. From a Christian point of view sin is in any case a bondage that should elicit a compassionate concern for the sinner. The purpose of identifying cognitive failures as sins is not to find a stick to beat the sinner, but rather to learn what we have to repent of. If we have a wrong attitude, if we are for the bad and against the good, if we do not recognize rights that other people have, if we see ourselves as the center of the universe, we have to repent of this—we have to acknowledge our wrongness and change our minds and our lives—regardless of whether it was our own voluntary action that got us into such a state. These questions of stance—of what we are for, what we are against, what we acknowledge and believe on certain points—have an importance, for the ethical quality of our lives, that is not entirely dependent on questions of what we cause, produce, or voluntarily do.

(3) False beliefs and other cognitive failures are sometimes morally objectionable at least in part because of bad *desires* that are manifested in them. One reason why it is morally offensive to hold too high an opinion of oneself is that that usually manifests a desire to aggrandize oneself at the expense of others. Indeed I believe that blameworthiness of cognitive failures arises much more from bad motives of this sort than from duties of self-culture that one has failed to perform (not that it is to be explained entirely by either or both of these causes). If I have failed to recognize another person's feelings, how much I should blame myself depends much more on whether I have the respect and concern that I should have for that person than on whether I was conscientiously trying to notice his or her feelings.

These motives—respect and concern for other people on the one hand, the desire to aggrandize oneself on the other—are involuntary in much the same way as beliefs are. One cannot develop the right sort of desires and concerns simply by deciding to have them. On the contrary, it is the testimony of moral experience that the improvement of one's desires and motives is difficult and often remains imperfect even with the most earnest efforts. Nonetheless I believe that bad desires and motives are sin, and to be repented of—but that is a subject for fuller discussion than can be given here.[4]

What concerns us now is the connection between bad motives and culpable cognitive failures. I have pointed out that cognitive failures may be culpable partly because they *manifest* a bad motive. It is worth noting that a bad motive, or morally offensive attitude, may be *constituted* in part by an offensive belief. Thus the belief that certain people lack certain rights is not just a *consequence* of the bad motive of disrespect or contempt for those people; it is part of what *constitutes* disrespect or contempt for them. As such it is as vicious morally as any other aspect of contempt.

II. The Importance of Being Right

Many morally offensive beliefs are also unreasonable, but that is not why they are *ethical* faults. Right ethical views can also be held in a very unreasonable way, and that does not necessarily keep it from being a credit to the person that he holds those beliefs. Perhaps there has been someone who accepted in principle a strict hedonistic act utilitarianism but also believed (inconsistently) that one ought not to punish an innocent person in order to procure a slight net increment in the sum or average of pleasure in the world. Suppose on being confronted with his inconsistency such a person concluded that one ought indeed to punish an innocent person if it were certain that that would slightly increase the sum of pleasure. I think this would be a change for the worse morally, even if it would make his system of beliefs more rational, because more consistent.

It is commonly more important for moral beliefs to be right than to be reasonable. And when they are wrong we may rightly blame them even if they are not unreasonable. I cannot prove that it is unreasonable to regard infanticide as a morally permissible method of population control; but I still think it a sin to hold that belief. (If any believers in infanticide should chance to read this statement, and think it rude, I ask them to bear in mind that I confess myself to be guilty of many of the sins discussed in this paper.)

We are so used to thinking of rationality as the paramount intellectual virtue that it may be useful to pass in review some of the areas of life in which it is morally or at least humanly important to be right in a way that is not accounted for by rationality. Let us begin with the learning of language. We would never have learned to speak or understand the speech of others at all if we had not had a marked ability to *guess correctly* what other people meant by the sounds they uttered. Children acquire a large body of beliefs about the meanings of words long before they have either the intellectual capacity or adequate evidence to justify those beliefs. In-

deed it is doubtful that we can ever have adequate evidence to justify a
large part of the beliefs that we rightly hold about other speakers' meanings. Even among adults communication would be gravely impoverished
if we understood each other's verbal and nonverbal signals only so far as
we could give a compelling justification for our interpretation. And the
ability to learn a new language quickly and well depends to no small
extent on one's willingness to trust one's hunches in these matters. Communication among human beings depends on a sort of natural empathy
which enables us, with remarkable reliability, to *guess* each other's meaning from very fragmentary evidence.

Belief that goes beyond the evidence is as important in *trusting* other
people as in understanding them. Trust in other people is based on a
conviction of their honesty and good will. When this conviction is strong,
it usually outruns any evidence for it that we could specify. It is important
that we often trust other people in circumstances quite different from any
in which we have previously known their honesty and good will to have
been tested. Sometimes we trust another person on very little evidence
indeed; and that is also of great value for human life.

Alas, one is sometimes deceived and disappointed in one's trust in other
people, so that the question whether one's trust is warranted does arise.
But I think the question whether trust is *rationally justified* is much less
important here, and less apt to be present to our minds, than the question
whether the other person is *in fact* trustworthy. If you are in fact honest
and loyal, you will (rightly) feel offended against, if modest grounds for
suspicion lead to distrust for you in someone who knows you rather well—
not because the other person seems *unreasonable,* but because he or she
ought to have *sensed* your trustworthiness. Similarly, if I trust A and not
B, being well acquainted with both, but can't explain why, that is terrible
if B is in fact trustworthy and A is treacherous; but it is at least less
terrible if my attitude is factually correct—that is, if B is indeed treacherous and A is trustworthy.

Self-knowledge is another area in which getting it right is important
and rationality will not carry us far enough. It is an ethical fault to be
blind to one's faults—to think oneself generous when really one is stingy,
or to believe that one is free of resentment or hatred or contempt toward
one's fellows when really one is full of them. Much of the philosophical
ink that has been spilled on this subject has coagulated around the question whether and to what extent it is correct to say that we *deceive* ourselves in these matters. We need not worry about that here. My question
is rather to what extent our problem with self-knowledge is one of rationality. It surely can be irrational to refuse to accept that one is, for

example, jealous, when confronted with all sorts of evidence from one's behavior. But I think that failure to recognize one's real desires and attitudes is very often a matter of blindness rather than irrationality. One has not reasoned badly, and one has not knowingly averted one's gaze from the evidence, but the facts have not registered. One has been influenced by a certain desire without feeling it; or it has never occurred to one that that ugly name could be applied to this attitude in oneself. This happens because we do not want to know—because we cannot stand to know—a certain fact about ourselves; but we are not conscious of what is going on. Here I think we are not irrational but blind. In most cases we ought to know what desires and attitudes we have, not by reasoning but simply because we have them. But sometimes we do not know it because we do not want to know it; and we are to blame for that.[5]

Let me try to place these reflections in the context of a wider view of the limitations of rationality—a view at once theological and somewhat skeptical. We are cognitively dependent creatures. We would like to be able to justify all our knowledge, deriving it by indubitably correct arguments from first principles certified by a luminous self-evidence. But we cannot. We are creatures to whom cognitive starting points, which we cannot justify, must be *given,* again and again.

This need permeates our empirical thinking. In relying on induction at all, and in trusting our judgments of simplicity or plausibility of hypotheses, we are guessing, relying on intellectual impulse or hunch; and we have to hope we are guessing right. Indeed we *believe* that we are guessing right; and it is some sort of cognitive disorder not to guess right. Theists will say that in guessing right in such matters we are understanding God's signals—the language by which God communicates to us his intentions as creator.[6]

And the dependence of our knowledge on guessing right is not limited to a few first principles. Daily and even hourly we have new occasions to judge the weight of evidence, to interpret the utterances and character and intentions of other people, to recognize our own feelings and attitudes. There is much in these occasions that we must simply guess or see; and rationality cannot guarantee that we will get it right. By nature or grace the right guess, the right cognitive impulse, must simply be given to us.

This applies also to ethical convictions and religious faith. Without going so far as to say that moral and religious truths are irrational, or rationally indefensible, I imagine we can agree that rationality alone will not assure us of reaching all that we ought to reach of them. Something more than rationality must be given to us here. As Christians we will say it is the testimony of the Holy Spirit; but presumably he may speak to us through a great variety of social influences and apparently natural inclinations, as well as through more dramatic experiences.

III. The Sin of Unbelief

Thus far I have said relatively little about specifically religious faith and unbelief. It is time to turn our attention to them, and particulary to the sin of unbelief, as it occurs in the experience of Christians. We might think of unbelief as occurring in two forms: (1) not believing God when he speaks to us (that is, not believing what he says); and (2) not believing in God (that is, not trusting him, or not believing that he exists at all, or not believing important truths about him). In fact, however, these forms of unbelief cannot be sharply separated. If we do not believe God when he speaks to us, it is probably because we do not trust him; and if we sin by not believing in God, it is what he says to us about himself that we do not believe.

Let us dwell a bit on this last point. I think the sin of unbelief always involves rejection of something God has said to the sinner. Simply not believing that God exists is not the sin of unbelief, if God has never spoken to you. Butterflies presumably do not believe in God, but they are not therefore guilty of the sin of unbelief. If we, unlike butterflies, are guilty of the sin of unbelief, it is not because we are supposed to be able to *figure out* divine truth for ourselves, but because God has spoken to us. For this reason it behooves us to be particularly reluctant to accuse others of the sin of unbelief. How do we know what God has said to them? For it is the *internal* testimony of the Holy Spirit that most concerns us here.

You may expect me to say something here about atheism. But I will not, because I have never been an atheist and I think it is not my business here to anatomize the sins that atheists may be committing. No, I will take a concrete example of unbelief as it is found in the Christian life.

It is suggested to me that I ought to follow a certain course of action. Perhaps my wife suggests it, or perhaps the thought arises in me spontaneously, or is prompted by something I hear in a sermon. Initially the thought comes to me with the force of a minor revelation. But the more I think about it, the more I think of good reasons for not acting on the idea. I come to the conclusion that it would be a mistake; yet I remain disturbed about it.

What is going on? Maybe God was telling me to follow that course of action, and I am not believing him. God's speech is not ineffectual; so we should expect that if we do not believe something he has said to us, his word will leave at least a trace of uneasiness in us. In the state that I described I may no longer be in a good position to tell whether it was God or a foolish impulse of my own that pressed me at first to do the action. What is clear is that if it was God, I do not want to hear him. And that is sin.

Why don't I want to hear God if he is telling me to follow that course of action? Quite possibly because I am *afraid*. Perhaps the course of action is one that would risk offending people whom I fear to offend. And in this fear we find a deeper level of the sin of unbelief. For why am I afraid? Don't I believe that God will bless my obedience if I sincerely try to do his will? Don't I believe that he can bring greater good out of any disasters that may befall me? Don't I believe that there is greater happiness to be found in venturing for God than in playing it safe for myself? Yes, I believe all those things. That is, I would sincerely assert them. I might even preach them in a sermon, or exert myself to defend them against philosophical attack. But obviously I do not believe them with all my heart.

This is, I think, the central form of the sin of unbelief in the Christian life. It is not a refusal to assent intellectually to theological truths, but a failure to trust in truths to which we do assent. Of course an attempt to resolve the conflict could lead, unhappily, to withdrawal of assent from the truths, rather than to trust in God; but more than intellectual assent is involved here.

The relationship between unbelief and fear is important. Trust can be understood in part as a sort of freedom from fear. It is a conceptual truth that if I fear that God will let me down, I do not entirely trust him. Conversely, perfect trust in God would free us from that fear, and from many others.

The emotional ingredient in faith, and in unbelief, is significant for their relation to the intellectual life. There ought to be room in our conception of faith for honest investigation of all questions, and for feeling the force of objections to our faith, even while we are sustained in that faith. Three things should be distinguished. (1) To recognize that God's goodness is in some sense less than 100 percent probable, that it is less certainly established, more open to doubt, than one's own existence, or than '2 + 2 = 4', is to see the element of venture in our faith. It is not necessarily to fall into the sin of unbelief. The sin is something else in our response to these objective facts about our epistemic situation. (2) We may *fear* that God will let us down. The fear adds something emotional, felt or unfelt, which pervasively poisons our attitudes and which normally does constitute some failure of trust in God. The certitude of faith has much more to do with confidence, or freedom from fear, which is partly an emotional state, than it has to do with judgments of certainty or great probability in any evidential sense. (3) To be complete, let us note that we might let the indecisiveness of the evidence affect our *action*. We might try to factor all the arguments, pro and con, into our decisions about what to do. In other words, we might hedge our bet on God's goodness. That would surely be a sin of unbelief.

There are, of course, cases in which evidence against beliefs that we hold ought to be factored into our decisions. If a hunter believes that the animal behind the bush is a deer, but recognizes that there is some reason to think it might be another hunter, the evidence against his belief ought certainly to influence his conduct. Some philosophers may hold that rationality, or even morality, requires us to factor into our decisions any uncertainty we recognize in the objective case for *any* belief we hold. But I think that is wrong. Our bet on God's love should not be hedged. Reasons to doubt other people's trustworthiness should sometimes be totally ignored. And our commitment to many ethical principles ought to be similarly unqualified. Suppose I see reason to doubt that there is any validity or binding force to morality at all; ought that uncertainty to be factored into my decision-making process? Surely not. So long as I do believe in morality, I must think that I ought absolutely to repudiate any hesitation to act on it, no matter what theoretical basis the hesitation may claim.

I have noted in section I that cognitive failures often owe their moral offensiveness at least in part to bad desires that are manifested in them. We may wonder whether a failure of trust in God is sinful on account of sinful desires that are manifested in it. This is a difficult question. The web of sin is a tangled mess of fears and desires which we cannot completely unravel. The fears that are obstacles to my believing what God says to me are not only fears of being let down by God; there are also fears of the frustration of my sinful desires. Perhaps to some extent I do not want to trust God because I sense that that threatens some idolatry that I have been cherishing. On the other hand, I wonder whether my sinful desires do not all *presuppose* a lack or weakness of trust in God's love. Could they stand in the face of a perfectly confident and vivid assurance of the riches of his goodness?

One motive that I think is particularly important in this context is lust for *control* of my own life and its circumstances. I would like to be able to plan my life and have it go according to plan. Or if I want to have some room in my life for the unplanned, the spontaneous and surprising, I would like the spontaneity to be my own caprice, and the surprises to be of certain sorts that please me. (Santa Claus is welcome anytime he cares to call.) This sort of control depends heavily on my having a stable and reliable view of myself and my world. It depends also on my having a trustworthy method of modifying and extending my picture of reality as new events occur. I suspect that much of our emotional attachment to *rationality* has to do with our counting on it as a crucial part of our intellectual equipment for controlling our lives. We rely on rationality for at least three functions: (1) to enable us to know where we are going as we plan, scheme, contrive, or indulge a whim; (2) to tell us how to manipulate situations and people to achieve our goals; and (3) to give us judgments of probabilities so that we can limit our risks and place our emotional investments in the safest and most promising areas.

The control of which I am speaking is obviously related to freedom and the satisfaction of desire, but must not be identified with them. The power of the lust for control shows itself, indeed, in the extent to which we may be willing to sacrifice freedom and desire in order to stay in control. We will adjust our desires to "reality," and restrict our projects to those that are favored by other people and our circumstances—all in order to avoid unpleasant surprises and the feeling that our life is out of our control.

The same motive may lead us to curtail our hopes. We adjust our plans easily to pleasant surprises, but unpleasant surprises threaten our control. From the standpoint of control, therefore, pessimism seems a stronger position than optimism. I think this fact is the main source of the intellectual machismo that prides itself on a sort of "tough-mindedness" that refuses to hope for very much. The desire for control tempts us to believe that if we hope for too much we will make fools of ourselves, whereas if we turn out to have hoped for too little we will only have proved to be "stronger" than we needed to be. This machismo is no more rational than the wishful thinking of which the hopeful are often accused. And when there is talk of "wishful thinking," we would do well to realize that if we have a nonrational motive for believing the best, most of us also have a nonrational motive for believing the worst. Pessimism is not happier than optimism; hope is happier than despair. But it is quite possible to prefer control to happiness.

What Christianity promises may seem "too good to be true"; the emotional meaning of this is that Christianity promises more than we can hope for without giving up control. The supreme threat to our control, however, is God himself. In Christian faith we are invited to trust a person so much greater than ourselves that we cannot understand him very fully. We have to trust his power and goodness in general, without having a blueprint of what he is going to do in detail. This is very disturbing because it entails a loss of our control of our own lives.

God promises life; and the life that he promises is encounter with the alien and new. It is grace and good surprises. In this context the continued lust for control of one's life, in preference to opening oneself to grace, is sin. But what is its relation to the sin of unbelief? Is the desire for control something that inhibits me from trusting God? I must say that in my experience it seems to be so. The feeling that it is stronger, more controlling, to expect evil than to expect good is a powerful enemy of faith. On the other hand, when I consider the question whether I would have this passion for controlling my life if I were not afraid to begin with, I am inclined to think that the lust for control *presupposes* a lack of trust in God. Perhaps the two sins support each other and neither is absolutely prior to the other.

IV. The Advantage of Faith over Sight

The opposition between trust and the desire to control one's own life is closely connected in my mind with the question, what is the good of faith or trust? The answer that Christian thinkers have most often given to the question is that as it is our highest good to be related in love to God, and as we have to believe that he exists and loves us in order to be related to him in that way, we need faith in God in order to attain our highest good. "For whoever would draw near to God must believe that he exists and that he rewards those who seek him" (Hebrews 11:6). And I would certainly agree that as the world is actually set up, we have to have faith in God in order to be rightly related to him here and now. But why should that be? Why should God set up a world in which it is faith rather than knowledge that is offered to us? The Bible indeed suggests that God particularly prizes a faith like that of Abraham, who "went out, not knowing where he was to go" (Hebrews 11:8); a faith that is tried by sufferings (I Peter 1:6–7); a faith that trusts him in the very blackness of death beyond which we cannot now *see* anything. Is there, then, some way in which faith is preferable to sight?

Well, suppose we always *saw* what people were like, and particularly what they would do in any situation in which we might have to do with them. How would we relate to people if we had such knowledge of them? I think we would manipulate them. I do not mean that we would necessarily treat people in a selfish or immoral way, but I think we could not help having an attitude of control toward them. And I think the necessity we would be under, to have such an attitude, would be conceptual and not merely causal. If I pursued my own ends in relation to you, knowing exactly how you would respond to every move, I would be manipulating you as much as I manipulate a typewriter or any other inanimate object. And if at some point I refrained from pursuing my own ends, in order to defer to some desire of yours, *I* would still be making the decision; I would be manipulating you in the service of your end that I had made my own. By the very nature of the case I could not escape from this manipulative role except insofar as I could forget or ignore what I knew about the responses you would make.

There is one loophole in this argument. I have assumed that my actions would be governed by teleological considerations; that is, I have assumed that my choices would be choices of ends to be pursued, or of means to those ends. But I do not believe that actions must, or should, always be governed by teleological considerations. Sometimes one ought to act on principle in spite of the probable or certain consequences. So even if I always knew how you would react to everything I might do, perhaps on some occasions that knowledge ought not to affect my choice of how to act in relation to you. And if in such a case I did conform my action to certain rules regardless of what I knew you would do in response, then I think I would not be manipulating you. But this affords only a very austere possibility of nonmanipulative relationships. We are not interested in personal relationships simply as occasions for doing our duty. We wish to aim at a relational *goal* that involves the cooperation of the other person. That is what I could not do without manipulating you if I always knew exactly, and with certainty, what your response would be.

Our actual uncertainty about what other people will do makes it possible to *depend* on another person in a way that is much more personal. It enables the other person to be more truly other. To the extent that I realize that I do not know how he will respond to my action, I cannot regard him as an extension of my faculty of action, as I regard my typewriter.

Even in the actual world, with all its uncertainties, trust is often manipulative. If I trust the bus driver, it is to take me exactly where I expect her to take me, with no unpleasant surprises en route. Even your trust in your doctor is apt to be manipulative, serving an end you have already settled on—namely, your health; and you will quite appropriately object if she does not tell you enough to make as many as possible of the crucial decisions for yourself. In cases like these the trust, and indeed the whole personal relationship, is not an end in itself, but a means to the individual ends of the parties involved.

There are other relationships, however, in which we open our lives to be influenced and partly shaped by the other person in ways that we cannot predict very precisely except that we have some confidence that they will be good. And even in that confidence we may be allowing the other person some part in defining our good. Uncertainty allows these relationships to be largely nonmanipulative, and I believe the relationships that seem most intensely personal are of this type. It is not easy to say exactly what is so good about the dependence—usually a mutual but often an unequal dependence—in these relationships. But I am sure that it is logically and not just causally necessary for whatever it is that we value so highly in the best personal relationships.

Some reference to Martin Buber seems to be in order at this point. It is one of the important differences between an I-It and an I-Thou relationship, as Buber conceives of them, that the former is implicitly or explicitly manipulative and the latter is not. One of the interesting claims that Buber makes is that the *I* of an I-Thou relationship or attitude is different from the *I* of I-It. I don't know how far that idea can be pushed, but I think the following is true. The nonmanipulative trust that uncertainty makes possible involves a sacrifice of some of our *control* over our own lives, but it does not necessarily make us less *free* on the whole. On the contrary, it seems to free us *to be ourselves in a different way*— perhaps because we do not see ourselves as responsible for the outcome in the same way as if we were clinging to a more controlling role.

God demands of us the greatest trust, the acceptance of the most complete dependence. In death he confronts each of us with a total loss of control over our own destiny. I do not believe that he has given us a map of Heaven or a system of salvation by works that would enable us to extend beyond the grave our scheming and contriving for our own personal future. But in relying not on themselves, "but on God who raises the dead" (II Corinthians 1:9), St. Paul and many other Christians testify that they have experienced his love and power in a way that they would not give up in exchange for control over their own destiny.

Extreme as our dependence on God is, I would not say that it is entirely lacking in mutuality. I believe that he also opens himself to be influenced by us; and this is particularly important in dealing with a *trial* of faith. If troubles impinge on a relationship of trust, they may seem to come from oneself, or from the person one trusts, or from outside the relationship.[7] It is when the difficulties appear to come from the trusted person that one's trust is in the fullest sense tried. In such a case it is most important where one goes for help. If you turn to a third party to be your champion against the person you trusted, there is a serious breakdown in the relationship of trust. But if you go to the person you trust, to work through the problem or conflict with him or her, your trust is tried but not yet broken. (I do not mean that this working through precludes the assistance of a third party who is not a partisan.)

The classic way to go to God to work through the problem or conflict with him when one's faith is tried is *prayer*. This will be petitionary prayer, or perhaps even a complaint addressed to God, as we find quite freely in the Psalms and the prophets, or an acknowledgment of the anger and fear one feels towards him. Prayer is not magic, and it is not to be believed that we can control God by our prayer. But I think a belief that God is open to be influenced by our prayer, in ways that we can neither predict nor control, is important to the function of prayer in working through a trial of faith. Without it we could hardly see the working through as real. I also think this belief is in accord with the nature of trust, which at its best is not an exchange of control for simple dependence, but an exchange of control for dependence in the context of an open relationship, in which there is real interaction, each party being open to be influenced by the other. Indeed the elimination of my influence on the person I trust would eliminate part of the venture of trust. I trust God some if I believe I will not be destroyed by what he does to me. I trust him more, not less, if I also believe I will not be destroyed by what I do to him in the relationship of trust.

Notes

*1. The present essay was written for presentation at a meeting of the Society of Christian Philosophers and is a product of the conviction that there is value in philosophizing sometimes in a way that presupposes faith. I hope that it will interest others as well as Christians, but what is said here about whose sins are under discussion should not be forgotten.

2. Alan Donagan, *The Theory of Morality* (Chicago: University of Chicago Press, 1977), p. 134.

3. Ibid., p. 135.

*4. See Robert Merrihew Adams, "Involuntary Sins," *The Philosophical Review*, 94 (1985): 3–31.

*5. It may be objected that I have been using a rather narrow, procedural sense of 'rationality', and that in a broader sense all the possible errors discussed in the last four paragraphs could be regarded as failures of rationality. I grant that this is true, if by 'rationality' we mean something as broad as *the proper func-*

tioning of our cognitive capacities. But the concept of rationality in that sense is so broad as to have little or no uncontroversial application in philosophical disputes. In particular, I do not see how it could be shown that lack or weakness of faith in God is not a failure of rationality in this sense. It is often claimed that God created us with a sense of his reality, and that we would all therefore believe in him if the divinely intended functioning of our cognitive capacities were not obstructed by the effect of original sin.

Other senses of 'rationality' could be considered in this context. But the concept of rationality is not essential to the main point that I am making here, namely, that there are many cases in which the principal test of good thinking is getting (or, perhaps, tending to get) the right answer. Why should there not also be matters of religious faith about which that is true?

6. This way of putting it is inspired by Bishop Berkeley's conception of a divine language in our sensations. See, e.g., the fourth dialogue of his *Alciphron*.

7. Here, and in the rest of this paragraph, I am drawing on ideas suggested in discussion by Paul Oppenheimer.

2

Kierkegaard's Arguments Against Objective Reasoning in Religion

It is sometimes held that there is something in the nature of religious faith itself that renders it useless or undesirable to reason objectively in support of such faith, even if the reasoning should happen to have considerable plausibility. Søren Kierkegaard's *Concluding Unscientific Postscript* is probably the document most commonly cited as representative of this view. In the present essay I shall discuss three arguments for the view. I call them the Approximation Argument, the Postponement Argument, and the Passion Argument; and I suggest they can all be found in the *Postscript*. I shall try to show that the Approximation Argument is a bad argument. The other two will not be so easily disposed of, however. I believe they show that Kierkegaard's conclusion, or something like it, does indeed follow from a certain conception of religiousness—a conception which has some appeal, although for reasons which I shall briefly suggest, I am not prepared to accept it.

Kierkegaard uses the word 'objective' and its cognates in several senses, most of which need not concern us here. We are interested in the sense in which he uses it when he says, "it is precisely a misunderstanding to seek an objective assurance," and when he speaks of "an objective uncertainty held fast in the appropriation-process of the most passionate inwardness" (pp. 41, 182).[1] Let us say that a piece of reasoning, *R*, is *objective reasoning* just in case every (or almost every) intelligent, fair-minded, and sufficiently informed person would regard *R* as showing or

Versions of this paper have been read to philosophical colloquia at Occidental College and California State University, Fullerton. I am indebted to participants in those discussions, to students in many of my classes, and particularly to Marilyn McCord Adams, Van Harvey, Thomas Kselman, William Laserow, and James Muyskens, for helpful comment on the ideas which are contained in this paper (or which would have been, had it not been for their criticisms).

tending to show (in the circumstances in which R is used, and to the extent claimed in R) that R's conclusion is true or probably true. Uses of 'objective' and 'objectively' in other contexts can be understood from their relation to this one; for example, an objective uncertainty is a proposition which cannot be shown by objective reasoning to be certainly true.

I. The Approximation Argument

"Is it possible to base an eternal happiness upon historical knowledge?" is one of the central questions in the *Postscript*, and in the *Philosophical Fragments* to which it is a "postscript." Part of Kierkegaard's answer to the question is that it is not possible to base an eternal happiness on objective reasoning about historical facts.

> For nothing is more readily evident than that the greatest attainable certainty with respect to anything historical is merely an *approximation*. And an approximation, when viewed as a basis for an eternal happiness, is wholly inadequate, since the incommensurability makes a result impossible (p. 25).

Kierkegaard maintains that it is possible, however, to base an eternal happiness on a belief in historical facts that is independent of objective evidence for them, and that that is what one must do in order to be a Christian. This is the Approximation Argument for the proposition that Christian faith cannot be based on objective reasoning.[2] (It is assumed that some belief about historical facts is an essential part of Christian faith, so that if religious faith cannot be based on objective historical reasoning, then Christian faith cannot be based on objective reasoning at all.) Let us examine the argument in detail.

Its first premise is Kierkegaard's claim that "the greatest attainable certainty with respect to anything historical is merely an approximation." I take him to mean that historical evidence, objectively considered, never completely excludes the possibility of error. "It goes without saying," he claims, "that it is impossible in the case of historical problems to reach an objective decision so certain that no doubt could disturb it" (p. 41). For Kierkegaard's purposes it does not matter how small the possibility of error is, so long as it is finitely small (that is, so long as it is not literally infinitesimal). He insists (p. 31) that his Approximation Argument makes no appeal to the supposition that the objective evidence for Christian historical beliefs is weaker than the objective evidence for any other historical belief. The argument turns on a claim about *all* historical evidence. The probability of error in our belief that there was an American Civil War in the nineteenth century, for instance, might be as small as $1/10^{2,000,000}$; that would be a large enough chance of error for Kierkegaard's argument.

It might be disputed, but let us assume for the sake of argument that there is some such finitely small probability of error in the objective grounds for all historical beliefs, as Kierkegaard held. This need not keep us from saying that we "know," and it is "certain," that there was an American Civil War. For such an absurdly small possibility of error is as good as no possibility of error at all, "for all practical intents and purposes," as we might say. Such a possibility of error is too small to be worth worrying about.

But would it be too small to be worth worrying about if we had an *infinite* passionate interest in the question about the Civil War? If we have an infinite passionate interest in something, there is no limit to how important it is to us. (The nature of such an interest will be discussed more fully in section III.) Kierkegaard maintains that in relation to an infinite passionate interest *no* possibility of error is too small to be worth worrying about. "In relation to an eternal happiness, and an infinite passionate interest in its behalf (in which latter alone the former can exist), an iota is of importance, of infinite importance . . ." (p. 28). This is the basis for the second premise of the Approximation Argument, which is Kierkegaard's claim that "an approximation, when viewed as a basis for an eternal happiness, is wholly inadequate" (p. 25). "An approximation is essentially incommensurable with an infinite personal interest in an eternal happiness" (p. 26).

At this point in the argument it is important to have some understanding of Kierkegaard's conception of faith, and the way in which he thinks faith excludes doubt. Faith must be decisive; in fact it seems to consist in a sort of decision-making. "The conclusion of belief is not so much a conclusion as a resolution, and it is for this reason that belief excludes doubt."[3] The decision of faith is a decision to disregard the possibility of error— to act on what is believed, without hedging one's bets to take account of any possibility of error.

To disregard the possibility of error is not to be unaware of it, or fail to consider it, or lack anxiety about it. Kierkegaard insists that the believer must be keenly *aware* of the risk of errror. "If I wish to preserve myself in faith I must constantly be intent upon holding fast the objective uncertainty, so as to remain out upon the deep, over seventy thousand fathoms of water, still preserving my faith" (p. 182).

For Kierkegaard, then, to ask whether faith in a historical fact can be based on objective reasoning is to ask whether objective reasoning can justify one in disregarding the possibility of error which (he thinks) historical evidence always leaves. Here another aspect of Kierkegaard's conception of faith plays its part in the argument. He thinks that in all genuine religious faith the believer is *infinitely* interested in the object of his faith. And he thinks it follows that objective reasoning cannot justify him in disregarding *any* possibility of error about the object of faith, and therefore cannot lead him all the way to religious faith where a historical fact is concerned. The farthest it could lead him is to the conclusion that *if* he had only a certain finite (though very great) interest in the matter, the possibility of error would be too small to be worth worrying about and he would be justified in disregarding it. But faith disregards a possibility of error that *is* worth worrying about, since an infinite interest is involved. Thus faith requires a "leap" beyond the evidence, a leap that cannot be justified by objective reasoning (cf. p. 90).

There is something right in what Kierkegaard is saying here, but his Approximation Argument is a bad argument. He is right in holding that grounds of doubt which may be insignificant for most practical purposes can be extremely troubling for the intensity of a religious concern, and that it may require great decisiveness, or something like courage, to overcome them religiously. But he is mistaken in holding that objective reasoning could not justify one in disregarding any possibility of error about something in which one is infinitely interested.

The mistake, I believe, lies in his overlooking the fact that there are at least two different reasons one might have for disregarding a possibility of error. The first is that the possibility is too small to be worth worrying about. The second is that the risk of not disregarding the possibility of error would be greater than the risk of disregarding it. Of these two reasons only the first is ruled out by the infinite passionate interest.

I will illustrate this point with two examples, one secular and one religious. A certain woman has a very great (though not infinite) interest in her husband's love for her. She rightly judges that the objective evidence available to her renders it 99.9 percent probable that he loves her truly. The intensity of her interest is sufficient to cause her some *anxiety* over the remaining 1/1,000 chance that he loves her not; for her this chance is not too small to be worth worrying about. (Kierkegaard uses a similar example to support his Approximation Argument; see p. 511). But she (very reasonably) wants to *disregard* the risk of error, in the sense of not hedging her bets, if he does love her. This desire is at least as strong as her desire not to be deceived if he does not love her. Objective reasoning should therefore suffice to bring her to the conclusion that she ought to disregard the risk of error, since by not disregarding it she would run 999 times as great a risk of frustrating one of these desires.

Or suppose you are trying to base your eternal happiness on your relation to Jesus, and therefore have an infinite passionate interest in the question whether he declared Peter and his episcopal successors to be infallible in matters of religious doctrine. You want to be committed to whichever is the true belief on this question, disregarding any possibility of error in it. And suppose, just for the sake of argument, that objective historical evidence renders it 99 percent probable that Jesus did declare Peter and his successors to be infallible—or 99 percent probable that he did not—for our present discussion it does not matter which. The 1 percent chance of error is enough to make you *anxious,* in view of your infinite interest. But objective reasoning leads to the conclusion that you ought to commit yourself to the more probable opinion, *disregarding* the risk of error, if your strongest desire in the matter is to be so committed to the true opinion. For the only other way to satisfy this desire would be to commit yourself to the less probable opinion, disregarding the risk of error in it. The first way will be successful if and only if the more probable opinion is true, and the second way if and only if the less probable opinion is true. Surely it is prudent to do what gives you a 99 percent chance of satisfying your strong desire, in preference to what gives you only a 1 percent chance of satisfying it.

In this argument your strong desire to be committed to the true opinion is presupposed. The reasonableness of this desire may depend on a belief for which no probability can be established by purely historical reasoning, such as the belief that Jesus is God. But any difficulties arising from this point are distinct from those urged in the Approximation Argument, which itself presupposes the infinite passionate interest in the historical question.

There is some resemblance between my arguments in these examples and Pascal's famous Wager argument. But whereas Pascal's argument turns on weighing an infinite interest against a finite one, mine turn on weighing a large chance of success against a small one. An argument closer to Pascal's will be discussed in section IV.

The reader may well have noticed in the foregoing discussion some unclarity about what sort of justification is being demanded and given for religious beliefs about historical facts. There are at least two different types of question about a proposition which I might try to settle by objective reasoning: (1) Is it probable that the proposition is true? (2) In view of the evidence which I have for and against the proposition, and my interest in the matter, is it prudent for me to have faith in the truth of the proposition, disregarding the possibility of error? Correspondingly, we may distinguish two ways in which a belief can be *based on* objective reasoning. The proposition believed may be the conclusion of a piece of objective reasoning, and accepted because it is that. We may say that such a belief is *objectively probable*. Or one might hold a belief or maintain a religious faith because of a piece of objective reasoning whose conclusion is that it would be prudent, morally right, or otherwise desirable for one to hold that belief or faith. In this latter case let us say that the belief is *objectively advantageous*. It is clear that historical beliefs can be objectively probable; and in the Approximation Argument, Kierkegaard does not deny Christian historical beliefs can be objectively probable. His thesis is, in effect, that in view of an infinite passionate interest in their subject matter, they cannot be objectively advantageous, and therefore cannot be fully justified objectively, even if they are objectively probable. It is this thesis that I have attempted to refute. I have not been discussing the question whether Christian historical beliefs are objectively probable.

II. The Postponement Argument

The trouble with objective historical reasoning, according to the Approximation Argument, is that it cannot yield complete certainty. But that is not Kierkegaard's only complaint against it as a basis for religious faith. He also objects that objective historical inquiry is never completely finished, so that one who seeks to base his faith on it postpones his religious commitment forever. In the process of historical research "new difficulties arise and are overcome, and new difficulties again arise. Each generation inherits from its predecessor the illusion that the method is quite impeccable, but the learned scholars have not yet succeeded . . . and so forth. . . . The infinite personal passionate interest of the subject . . . vanishes more and more, because the decision is postponed, and postponed as following directly upon the result of the learned inquiry" (p. 28). As soon as we take "an historical document" as "our standard for the determination of Christian truth," we are "involved in a parenthesis whose conclusion is everlastingly prospective" (p. 28)—that is, we are involved in a religious digression which keeps religious commitment forever in the future.[4]

Kierkegaard has such fears about allowing religious faith to rest on *any* empirical reasoning. The danger of postponement of commitment arises not only from the uncertainties of historical scholarship, but also in connection with the design argument for God's existence. In the *Philosoph-*

ical Fragments Kierkegaard notes some objections to the attempt to prove God's existence from evidence of "the wisdom in nature, the goodness, the wisdom in the governance of the world," and then says, "even if I began I would never finish, and would in addition have to live constantly in suspense, lest something so terrible should suddenly happen that my bit of proof would be demolished."[5] What we have before us is a quite general sort of objection to the treatment of religious beliefs as empirically testable. On this point many analytical philosophers seem to agree with Kierkegaard. Much discussion in recent analytical philosophy of religion has proceeded from the supposition that religious beliefs are not empirically testable. I think it is far from obvious that that supposition is correct; and it is interesting to consider arguments that may be advanced to support it.

Kierkegaard's statements suggest an argument that I call the Postponement Argument. Its first premise is that one cannot have an authentic religious faith without being totally committed to it. In order to be totally committed to a belief, in the relevant sense, one must be determined not to abandon the belief under any circumstances that one recognizes as epistemically possible.

The second premise is that one cannot yet be totally committed to any belief which one bases on an inquiry in which one recognizes any possibility of a future need to revise the results. Total commitment to any belief so based will necessarily be postponed. I believe that this premise, suitably interpreted, is true. Consider the position of someone who regards himself as committed to a belief on the basis of objective evidence, but who recognizes some possibility that future discoveries will destroy the objective justification of the belief. We must ask how he is disposed to react in the event, however unlikely, that the objective basis of his belief is overthrown. Is he prepared to abandon the belief in that event? If so, he is not totally committed to the belief in the relevant sense. But if he is determined to cling to his belief even if its objective justification is taken away, then he is not basing the belief on the objective justification—or at least he is not basing it solely on the justification.[6]

The conclusion to be drawn from these two premises is that authentic religious faith cannot be based on an inquiry in which one recognizes any possibility of a future need to revise the results. We ought to note that this conclusion embodies two important restrictions on the scope of the argument.

In the first place, we are not given an argument that authentic religious faith cannot *have* an objective justification that is subject to possible future revision. What we are given is an argument that the authentic believer's holding of his religious belief cannot *depend* entirely on such a justification.

In the second place, this conclusion applies only to those who *recognize* some epistemic possibility that the objective results which appear to support their belief may be overturned. I think it would be unreasonable to require, as part of total commitment, a determination with regard to one's response to circumstances that one does not recognize as possible at all. It may be, however, that one does not recognize such a possibility when one ought to.

Kierkegaard needs one further premise in order to arrive at the conclusion that authentic religious faith cannot without error be based on any objective empirical reasoning. This third premise is that in every objective empirical inquiry there is always, objectively considered, some epistemic possibility that the results of the inquiry will need to be revised in view of new evidence or new reasoning. I believe Kierkegaard makes this assumption; he certainly makes it with regard to historical inquiry. From this premise it follows that one is in error if in any objective empirical inquiry one does not recognize any possibility of a future need to revise the results. But if one does recognize such a possibility, then according to the conclusion already reached in the Postponement Argument, one cannot base an authentic religious faith on the inquiry.

Some philosophers might attack the third premise of this argument; and certainly it is controversial. But I am more inclined to criticize the first premise. There is undoubtedly something plausible about the claim that authentic religious faith must involve a commitment so complete that the believer is resolved not to abandon his belief under any circumstances that he regards as epistemically possible. If you are willing to abandon your ostensibly religious beliefs for the sake of objective inquiry, mightn't we justly say that objective inquiry is your real religion, the thing to which you are most deeply committed?

There is also something plausible to be said on the other side, however. It has commonly been thought to be an important part of religious ethics that one ought to be humble, teachable, open to correction, new inspiration, and growth of insight, even (and perhaps especially) in important religious beliefs. That view would have to be discarded if we were to concede to Kierkegaard that the heart of commitment in religion is an unconditional determination not to change in one's important religious beliefs. In fact I think there is something radically wrong with this conception of religious commitment. Faith ought not to be thought of as unconditional devotion to a belief. For in the first place the object of religious devotion is not a belief or attitude of one's own, but God. And in the second place it may be doubted that religious devotion to God can or should be completely unconditional. God's love for sinners is sometimes said to be completely unconditional, not being based on any excellence or merit of theirs. But religious devotion to God is generally thought to be based on his goodness and love. It is the part of the strong, not the weak, to love unconditionally. And in relation to God we are weak.

III. The Passion Argument

In Kierkegaard's statements of the Approximation Argument and the Postponement Argument it is assumed that a system of religious beliefs might be objectively probable. It is only for the sake of argument, however, that Kierkegaard allows this assumption. He really holds that religious faith, by its very nature, needs objective *im*probability. "Anything that is almost probable, or probable, or extremely and emphatically probable, is something [one] can almost know, or as good as know, or extremely and emphatically almost *know*—but it is impossible to *believe*" (p. 189). Nor will Kierkegaard countenance the suggestion that religion ought to go beyond belief to some almost-knowledge based on probability. "Faith is the highest passion in a man. There are perhaps many in every generation who do not even reach it, but no one gets further."[7] It would be a betrayal of religion to try to go beyond faith. The suggestion that faith might be replaced by "probabilities and guarantees" is for the believer "a temptation to be resisted with all his strength" (p. 15). The attempt to establish religious beliefs on a foundation of objective probability is therefore no service to religion, but inimical to religion's true interests. The approximation to certainty which might be afforded by objective probability is rejected, not only for the reasons given in the Approximation Argument and Postponement Argument, but also from a deeper motive, "since on the contrary it behooves us to get rid of introductory guarantees of security, proofs from consequences, and the whole mob of public pawnbrokers and guarantors, so as to permit the absurd to stand out in all its clarity—in order that the individual may believe if he wills it; I merely say that it must be strenuous in the highest degree so to believe" (p. 190).

As this last quotation indicates, Kierkegaard thinks that religious belief ought to be based on a strenuous exertion of the will—a passionate striving. His reasons for thinking that objective probability is religiously undesirable have to do with the place of passion in religion, and constitute what I call the Passion Argument. The first premise of the argument is that the most essential and the most valuable feature of religiousness is passion, indeed an infinite passion, a passion of the greatest possible intensity. The second premise is that an infinite passion requires objective improbability. And the conclusion therefore is that that which is most essential and most valuable in religiousness requires objective improbability.

My discussion of this argument will have three parts. (a) First I will try to clarify, very briefly, what it is that is supposed to be objectively improbable. (b) Then we will consider Kierkegaard's reasons for holding that infinite passion requires objective improbability. In so doing we will also gain a clearer understanding of what a Kierkegaardian infinite passion is. (c) Finally I will discuss the first premise of the argument—although issues will arise at that point which I do not pretend to be able to settle by argument.

(a) What are the beliefs whose improbability is needed by religious passion? Kierkegaard will hardly be satisfied with the improbability of just any one belief; it must surely be at least an important belief. On the other hand it would clearly be preposterous to suppose that every belief involved in Christianity must be objectively improbable. (Consider, for example, the belief that the man Jesus did indeed live.) I think that what is demanded in the Passion Argument is the objective improbability of at least one belief which must be true if the goal sought by the religious passion is to be attained.

(b) We can find in the *Postscript* suggestions of several reasons for thinking that an infinite passion needs objective improbability. The two that seem to be most interesting have to do with (i) the risks accepted and (ii) the costs paid in pursuance of a passionate interest.

(i) One reason that Kierkegaard has for valuing objective improbability is that it increases the *risk* attaching to the religious life, and risk is so essential for the expression of religious passion that "without risk there is no faith" (p. 182). About the nature of an eternal happiness, the goal of religious striving, Kierkegaard says "there is nothing to be said . . . except that it is the good which is attained by venturing everything absolutely" (p. 382).

> But what then does it mean to venture? A venture is the precise correlative of an uncertainty; when the certainty is there the venture becomes impossible. . . . If what I hope to gain by venturing is itself certain, I do not risk or venture, but make an exchange. . . . No, if I am in truth resolved to venture, in truth resolved to strive for the attainment of the highest good, the uncertainty must be there, and I must have room to move, so to speak.

But the largest space I can obtain, where there is room for the most vehement gesture of the passion that embraces the infinite, is uncertainty of
knowledge with respect to an eternal happiness, or the certain knowledge
that the choice is in the finite sense a piece of madness: now there is room,
now you can venture! (pp. 380–82)

How is it that objective improbability provides the largest space for the
most vehement gesture of infinite passion? Consider two cases. (A) You
plunge into a raging torrent to rescue from drowning someone you love,
who is crying for help. (B) You plunge into a raging torrent in a desperate
attempt to rescue someone you love, who appears to be unconscious and
may already have drowned. In both cases you manifest a passionate interest in saving the person, risking your own life in order to do so. But
I think Kierkegaard would say there is more passion in the second case
than in the first. For in the second case you risk your life on what is,
objectively considered, a smaller chance that you will be able to save
your loved one. A greater passion is required for a more desperate attempt.

A similar assessment may be made of the following pair of cases. (A')
You stake everything on your faith in the truth of Christianity, knowing
that it is objectively 99 percent probable that Christianity is true. (B')
You stake everything on your faith in the truth of Christianity, knowing
that the truth of Christianity is, objectively, possible but so improbable
that its probability is, say, as small as $1/10^{2,000,000}$. There is passion in
both cases, but Kierkegaard will say that there is more passion in the
second case than in the first. For to venture the same stake (namely,
everything) on a much smaller chance of success shows greater passion.

Acceptance of risk can thus be seen as a *measure* of the intensity of
passion. I believe this provides us with one way of understanding what
Kierkegaard means when he calls religious passion "infinite." An *infinite*
passionate interest in x is an interest so strong that it leads one to make
the greatest possible sacrifices in order to obtain x, on the smallest possible chance of success. The infinity of the passion is shown in that there
is no sacrifice so great one will not make it, and no chance of success
so small one will not act on it. A passion which is infinite in this sense
requires, by its very nature, a situation of maximum risk for its expression.

It will doubtless be objected that this argument involves a misunderstanding of what a passionate interest is. Such an interest is a disposition.
In order to have a great passionate interest it is not necessary actually to
make a great sacrifice with a small chance of success; all that is necessary
is to have such an intense interest that one *would* do so if an appropriate

occasion should arise. It is therefore a mistake to say that there *is* more passion in case (B) than in case (A), or in (B') than in (A'). More passion is *shown* in (B) than in (A), and in (B') than in (A'); but an equal passion may exist in cases in which there is no occasion to show it.

This objection may well be correct as regards what we normally mean by "passionate interest." But that is not decisive for the argument. The crucial question is what part dispositions, possibly unactualized, ought to play in religious devotion. And here we must have a digression about the position of the *Postscript* on this question—a position that is complex at best and is not obviously consistent.

In the first place I do not think that Kierkegaard would be prepared to think of passion, or a passionate interest, as primarily a disposition that might remain unactualized. He seems to conceive of passion chiefly as an intensity in what one actually does and feels. "Passion is momentary" (p. 178), although capable of continual repetition. And what is momentary in such a way that it must be repeated rather than protracted is presumably an occurrence rather than a disposition. It agrees with this conception of passion that Kierkegaard idealizes a life of "persistent striving," and says that the religious task is to "exercise" the God-relationship and to give "existential expression" to the religious choice (pp. 110, 364, 367).

All of this supports the view that what Kierkegaard means by "an infinite passionate interest" is a pattern of actual decision-making in which one continually exercises and expresses one's religiousness by making the greatest possible sacrifices on the smallest possible chance of success. In order to actualize such a pattern of life one needs chances of success that are as small as possible. That is the room that is required for "the most vehement gesture" of infinite passion.

But on the other hand Kierkegaard does allow a dispositional element in the religious life, and even precisely in the making of the greatest possible sacrifices. We might suppose that if we are to make the greatest possible sacrifices in our religious devotion, we must do so by abandoning all worldly interests and devoting all our time and attention to religion. That is what monasticism attempts to do, as Kierkegaard sees it; and (in the *Postscript,* at any rate) he rejects the attempt, contrary to what our argument to this point would have led us to expect of him. He holds that "resignation" (pp. 353, 367) or "renunciation" (pp. 362, 386) of *all* finite ends is precisely the first thing that religiousness requires; but he means a renunciation that is compatible with pursuing and enjoying finite ends (pp. 362–71). This renunciation is the practice of a sort of detachment; Kierkegaard uses the image of a dentist loosening the soft tissues around a tooth, while it is still in place, in preparation for pulling it (p. 367). It is partly a matter of not treating finite things with a desperate seriousness, but with a certain coolness or humor, even while one pursues them (pp. 368, 370).

This coolness is not just a disposition. But the renunciation also has a dispositional aspect. "Now if for any individual an eternal happiness is his highest good, this will mean that all finite satisfactions are volitionally relegated to the status of what may have to be renounced in favor of an eternal happiness" (p. 350). The volitional relegation is not a disposition but an act of choice. The object of this choice, however, appears to be a dispositional state—the state of being such that one *would* forgo any finite satisfaction *if* it *were* religiously necessary or advantageous to do so.

It seems clear that Kierkegaard, in the *Postscript*, is willing to admit a dispositional element at one point in the religious venture, but not at another. It is enough in most cases, he thinks, if one is *prepared* to cease for the sake of religion from pursuing some finite end; but it is not enough that one *would* hold to one's belief in the face of objective improbability. The belief must actually be improbable, although the pursuit of the finite need not actually cease. What is not clear is a reason for this disparity. The following hypothesis, admittedly somewhat speculative as interpretation of the text, is the best explanation I can offer.

The admission of a dispositional element in the religious renunciation of the finite is something to which Kierkegaard seems to be driven by the view that there is no alternative to it except idolatry. For suppose one actually ceases from all worldly pursuits and enters a monastery. In the monastery one would pursue a number of particular ends (such as getting up in the middle of the night to say the offices) which, although religious in a way ("churchy," one might say), are still finite. The absolute *telos* or end of religion is no more to be identified with them than with the ends pursued by an alderman (pp. 362–71). To pretend otherwise would be to make an idolatrous identification of the absolute end with some finite end. An existing person cannot have sacrificed everything by actually having ceased from pursuing *all* ends. For as long as he lives and acts he is pursuing some finite end. Therefore his renouncing *everything* finite must be at least partly dispositional.

Kierkegaard does not seem happy with this position. He regards it as of the utmost importance that the religious passion should come to expression. The problem of finding an adequate expression for a passion for an infinite end, in the face of the fact that in every concrete action one will be pursuing some finite end, is treated in the *Postscript* as the central problem of religion (see especially pp. 386–468). If the sacrifice of everything finite must remain largely dispositional, then perhaps it is all the more important to Kierkegaard that the smallness of the chance for which it is sacrificed should be fully actual, so that the infinity of the religious passion may be measured by an actuality in at least one aspect of the religious venture.

(ii) According to Kierkegaard, as I have argued, the intensity of a passion is measured in part by the smallness of the chances of success that one acts on. It can also be measured in part by its *costliness*—that is, by how much one gives up or suffers in acting on those chances. This second measure can also be made the basis of an argument for the claim that an infinite passion requires objective improbability. For the objective improbability of a religious belief, if recognized, increases the costliness of holding it. The risk involved in staking everything on an objectively improbable belief gives rise to an anxiety and mental suffering whose acceptance is itself a sacrifice. It seems to follow that if one is not staking everything on a belief one sees to be objectively improbable, one's passion is not infinite in Kierkegaard's sense, since one's sacrifice could be greater if one did adhere to an improbable belief.

Kierkegaard uses an argument similar to this. For God to give us objective knowledge of himself, eliminating paradox from it, would be "to lower the price of the God-relationship."

> And even if God could be imagined willing, no man with passion in his heart could desire it. To a maiden genuinely in love it could never occur that she had bought her happiness too dear, but rather that she had not bought it dear enough. And just as the passion of the infinite was itself the truth, so in the case of the highest value it holds true that the price is the value, that a low price means a poor value . . . (p. 207).

Kierkegaard here appears to hold, first, that an increase in the objective probability of religious belief would reduce its costliness, and second, that the value of a religious life is measured by its cost. I take it his reason for the second of these claims is that passion is the most valuable thing in a religious life and passion is measured by its cost. If we grant Kierkegaard the requisite conception of an infinite passion, we seem once again to have a plausible argument for the view that objective improbability is required for such a passion.

(c) We must therefore consider whether infinite passion, as Kierkegaard conceives of it, ought to be part of the religious ideal of life. Such a passion is a striving, or pattern of decision-making, in which, with the greatest possible intensity of feeling, one continually makes the greatest possible sacrifices on the smallest possible chance of success. This seems to me an impossible ideal. I doubt that any human being could have a passion of this sort, because I doubt that one could make a sacrifice so great that a greater could not be made, or have a (nonzero) chance of success so small that a smaller could not be had.

But even if Kierkegaard's ideal is impossible, one might want to try to approximate it. Intensity of passion might still be measured by the greatness of sacrifices made and the smallness of chances of success acted on, even if we cannot hope for a greatest possible or a smallest possible here. And it could be claimed that the most essential and valuable thing in religiousness is a passion that is very intense (though it cannot be infinite) by this standard—the more intense the better. This claim will not support an argument that objective improbability is absolutely required for religious passion. For a passion could presumably be very intense, involving great sacrifices and risks of some other sort, without an objectively improbable belief. But it could still be argued that objectively improbable religious beliefs enhance the value of the religious life by increasing its sacrifices and diminishing its chances of success, whereas objective probability detracts from the value of religious passion by diminishing its intensity.

The most crucial question about the Passion Argument, then, is whether maximization of sacrifice and risk are so valuable in religion as to make objective improbability a desirable characteristic of religious beliefs. Certainly much religious thought and feeling places a very high value on sacrifice and on passionate intensity. But the doctrine that it is desirable to increase without limit, or to the highest possible degree (if there is one) the cost and risk of a religious life is less plausible (to say the least) than the view that *some* degree of cost and risk may add to the value of a religious life. The former doctrine would set the religious interest at enmity with all other interests, or at least with the best of them. Kierkegaard is surely right in thinking that it would be impossible to live without pursuing some finite ends. But even so it would be possible to exchange the pursuit of better finite ends for the pursuit of worse ones— for example, by exchanging the pursuit of truth, beauty, and satisfying personal relationships for the self-flagellating pursuit of pain. And a way of life would be the costlier for requiring such an exchange. Kierkegaard does not, in the *Postscript,* demand it. But the presuppositions of his Passion Argument seem to imply that such a sacrifice would be religiously desirable. Such a conception of religion is demonic. In a tolerable religious ethics some way must be found to conceive of the religious interest as inclusive rather than exclusive of the best of other interests— including, I think, the interest in having well-grounded beliefs.

IV. Pascal's Wager and Kierkegaard's Leap

Ironically, Kierkegaard's views about religious passion suggest a way in which his religious beliefs could be based on objective reasoning—not on reasoning which would show them to be objectively probable, but on reasoning which shows them to be objectively advantageous. Consider the situation of a person whom Kierkegaard would regard as a genuine Christian believer. What would such a person want most of all? He would want above all else to attain the truth through Christianity. That is, he would desire both that Christianity be true and that he himself be related to it as a genuine believer. He would desire that state of affairs (which we may call S) so ardently that he would be willing to sacrifice everything else to obtain it, given only the smallest possible chance of success.

We can therefore construct the following argument, which has an obvious analogy to Pascal's Wager. Let us assume that there is, objectively, some chance, however small, that Christianity is true. This is an assumption which Kierkegaard accepts (p. 31), and I think it is plausible. There are two possibilities, then: either Christianity is true, or it is false. (Others might object to so stark a disjunction, but Kierkegaard will not.) If Christianity is false it is impossible for anyone to obtain S, since S includes the truth of Christianity. It is only if Christianity is true that anything one does will help one or hinder one in obtaining S. And if Christianity is true, one will obtain S just in case one becomes a genuine Christian believer. It seems obvious that one would increase one's chances of becoming a genuine Christian believer by becoming one now (if one can), even if the truth of Christian beliefs is now objectively uncertain or improbable. Hence it would seem to be advantageous for anyone who can to become a genuine Christian believer now, if he wants S so much that he would be willing to sacrifice everything else for the smallest possible chance of obtaining S. Indeed I believe that the argument I have given for this conclusion is a piece of objective reasoning, and that Christian belief is therefore *objectively* advantageous for anyone who wants S as much as a Kierkegaardian genuine Christian must want it.

Of course this argument does not tend at all to show that it is objectively probable that Christianity is true. It only gives a practical, prudential reason for believing, to someone who has a certain desire. Nor does the argument do anything to prove that such an absolutely overriding desire for S is reasonable.[8] It does show, however, that just as Kierkegaard's position has more logical structure than one might at first think, it is more difficult than he probably realized for him to get away entirely from objective justification.

Notes

1. Søren Kierkegaard, *Concluding Unscientific Postscript,* trans. David F. Swenson; introduction, notes, and completion of translation by Walter Lowrie (Princeton, N.J.: Princeton University Press, 1941). Page references in parentheses in the body of the present paper are to this work.

2. The argument is not original with Kierkegaard. It can be found in works of G. E. Lessing and D. F. Strauss that Kierkegaard had read. See especially Thulstrup's quotation and discussion of a passage from Strauss in the commentary portion of Søren Kierkegaard, *Philosophical Fragments,* trans. David F. Swenson, 2d ed., translation revised by Howard V. Hong, with introduction and commentary by Niels Thulstrup (Princeton, N.J.: Princeton University Press, 1962), pp. 149–51.

3. Kierkegaard, *Philosophical Fragments,* p. 104; cf. pp. 102–3.

4. Essentially the same argument can be found in a plea, which has had great influence among more recent theologians, for making Christian faith independent of the results of critical historical study of the Bible: Martin Kähler's famous lecture, first delivered in 1892, *Der sogenannte historische Jesus und der geschichtliche biblische Christus* (Munich: Christus Kaiser Verlag, 1961), p. 50f.

5. Kierkegaard, *Philosophical Fragments,* p. 52.

6. Kierkegaard notes the possibility that in believing in God's existence "I make so bold as to defy all objections, even those that have not yet been made." But in that case he thinks the belief is not really based on the evidence of God's work in the world; "it is not from the works that I make my proof" (*Philosophical Fragments,* p. 52).

7. Søren Kierkegaard, *Fear and Trembling,* trans. Walter Lowrie, 2d ed. (Princeton, N.J.: Princeton University Press, 1970; published in one volume with *The Sickness unto Death*), p. 131. Cf. *Postscript,* p. 31f.

8. It is worth noting, though, that a similar argument might still provide some less overriding justification of belief to someone who had a strong, but less overriding, desire for S.

3

The Leap of Faith

One of the main arguments of the *Concluding Unscientific Postscript* has two premises, stated by Kierkegaard in these words:

[1] The greatest attainable certainty with respect to anything historical is merely an *approximation*.

[2] And an approximation, when viewed as a basis for an eternal happiness, is wholly inadequate (p. 25).[1]

The conclusion, clear enough but not stated so succinctly in the context, is that

[3] Therefore an eternal happiness cannot be based on a (rational) certainty about anything historical.

In an earlier paper[2] I have dubbed this the "Approximation Argument," proposed an interpretation of it, and criticized the argument under that interpretation. I now think another interpretation is possible, which is at least partly liable to a similar criticism, but may lead us deeper into Kierkegaard's real contribution to our thinking about the nature of faith. I do not think it is necessary to choose between the interpretations; both seem to correspond to intentions that are fairly clear in the text.

The interpretations disagree on the reference of 'certainty', and therefore of 'approximation' in Kierkegaard's formulation of the argument. My first interpretation took these terms to refer to the degree to which the belief in question is justified by the historical research that has been accomplished. On this reading, the argument can be restated as follows:

(1a) The greatest degree to which a belief can be justified by objective historical reasoning is only an approximation to certainty (that is, a probability of less than 100 percent).

(2a) A degree of justification that only approximates certainty is wholly inadequate as a basis for an eternal happiness.

(3a) Therefore an eternal happiness cannot be based on objective historical reasoning.

My criticism of this version of the argument focused on premise (2a). (2a) is supported by the contention that for the ("infinite") intensity of a religious person's interest in an eternal happiness, no chance of error is "too small to be worth worrying about," and hence a probability of less than 100 percent cannot justify, for such an interest, the totally unreserved reliance that religious faith requires. My objection to this reasoning is that it presupposes erroneously that the only good reason for disregarding a risk of error is that the risk is too small to be worth worrying about. One would have a good reason of a different sort for disregarding a risk of error that *is* large enough to be worth worrying about if disregarding it were the likeliest way to attain one's chief ends. And on the showing of Kierkegaard's Approximation Argument, it might well be rational for a would-be Christian to disregard the 30 percent chance of error, if objective historical reasoning showed it 70 percent probable that Jesus rose from the dead. For that would be the likeliest way of attaining her chief ends, in that situation, if it was an end of overriding importance, for her, to believe unreservedly in Jesus' resurrection if and only if it really happened.

The other interpretation of the Approximation Argument takes 'certainty' and 'approximation' in Kierkegaard's formulation of the argument to refer, not to the degree of justification of the belief in question, but to the belief itself. The issue, on this reading, is not how close the probability of the belief comes to 100 percent, but how close the belief comes to complete conviction. In this connection it will be useful to look at one of the passages in which Kierkegaard develops the notion of a "leap" of faith:

> What if instead of talking or dreaming about an absolute beginning, we talked about a leap. To be content with a "mostly," an "as good as," a "you could almost say that," a "when you sleep on it until tomorrow, you can easily say that," suffices merely to betray a kinship with Trop, who, little by little, reached the point of assuming that almost having passed his examinations, was the same as having passed them. . . . Reflection can be halted only by a leap . . . When the subject does not put an end to his reflection, he is made infinite in reflection, i.e., he does not arrive at a decision (p. 105).

It would of course be merely ridiculous to say, 'When you sleep on it until tomorrow, you can easily say that Jesus rose from the dead'. But there certainly have been scholars who have aspired to be in a position to say, 'Probably Jesus rose from the dead'—and philosophers who have been prepared to identify belief in general, and religious belief in particular, with an assignment of probabilities.[3] Kierkegaard's central point, in this passage, is that that is not enough for religious faith. 'Probably Jesus rose from the dead' and 'Probably God is love' are not affirmations of faith. To get from this probability assignment to the simple affirmation of faith, 'Jesus rose from the dead', a transition is needed, which Kierkegaard calls a "leap." This leap from probability assignment to full belief is needed when the probability assigned is high, as well as when it is low (a feature of Kierkegaard's position that often is overlooked). The leap, according to Kierkegaard, must be made by a "decision," which puts an end to reflection.

There are contexts in which a probability assignment is all the belief that is required of us. In some cases, indeed, a careful calculation of the probabilities, a strict proportioning to them of our assent, and a factoring of all the risks and probabilities into our practical decisions are all the belief it is desirable for us to have. This is true of an investor's beliefs about the future prices of securities, and of a doctor's beliefs about the effects of various possible treatments on her patients. If 'Interest rates will probably decline in the next six months' sounds too indefinite in the mouth of an investment advisor, it is because we want a more precise estimate of *how* probable the decline is, not a firmer conviction of the fact of the decline.

But there are also contexts in which more conviction is demanded. 'Probably so', in answer to the question, 'Do you love me?' is not exactly an affirmation of love. In answer to 'Is the moral law binding on us?' it is apt to leave the impression that the respondent is insufficiently committed to morality. To factor into one's investment decisions whatever chance of error one sees in one's estimate of the probable course of interest rates is just what is expected of the prudent investor; but the instant I factor into my practical deliberations a "7-percent chance that morality is just an illusion," I am not living morally but amorally.

Another context in which more decisiveness is required is repentance. 'Probably I was wrong to do that to you' is not much of an apology. And even if I say it only to myself, the 'probably' is apt to express a reservation that is incompatible with true contrition.

Kierkegaard is surely right in placing religious faith in this category of beliefs for which 'probably' is not enough. 'Probably Jesus rose from the dead' is indeed not an affirmation of faith. A "leap" from probability assessment, however favorable, to a different kind of conviction is required.

Against this background we can formulate our second version of the
Approximation Argument:

(1b) The strongest belief that can be based on objective historical reasoning
is a probability assignment of less than 100 percent.

(2b) Any probability assignment of less than 100 percent is wholly inadequate
as a form of religious faith, as a basis for an eternal happiness.

(3b) Therefore an eternal happiness cannot be based on objective historical
reasoning.

In the first interpretation the second premise was the object of my attack;
here the second premise seems absolutely correct. As I have been arguing, religious faith is more than a probability assignment. (1b), however, may be liable to the same sort of criticism as (2a). Each seems to
depend on a questionable assumption about what would be required to
justify an unreserved conviction. In the case of (1b), the assumption is
that if objective historical reasoning discovers a probability of no more
than *n* percent for a proposition *p*, then the strongest form of belief in *p*
that such reasoning can justify is a mere probability assignment—the belief that *p* is *n* percent probable. But this is an error. Suppose that objective historical reasoning shows it 98.5 percent probable, on the evidence you have, that your past behavior satisfies a description that, on
ethical principles to which you are committed, implies that you have seriously wronged another person. Shall we conclude that the strongest conviction of guilt that objective historical reasoning could justify for you
could only take the form, 'Probably I seriously wronged him' or 'Almost
certainly I seriously wronged him'? No. The moral importance of contrition, and its nature, are such that reasoning that establishes for you that
it is 98.5 percent probable that you have seriously wronged someone will
also justify the transition or "leap" from that probability assignment to
the simple belief or unreserved conviction expressed by 'I have seriously
wronged him'.

Similarly, in view of the nature and importance of religious faith, reasoning that established a high probability that God raised Jesus from the
dead could also justify a transition from that probability assignment to
unreserved belief in Jesus' resurrection. This is not to deny that a "leap"
is involved here, from a probability assignment to a belief of a different
nature. But it appears that the leap could be rationally justified. Especially
if the leap is a decision, as Kierkegaard suggests—a decision to live on
the assumption that the religious claim is true, disregarding any chance
that it is false—it seems that that decision could be justified rationally by
evidence that the claim is probably true and that, if it is true, one can

attain one's chief ends in the matter only by accepting the decision without reservation.

Perhaps the second version of the Approximation Argument can be defended from this attack by another interpretation, this time of (1b). I have treated 'based on' in (1b) as equivalent to 'justified by'. But we could construe it more genetically as meaning 'attained through'. This would be more closely connected with 'attainable' in Kierkegaard's formulation of [1]. (1b) would then be a claim about what is psychologically possible: that the strongest belief that can be reached through a process of objective historical reasoning is a mere probability assignment of less than 100 percent.

This is not a very plausible claim, as it stands. Surely it is psychologically possible, on the basis of objective historical reasoning, to make a leap of the sort that Kierkegaard seems to be demanding—a voluntary decision to live on the assumption of the truth of a proposition rendered probable by the reasoning, and to disregard any risk of error. But maybe Kierkegaard's emphasis on voluntary decision is misleading here. For it is plausible to suppose that religious faith involves something more, something even harder to reach by a process of reasoning. 'Probably so' cannot be turned into an affirmation of faith by adding, 'And I have therefore decided to act resolutely on the assumption that it is so'. What may still be lacking in such a resolution is a deeply *felt* conviction that the proposition believed is true. There is a pattern of emotionality, as well as a pattern of voluntary actions, that belongs to a religious way of life. The ideal of religious faith therefore has an emotional aspect. Peace, joy, gratitude, and the freedom to love are supposed to flow from a confidently held conviction that God is good. In this faith one is to respond emotionally to the divine goodness in which one believes, rather than to the balance of the evidence that one sees for it and against it. Most believers will have some emotional response to grounds that they see for doubting; but ideally, at least, the believer's emotional response to what she believes in faith will be greater than is proportionate to the degree to which objective reasoning or evidence renders the belief probable for her.

Can such confidence "with respect to anything historical" be produced by objective reasoning? Not by objective reasoning alone, I should say. One is not likely to sustain the confidence of religious faith without seeing *some* grounds for one's belief. And it may be possible to argue cogently, on rational grounds, that it is *desirable* in some cases for the confidence of a religious belief to exceed the degree of probability rationally assigned to it. But the confidence itself is an elemental religious phenomenon which at least partly precedes rather than follows rational justification.

That conclusion may not concede very much to Kierkegaard. Can we go farther, and hold that objective rational investigation is incompatible, psychologically, with the confidence of religious faith? Construed broadly, this claim seems to be empirically false. There are surely (many religious) believers who have maintained a strong and steady confidence in their faith while examining with as much objectivity as most of us are capable of, the evidence for and against their religious convictions. But in such an investigation, it is only judgments about the value of various pieces of evidence that are fully up for grabs. The possibility of actually giving up her central religious convictions is felt by the believer as remote.

There is another type of inquiry into the grounds of religious belief, however, in which one feels that one's faith is at risk throughout the process—or perhaps even that faith does not really belong to one until the process is complete. That is in fact the kind of investigation against which many of Kierkegaard's protests appear to be directed, and he would be on firmer ground in holding that while the investigation lasts,[4] the investigator cannot have a fully confident religious faith.

Notes

1. Page references in parentheses are to Søren Kierkegaard, *Concluding Unscientific Postscript*, trans. D. F. Swenson and W. Lowrie (Princeton, N.J.: Princeton University Press, 1941).

2. See chapter 2 in the present volume.

3. Such a view is adopted by Richard Swinburne, *Faith and Reason* (Oxford: Clarendon Press, 1981), chapters 1 and 4.

4. Kierkegaard maintains, of course, that on its own terms, investigation is never complete. Here the second interpretation of the Approximation Argument merges with what, in my earlier paper, I called "the Postponement Argument"— though here it is emotional confidence rather than voluntary commitment that is seen as postponed.

PART TWO

THE PROBLEM
OF EVIL

4

Must God Create the Best?

Many philosophers and theologians have accepted the following proposition:

> (P) If a perfectly good moral agent created any world at all, it would have to be the very best world that he could create.

The best world that an omnipotent God could create is the best of all logically possible worlds. Accordingly, it has been supposed that if the actual world was created by an omnipotent, perfectly good God, it must be the best of all logically possible worlds.

   In this paper I shall argue that ethical views typical of the Judeo-Christian religious tradition do not require the Judeo-Christian theist to accept (P). He must hold that the actual world is a good world. But he need not maintain that it is the best of all possible worlds, or the best world that God could have made.[1]

   The position which I am claiming that he can consistently hold is that *even if* there is a best among possible worlds, God could create another instead of it, and still be perfectly good. I do not in fact see any good reason to believe that there is a best among possible worlds. Why can't it be that for every possible world there is another that is better? And if there is no maximum degree of perfection among possible worlds, it would be unreasonable to blame God, or think less highly of his goodness, be-

Among the many to whom I am indebted for help in working out the thoughts contained in this paper, and for criticisms of earlier drafts of it, I must mention Marilyn McCord Adams, Richard Brandt, Eric Lerner, the members of my graduate class on theism and ethics in the fall term of 1970 at the University of Michigan, and the editors of the *Philosophical Review*.

cause he created a world less excellent thàn he could have created.[2] But I do not claim to be able to prove that there is no best among possible worlds, and in this essay I shall assume for the sake of argument that there is one.

Whether we accept proposition (*P*) will depend on what we believe are the requirements for perfect goodness. If we apply an act-utilitarian standard of moral goodness, we will have to accept (*P*). For by act-utilitarian standards it is a moral obligation to bring about the best state of affairs that one can. It is interesting to note that the ethics of Leibniz, the best-known advocate of (*P*), is basically utilitarian.[3] In his *Theodicy* (pt. I, sec. 25) he maintains, in effect, that men, because of their ignorance of many of the consequences of their actions, ought to follow a rule-utilitarian code, but that God, being omniscient, must be a perfect act utilitarian in order to be perfectly good.

I believe that utilitarian views are not typical of the Judeo-Christian ethical tradition, although Leibniz is by no means the only Christian utilitarian. In this essay I shall assume that we are working with standards of moral goodness which are not utilitarian. But I shall not try either to show that utilitarianism is wrong or to justify the standards that I take to be more typical of Judeo-Christian religious ethics. To attempt either of these tasks would unmanageably enlarge the scope of the paper. What I can hope to establish here is therefore limited to the claim that the rejection of (*P*) is consistent with Judeo-Christian religious ethics.

Assuming that we are not using utilitarian standards of moral goodness, I see only two types of reason that could be given for (*P*). (1) It might be claimed that a creator would necessarily wrong someone (violate someone's rights), or be less kind to someone than a perfectly good moral agent must be, if he knowingly created a less excellent world instead of the best that he could. Or (2) it might be claimed that even if no one would be wronged or treated unkindly by the creation of an inferior world, the creator's choice of an inferior world must manifest a defect of character. I will argue against the first of these claims in section II. Then I will suggest, in section III, that God's choice of a less excellent world could be accounted for in terms of his grace, which is considered a virtue rather than a defect of character in Judeo-Christian ethics. A counterexample, which is the basis for the most persuasive objections to my position that I have encountered, will be considered in sections IV and V.

II

Is there someone *to* whom a creator would have an obligation to create the best world he could? Is there someone whose rights would be violated, or who would be treated unkindly, if the creator created a less excellent world? Let us suppose that our creator is God, and that there does not exist any being, other than himself, which he has not created. It follows that if God has wronged anyone, or been unkind to anyone, in creating whatever world he has created, this must be one of his own creatures. To which of his creatures, then, might God have an obligation to create the best of all possible worlds? (For that is the best world he could create.)

Might he have an obligation to the creatures in the best possible world, to create them? Have they been wronged, or even treated unkindly, if God has created a less excellent world, in which they do not exist, instead of creating them? I think not. The difference between actual beings and merely possible beings is of fundamental moral importance here. The moral community consists of actual beings. It is they who have actual rights, and it is to them that there are actual obligations. A merely possible being cannot be (actually) wronged or treated unkindly. A being who never exists is not wronged by not being created, and there is no obligation to any possible being to bring it into existence.

Perhaps it will be objected that we believe we have obligations to future generations, who are not yet actual and may never be actual. We do say such things, but I think what we mean is something like the following. There is not merely a logical possibility, but a probability greater than zero, that future generations will really exist; and *if* they will in fact exist, we will have wronged them if we act or fail to act in certain ways. On this analysis we cannot have an obligation to future generations to bring them into existence.

I argue, then, that God does not have an obligation to the creatures in the best of all possible worlds to create them. If God has chosen to create a world less excellent than the best possible, he has not thereby wronged any creatures whom he has chosen not to create. He has not even been unkind to them. If any creatures are wronged, or treated unkindly, by such a choice of the creator, they can only be creatures that exist in the world he has created.

I think it is fairly plausible to suppose that God could create a world which would have the following characteristics:

(1) None of the individual creatures in it would exist in the best of all possible worlds.

(2) None of the creatures in it has a life which is so miserable on the whole that it would be better for that creature if it had never existed.

(3) Every individual creature in the world is at least as happy on the whole as it would have been in any other possible world in which it could have existed.

It seems obvious that if God creates such a world he does not thereby wrong any of the creatures in it, and does not thereby treat any of them with less than perfect kindness. For none of them would have been benefited by his creating any other world instead.[4]

If there are doubts about the possibility of God's creating such a world, they will probably have to do with the third characteristic. It may be worthwhile to consider two questions, on the supposition (which I am not endorsing) that no possible world less excellent than the best would have characteristic (3), and that God has created a world which has characteristics (1) and (2) but not (3). In such a case must God have wronged one of his creatures? Must he have been less than perfectly kind to one of his creatures?

I do not think it can reasonably be argued that in such a case God must have wronged one of his creatures. Suppose a creature in such a case were to complain that God had violated its rights by creating it in a world in which it was less happy on the whole than it would have been in some other world in which God could have created it. The complaint might express a claim to special treatment: "God ought to have created *me* in more favorable circumstances (even though that would involve his creating some *other* creature in less favorable circumstances than he could have created it in)." Such a complaint would not be reasonable, and would not establish that there had been any violation of the complaining creature's rights.

Alternatively, the creature might make the more principled complaint, "God has wronged me by not following the principle of refraining from creating any world in which there is a creature that would have been happier in another world he could have made." This also is an unreasonable complaint. For if God followed the stated principle, he would not create any world that lacked characteristic (3). And we are assuming that no world less excellent than the best possible would have characteristic (3). It follows that if God acted on the stated principle he would not create any world less excellent than the best possible. But the complaining creature would not exist in the best of all possible worlds; for we are assuming that this creature exists in a world which has characteristic (1). The complaining creature, therefore, would never have existed if God had followed the principle that is urged in the complaint. There could not possibly be any advantage to this creature from God's having followed that principle; and the creature has not been wronged by God's not following the principle. (It would not be better for the creature if it had never existed; for we are assuming that the world God created has characteristic (2).)

The question of whether in the assumed case God must have been unkind to one of his creatures is more complicated than the question of whether he must have wronged one of them. In fact it is too complicated to be discussed adequately here. I will just make three observations about it.

The first is that it is no clearer that the best of all possible worlds would possess characteristic (3) than that some less excellent world would possess it. In fact it has often been supposed that the best possible world might not possess it. The problem we are now discussing can therefore arise also for those who believe that God has created the best of all possible worlds.

My second observation is that if kindness to a person is the same as a tendency to promote his happiness, God has been less than perfectly (completely, unqualifiedly) kind to any creature whom he could have made somewhat happier than he has made it. (I shall not discuss here whether kindness to a person is indeed the same as a tendency to promote his happiness; they are at least closely related.)

But in the third place I would observe that such qualified kindness (if that is what it is) toward some creatures is consistent with God's being perfectly good, and with his being very kind to all his creatures. It is consistent with his being very kind to all his creatures because he may have prepared for all of them a very satisfying existence even though some of them might have been slightly happier in some other possible world. It is consistent with his being perfectly good because even a perfectly good moral agent may be led, by other considerations of sufficient weight, to qualify his kindness or beneficence toward some person. It has sometimes been held that a perfectly good God might cause or permit a person to have less happiness than he might otherwise have had, in order to punish him, or to avoid interfering with the freedom of another person, or in order to create the best of all possible worlds. I would suggest that the desire to create and love all of a certain group of possible creatures (assuming that all of them would have satisfying lives on the whole) might be an adequate ground for a perfectly good God to create them, even if his creating *all* of them must have the result that some of them are less happy than they might otherwise have been. And they need not be the best of all possible creatures, or included in the best of all possible worlds, in order for this qualification of his kindness to be consistent with his perfect goodness. The desire to create *those* creatures is as legitimate a ground for him to qualify his kindness toward some, as the desire to create the best of all possible worlds. This suggestion seems to me to be in keeping with the aspect of the Judeo-Christian moral ideal which will be discussed in section III.

These matters would doubtless have to be discussed more fully if we were considering whether the *actual* world can have been created by a perfectly good God. For our present purposes, however, enough may have been said—especially since, as I have noted, it seems a plausible assumption that God could make a world having characteristics (1), (2), and (3). In that case he could certainly make a less excellent world than the best of all possible worlds without wronging any of his creatures or failing in kindness to any of them. (I have, of course, *not* been arguing that there is *no* way in which God could wrong anyone or be less kind to anyone than a perfectly good moral agent must be.)

III

Plato is one of those who held that a perfectly good creator would make the very best world he could. He thought that if the creator chose to make a world less good than he could have made, that could be understood only in terms of some defect in the creator's character. Envy is the defect that Plato suggests.[5] It may be thought that the creation of a world inferior to the best that he could make would manifest a defect in the creator's character even if no one were thereby wronged or treated unkindly. For the perfectly good moral agent must not only be kind and refrain from violating the rights of others, but must also have other virtues. For instance, he must be noble, generous, high-minded, and free from envy. He must satisfy the moral ideal.

There are differences of opinion, however, about what is to be included in the moral ideal. One important element in the Judeo-Christian moral ideal is *grace*. For present purposes, grace may be defined as a disposition to love which is not dependent on the merit of the person loved. The gracious person loves without worrying about whether the person he loves is worthy of his love. Or perhaps it would be better to say that the gracious person sees what is valuable in the person he loves, and does not worry about whether it is more or less valuable than what could be found in someone else he might have loved. In the Judeo-Christian tradition it is typically believed that grace is a virtue which God does have and men ought to have.

A God who is gracious with respect to creating might well choose to create and love less excellent creatures than he could have chosen. This is not to suggest that grace in creation consists in a preference for imperfection as such. God could have chosen to create the best of all possible creatures, and still have been gracious in choosing them. God's graciousness in creation does not imply that the creatures he has chosen to create must be less excellent than the best possible. It implies, rather, that even if they are the best possible creatures, that is not the ground for his choosing them. And it implies that there is nothing in God's nature or character which would require him to act on the principle of choosing the best possible creatures to be the object of his creative powers.[6]

Grace, as I have described it, is not part of everyone's moral ideal. For instance, it was not part of Plato's moral ideal. The thought that it may be the expression of a virtue, rather than a defect of character, in a creator, *not* to act on the principle of creating the best creatures he possibly could, is quite foreign to Plato's ethical viewpoint. But I believe that thought is not at all foreign to a Judeo-Christian ethical viewpoint.

This interpretation of the Judeo-Christian tradition is confirmed by the religious and devotional attitudes toward God's creation which prevail in the tradition. People who worship God do not normally praise him for his moral rectitude and good judgment in creating *us*. They thank God for their existence as for an undeserved personal favor. Religious writings frequently deprecate the intrinsic worth of human beings, considered apart from God's love for them, and express surprise that God should concern himself with them at all.

> When I look at thy heavens, the work of thy fingers, the
>   moon and the stars which thou hast established;
> What is man that thou art mindful of him, and the son of
>   man that thou dost care for him?
> Yet thou hast made him little less than God, and dost crown
>   him with glory and honor.
> Thou hast given him dominion over the works of thy hands;
>   thou hast put all things under his feet (Psalm 8:3–6).

Such utterances seem quite incongruous with the idea that God created us because if he had not he would have failed to bring about the best possible state of affairs. They suggest that God has created human beings and made them dominant on this planet although he could have created intrinsically better states of affairs instead.

I believe that in the Judeo-Christian tradition the typical religious attitude (or at any rate the attitude typically encouraged) toward the fact of our existence is something like the following. "I am glad that I exist, and I thank God for the life he has given me. I am also glad that other people exist, and I thank God for them. Doubtless there could be more excellent creatures than we. But I believe that God, in his grace, created us and loves us; and I accept that gladly and gratefully." (Such an attitude need not be complacent; for the task of struggling against certain evils may be seen as precisely a part of the life that the religious person is to accept and be glad in.) When people who have or endorse such an attitude say that God is perfectly good, we will not take them as committing themselves to the view that God is the kind of being who would not create any other world than the best possible. For they regard grace as an important part of perfect goodness.

IV

On more than one occasion when I have argued for the positions I have taken in sections II and III, a counterexample of the following sort has been proposed. It is the case of a person who, knowing that he intends to conceive a child and that a certain drug invariably causes severe mental retardation in children conceived by those who have taken it, takes the drug and conceives a severely retarded child. We all, I imagine, have a strong inclination to say that such a person has done something wrong. It is objected to me that our moral intuitions in this case (presumably including the moral intuitions of religious Jews and Christians) are inconsistent with the views I have advanced above. It is claimed that consistency requires me to abandon those views unless I am prepared to make moral judgments that none of us are in fact willing to make.

I will try to meet these objections. I will begin by stating the case in some detail, in the most relevant form I can think of. Then I will discuss objections based on it. In this section I will discuss an objection against what I have said in section II, and a more general objection against the rejection of proposition (P) will be discussed in section V.

Let us call this case (A). A certain couple become so interested in retarded children that they develop a strong desire to have a retarded child of their own—to love it, to help it realize its potentialities (such as they are) to the full, to see that it is as happy as it can be. (For some reason it is impossible for them to *adopt* such a child.) They act on their desire. They take a drug which is known to cause damaged genes and abnormal chromosome structure in reproductive cells, resulting in severe mental retardation of children conceived by those who have taken it. A severely retarded child is conceived and born. They lavish affection on the child. They have ample means, so that they are able to provide for special needs, and to insure that others will never be called on to pay for the child's support. They give themselves unstintedly, and do develop the child's capacities as much as possible. The child is, on the whole, happy, though incapable of many of the higher intellectual, aesthetic, and social joys.

It suffers some pains and frustrations, of course, but does not feel miserable on the whole.

The first objection founded on this case is based, not just on the claim that the parents have done something wrong (which I certainly grant), but on the more specific claim that they have *wronged the child*. I maintained, in effect, in section II that a creature has not been wronged by its creator's creating it if both of the following conditions are satisfied.[7] (4) The creature is not, on the whole, so miserable that it would be better for him if he had never existed. (5) No being who came into existence in better or happier circumstances would have been the same individual as the creature in question. If we apply an analogous principle to the parent-child relationship in case (A), it would seem to follow that the retarded child has not been wronged by its parents. Condition (4) is satisfied: The child is happy rather than miserable on the whole. And condition (5) also seems to be satisfied. For the retardation in case (A), as described, is not due to prenatal injury but to the genetic constitution of the child. Any normal child the parents might have conceived (indeed any normal child at all) would have had a different genetic constitution, and would therefore have been a different person, from the retarded child they actually did conceive. But—it is objected to me—we do regard the parents in case (A) as having wronged the child, and therefore we cannot consistently accept the principle that I maintained in section II.

My reply is that if conditions (4) and (5) are really satisfied the child cannot have been wronged by its parents' taking the drug and conceiving it. If we think otherwise we are being led, perhaps by our emotions, into a confusion. If the child is not worse off than if it had never existed, and if *its* never existing would have been a sure consequence of its not having been brought into existence as retarded, I do not see how *its* interests can have been injured, or *its* rights violated, by the parents' bringing it into existence as retarded.

It is easy to understand how the parents might come to feel that they had wronged the child. They might come to feel guilty (and rightly so), and the child would provide a focus for the guilt. Moreover, it would be easy, psychologically, to assimilate case (A) to cases of culpability for prenatal injury, in which it is more reasonable to think of the child as having been wronged.[8] And we often think very carelessly about counterfactual personal identity, asking ourselves questions of doubtful intelligibility, such as, "What if I had been born in the Middle Ages?" It is very easy to fail to consider the objection, "But that would not have been the same person."

It is also possible that an inclination to say that the child has been wronged may be based, at least in part, on a doubt that conditions (4) and (5) are really satisfied in case (A). Perhaps one is not convinced that in real life the parents could ever have a reasonable confidence that the child would be happy rather than miserable. Maybe it will be doubted that a few changes in chromosome structure, and the difference between damaged and undamaged genes, are enough to establish that the retarded child is a different person from any normal child that the couple could have had. Of course, if conditions (4) and (5) are not satisfied, the case does not constitute a counterexample to my claims in section II. But I would not rest any of the weight of my argument on doubts about the satisfaction of the conditions in case (A), because I think it is plausible to suppose that they would be satisfied in case (A) or in some very similar case.

V

Even if the parents in case (A) have not wronged the child, I assume that they have done something wrong. It may be asked *what* they have done wrong, or *why* their action is regarded as wrong. And these questions may give rise to an objection, not specifically to what I said in section II, but more generally to my rejection of proposition (P). For it may be suggested that what is wrong about the action of the parents in case (A) is that they have violated the following principle:

(Q) It is wrong to bring into existence, knowingly, a being less excellent than one could have brought into existence.[9]

If we accept this principle we must surely agree that it would be wrong for a creator to make a world that was less excellent than the best he could make, and therefore that a perfectly good creator would not do such a thing. In other words, (Q) implies (P).

I do not think (Q) is a very plausible principle. It is not difficult to think of counterexamples to it.

Case (B): A man breeds goldfish, thereby bringing about their existence. We do not normally think it is wrong, or even prima facie wrong, for a man to do this, even though he could equally well have brought about the existence of more excellent beings, more intelligent and capable of higher satisfactions. (He could have bred dogs or pigs, for example.) The deliberate breeding of human beings of subnormal intelligence is morally offensive; the deliberate breeding of species far less intelligent than retarded human children is not morally offensive.

Case (C): Suppose it has been discovered that if intending parents take a certain drug before conceiving a child, they will have a child whose abnormal genetic consitution will give it vastly superhuman intelligence and superior prospects of happiness. Other things being equal, would it be wrong for intending parents to have normal children instead of taking the drug? There may be considerable disagreement of moral judgment about this. I do not think that parents who chose to have normal children rather than take the drug would be doing anything wrong, nor that they would necessarily be manifesting any weakness or defect of moral character. Parents' choosing to have a normal rather than a superhuman child would not, at any rate, elicit the strong and universal or almost universal disapproval that would be elicited by the action of the parents in case (A). Even with respect to the offspring of human beings, the principle we all confidently endorse is not that it is wrong to bring about, knowingly and voluntarily, the procreation of offspring less excellent than could have been procreated, but that it is wrong to bring about, knowingly and voluntarily, the procreation of a human offspring which is deficient by comparison with normal human beings.

Such counterexamples as these suggest that our disapproval of the action of the parents in case (A) is not based on principle (Q), but on a less general and more plausible principle such as the following:

> (R) It is wrong for human beings to cause, knowingly and voluntarily, the procreation of an offspring of human parents which is notably deficient, by comparison with normal human beings, in mental or physical capacity.

One who rejects (Q) while maintaining (R) might be held to face a problem of explanation. It may seem arbitrary to maintain such a specific moral principle as (R), unless one can explain it as based on a more general principle, such as (Q). I believe, however, that principle (R) might well be explained in something like the following way in a theological ethics in the Judeo-Christian tradition, consistently with the rejection of (Q) and (P).[10]

God, in his grace, has chosen to have human beings among his creatures. In creating us he has certain intentions about the qualities and goals of human life. He has these intentions for us, not just as individuals, but as members of a community which in principle includes the whole human race. And his intentions for human beings as such extend to the offspring (if any) of human beings. Some of these intentions are to be realized by human voluntary action, and it is our duty to act in accordance with them.

It seems increasingly possible for human voluntary action to influence the genetic constitution of human offspring. The religious believer in the

Judeo-Christian tradition will want to be extremely cautious about this. For he is to be thankful that we exist as the beings we are, and will be concerned lest he bring about the procreation of human offspring who would be deficient in their capacity to enter fully into the purposes that God has for human beings as such. We are not God. We are his creatures, and we belong to him. Any offspring we have will belong to him in a much more fundamental way than they can belong to their human parents. We have not the right to try to have as our offspring just any kind of being whose existence might on the whole be pleasant and of some value (for instance, a being of very low intelligence but highly specialized for the enjoyment of aesthetic pleasures of smell and taste). If we do intervene to affect the genetic constitution of human offspring, it must be in ways which seem likely to make them *more* able to enter fully into what we believe to be the purposes of God for human beings as such. The deliberate procreation of children deficient in mental or physical capacity would be an intervention which could hardly be expected to result in offspring more able to enter fully into God's purposes for human life. It would therefore be sinful, and inconsistent with a proper respect for the human life which God has given us.

On this view of the matter, our obligation to refrain from bringing about the procreation of deficient human offspring is rooted in our obligation to God, as his creatures, to respect his purposes for human life. In adopting this theological rationale for the acceptance of principle (*R*), one in no way commits oneself to proposition (*P*). For one does not base (*R*) on any principle to the effect that one must always try to bring into existence the most excellent things that one can. And the claim that, because of his intentions for human life, we have an obligation to God not to try to have as our offspring beings of certain sorts does not imply that it would be wrong for God to create such beings in other ways. Much less does it imply that it would be wrong for God to create a world less excellent than the best possible.

In this essay I have argued that a creator would not necessarily wrong anyone, or be less kind to anyone than a perfectly good moral agent must be, if he created a world of creatures who would not exist in the best world he could make. I have also argued that from the standpoint of Judeo-Christian religious ethics, a creator's choice of a less excellent world need not be regarded as manifesting a defect of character. It could be understood in terms of his *grace*, which (in that ethics) is considered an important part of perfect goodness. In this way I think the rejection of proposition (*P*) can be seen to be congruous with the attitude of gratitude and respect for human life as God's gracious gift which is encouraged in the Judeo-Christian religious tradition. And that attitude (rather than any belief that one ought to bring into existence only the best beings one can) can be seen as a basis for the disapproval of the deliberate procreation of deficient human offspring.

Notes

1. What I am saying in this paper is obviously relevant to the problem of evil. But I make no claim to be offering a complete theodicy here.

2. Leibniz held (in his *Theodicy*, pt. 1, sec. 8) that if there were no best among possible worlds, a perfectly good God would have created nothing at all. But Leibniz is mistaken if he supposes that in this way God could avoid choosing an alternative less excellent than others he could have chosen. For the existence of no created world at all would surely be a less excellent state of affairs than the existence of some of the worlds that God could have created.

3. See Gaston Grua, *Jurisprudence universelle et théodicée selon Leibniz* (Paris, 1953), pp. 210–18.

4. Perhaps I can have a right to something which would not benefit me (e.g., if it has been promised to me). But if there are such nonbeneficial rights, I do not see any plausible reason for supposing that a right not to be created could be among them.

5. *Timaeus*, 29E–30A.

*6. This argument may be stated more adequately as follows. It would be inconsistent to hold both (i) that grace, as a disposition to love that is not dependent on the merit of the beloved, is one of the best virtues, and (ii) that a creator's choosing to create and love less excellent creatures than he could have chosen must necessarily manifest some imperfection in the creator's character. For (ii) can hardly be asserted except on the basis of the assumption (iii) that it would be an imperfection to choose objects to be created and loved on any basis other than merit; and (iii) is a denial of (i).

I put the argument, this time, in terms of "imperfection" rather than "defect" because I agree with Philip L. Quinn's claim that a being could be free of moral defects without being morally perfect or "superlatively good" as God is supposed to be [Quinn, "God, Moral Perfection, and Possible Worlds," a critique of the present paper, in *God: The Contemporary Discussion*, ed. Frederick Sontag and M. Darrol Bryant (New York: Rose of Sharon Press, 1982), p. 208f.]. Quinn's illuminating essay leaves me unconvinced on the main issue, however. He thinks it is "a fairly obvious truth" (iv) that necessarily, "if x is an omnipotent moral agent and x actualizes w'" (a morally less excellent world than x could have actualized), then it is possible for there to be "a better moral agent" than x is in w' (p. 213). This does not seem at all obvious to me. It articulates a consequentialist position on the ethics of creation. Moreover, (iv) is very similar to (iii), and like (iii), it seems out of keeping with (i), which I believe to be true.

Why must the excellence of a creator, or even of the creative action, be measured by the excellence of the creation, if love that is not dependent on the merit of its object is a great virtue?

7. I am not holding that these are necessary conditions, but only that they are jointly sufficient conditions, for a creature's not being wronged by its creator's creating it. I have numbered these conditions in such a way as to avoid confusion with the numbered characteristics of worlds in section II.

8. It may be questioned whether even the prenatally injured child is the same person as any unimpaired child that might have been born. I am inclined to think it is the same person. At any rate there is *more* basis for regarding it as the same person as a possible normal child than there is for so regarding a child with abnormal genetic constitution.

9. Anyone who was applying this principle to human actions would doubtless insert an "other things being equal" clause. But let us ignore that, since such a clause would presumably provide no excuse for an agent who was deciding an issue so important as what world to create.

10. I am able to give here, of course, only a very incomplete sketch of a theological position on the issue of "biological engineering."

5

Existence, Self-interest, and the Problem of Evil

Leibniz once wrote, "You will insist that you can complain, why didn't God give you more strength [to resist temptation]. I answer: if He had done that, you would not be you, for He would not have produced you but another creature" (Leibniz, 1948: 327). This can be understood in terms of Leibniz's opinion that every possible individual exists in only one possible world. Since the least difference in events makes a different possible world, it follows that none of us actual individuals could have existed if any actual evil failed to occur. On this view it seems that we are benefited by each and every evil that happens, if our existence is a good to us, and that God is good to us in permitting them, since we could not exist without them.

If all evils that happen are good for the individuals to whom they happen, that is reason enough for a perfectly good being to cause or permit them. Indeed it provides a complete theodicy. Leibniz would not think so, since he thought that a perfectly good God must create only the best of all possible worlds. I have argued elsewhere (Adams, 1972 [see chapter 4 in this volume]) that Leibniz was wrong about that, but I am no more able than he to accept this complete theodicy. For I think his thesis that each individual exists in only one possible world is quite implausible.

But it is true (as I shall argue) that we would not be ourselves without

Only a little remains in this paper from "Self-Identity, Self-Interest, and the Problem of Evil," which I read at the Western Division of the A.P.A. in 1974 but never published. Marilyn McCord Adams, Robert Audi, Derek Parfit, Alvin Plantinga, and Keith Yandell read that paper and gave me extensive comments which helped greatly in preparing this one. I am also indebted to William Hasker and Peter McAllen for comments on some of the points in the earlier paper. Much of the work for the present paper was supported by a fellowship from the National Endowment for the Humanities, which is gratefully acknowledged.

many and great evils. I will try to show that although it does not yield a complete theodicy, this fact has three contributions to make to a response to the problem of evil.

I. We Owe Our Existence to Prior Evils

The first contribution is a proof that if our lives will have been worth living on the whole, we cannot have been injured by most of the evils that preceded our coming to be, and God has not been unfair to us in causing or permitting them, although (or indeed because) they have shaped our lives. Leibniz makes this point too, without presupposing anything implausible about trans-world identity. To those who are angry at God for not replacing Adam and Eve, after their fall, with better creatures, "so that the stain should not be transmitted to their posterity," he replies that

> if God had thus removed sin, a very different series of things, very different combinations of circumstances and people and marriages, and very different people would have emerged, and hence if sin had been taken away or extinguished they themselves would not be in the world. And therefore they have no reason to be angry at Adam or Eve for sinning, much less at God for permitting the sin, since they ought rather to set their own existence to the credit of this very toleration of sins (Leibniz, 1967: 128).

Leibniz goes on to compare the complainers with someone of half-noble birth who is "angry with his father for marrying a lower-born wife, not thinking that another person would be in the world instead of him if his father had married a different wife."

Leibniz is right about this. Even if I could have existed without some of the evils of the actual world (for example, those that will occur tomorrow), I could not have existed without past evils that have profoundly affected the course of human history, and especially the "combinations of . . . people and marriages." We do not have to go all the way back to Adam and Eve to find evils that were necessary for our existence. If it had not been for the First World War, for example, my parents would probably never have met and married, and I would not have been born. A multiplicity of interacting chances, including evils great and small, affect which people mate, which gametes find each other, and which children come into being. The farther back we go in history, the larger the proportion of evils to which we owe our being; for the causal nexus relevant to our individual genesis widens as we go back in time. We almost certainly would never have existed had there not been just about the same evils as actually occurred in a large part of human history.

I think it follows that God has not wronged *us* in causing or permitting those evils, if he is going to see to it that we will have lives that are worth living on the whole. What right could I have against satisfying the necessary conditions of my coming to be, and how could I be injured by satisfying them, if my life will be worth living? It seems also to follow, as Leibniz notes, that we have not been injured by humans, such as Adam and Eve, who perpetrated evils that were necessary for our existence.

Of course it is not we but our ancestors whom one is most tempted to regard as wronged by evil *events* that preceded our coming to be. But those events have consequences in our own time that appear harmful to us. And more broadly, we may be tempted to complain, on our own account, of evil *conditions,* or features of the natural and historical order, that are far older than we are. By nature and historical situation human beings are subject to disease and death, exposed to earthquake and hurricane, and surrounded by potential enemies. Had it not been so, we would never have existed. We may ask why God does not intervene in the natural and historical process in our lifetime to protect us from the consequences of these facts. But it is important for theodicy to realize that that is what is being asked. If we have lives that are worth living on the whole, we cannot have been wronged by the creation of a natural and historical order that has these features; for we could not have existed without them.

It will be objected that even if evils were *causally* necessary for our existence, an *omnipotent* deity could have created us without them, and may have wronged us by not doing so. But I think that is wrong, for three reasons.

(1) God's reasons for creating us individually are presumably bound up with his other plans for the world, which would have been different if he had prevented the evils in question. I see no reason why he would or should have created us in particular if he had prevented them—and hence no reason why he has wronged us by not doing so.

(2) I do not think it would have been possible, in the metaphysical or broadly logical sense that is relevant here, for me to exist in a world that differed much from the actual world in the evils occurring in the parts of history that contain my roots. We are sure that once begun, my life could have continued in many different ways that it actually did not, and would still have been mine. But I think that case is at least close to being the only one in which it is intuitively clear that I could have existed in circumstances very different from those that actually obtain. My identity is established by my beginning. It has been suggested that no one who was not produced from the same individual egg and sperm cells as I was could have been me (cf. Kripke, 1974: 312–4). If so, the identity of those

gametes presumably depends in turn on their beginnings and on the identity of my parents, which depends on the identity of the gametes from which they came, and so on. It seems to me implausible to suppose that the required identities could have been maintained through generations in which the historical context differed radically from the actual world by the omission of many, or important, evils. Even if the identity of the parents be presupposed, could it be the same individual sperm cell, and not just one like it, originating in such a different context?

(3) Even if I could, metaphysically or logically, have existed without most past evils and their consequences in my experience, I doubt that that existence could have been mine in such a way as to matter much from the point of view of my self-interest, because it would not bear what I shall call in section III "the self-interest relation" to my actual life.

If this argument is to establish that God has not wronged any created person by allowing evils that were necessary for that person's existence, it obviously must be assumed that every created person will have, in the end and on the whole, a life history that is good for him, or at least worth living (unless perhaps he has brought something worse on himself through some free and commensurate fault of his own). This assumption is normally a part of theistic faith. Indeed it is one of the principal things that such faith has to say about the problem of evil. Given the apparent unhappiness of some people's lives between birth and death, the assumption seems unlikely to be true unless there is life after death, at least for some of us. But that too is commonly a part of theistic faith. We should not expect theodicy to be unaffected by the addition or subtraction of such eschatological beliefs. Without them, indeed, the traditional belief in divine omnipotence that forms part of most formulations of the problem of evil loses much of its motivation. For the possibility of miracle is probably the biggest stake that religion has in the belief that God's power is not subject to the laws of nature. And resurrection and final salvation from natural evil are the chief miracle, of which any others believed in are foretastes.

II. The Ethics of Creation

What goals should we have for the future of the world, and how should we pursue them? These questions provide us with interesting analogies to moral issues about God's decisions in creating. In evaluating actions that shape the future we can consider (1) the interests of future individuals, (2) the interests of individuals that now exist, and (3) the kind of society to which the actions will lead. These considerations will illuminate (1) a possible objection to the argument of section I, (2) the second contribution made to theodicy by the fact that we owe our existence to evils, and (3) the structure of a theodicy to which that fact contributes.

(1) The argument of section I has the consequence that considerations of what would be advantageous, or just, to members of future generations give less guidance for action than is commonly thought. For almost every action or social decision that has any effect at all on individuals who will be born several years later affects their identity. An energy policy, for example, would affect people's lives pervasively—where they go, when they go, how far they go, how they earn their living, how they spend their time. And these things in turn would affect their reproductive history—whom they marry, when they conceive, and therefore what children they have. After at most a few decades, virtually no individual would be born who would have been born without the policy. Suppose that we continue to squander the earth's resources, leaving no oil or coal at all for those who will live in the year 2140. Our descendants then may be tempted to think we have been unfair to them in using more than our share. But if their lives are worth living it would not have been better for them if we had followed a policy of fuel conservation. For they would not have existed in that case. It is hard to see how they can have been injured or treated unjustly by our not acting in a way that would have prevented their existence.

If it followed further that there is nothing wrong with squandering the earth's resources, that consequence would discredit my argument. But it does not follow. Squandering may even be unfair to future individuals if it increases the probability of their having lives so miserable that one would wish for their sake that they had not existed. Theists may believe that God will not permit such a result in the long run, but we probably have no right to presume on his goodness in this context. We should try not to have descendants who will have reason to be sorry they ever existed. But this principle alone will hardly provide adequate guidance for decisions that shape the future. The chief reason why we ought to conserve is to be found in the concern we ought to have about the kind of society to which our actions will lead in the future.

(2) We can see here that it would be a mistake to suppose that we ought to do *whatever* is best for those persons who could be individually disadvantaged by our decision, who will be chiefly or exclusively persons that now exist (cf. Parfit, 1984: chap. 16). For it is sometimes right to impose net costs on existing individuals for the sake of a fairly distant future, even though no future individual would be disadvantaged by our not paying the costs. It might be, for example, that we ought to conserve

coal as well as other fuels, for the sake of the twenty-second century, to the net disadvantage of persons now living, even if (for reasons indicated above) no twenty-second century individual would be disadvantaged by our using more coal.

Similarly I think a society (or the whole human race) might well be justified in following a policy designed to perpetuate itself by maintaining an appropriate population size even though it was correctly believed that it would be advantageous, on average, to existing members of the society to let it die out gradually, over several generations, by reducing the birth rate and the attendant economic burdens. Perhaps only a minority want to be parents, and they are willing to have enough children to maintain the population, but only if the whole community takes responsibility for the children's education and economic support. Naturally the costs will be felt more keenly by some existing individuals than by others, even if the tax policies are as fair as possible. But if the policies have been in effect for several generations, any charge that it is unfair to impose such a burden on present individuals at all can be answered, not only by the necessity of the burden for a desirable goal of the society, but also by the following argument.

None of the present members of the society would have existed without the actual population policy (for reasons that the reader should by now be able to supply). Even those who bear the heaviest net disutility from its continuation will therefore have benefited by the policy on the whole, provided their lives are worth living. They owe their existence to similar burdens borne earlier by others. This is a reason for thinking that continuing the policy is not unfair to them. Not that discontinuing the policy would be unfair to the children who would not be born; for only those who at some time exist can be wronged, harmed, or badly treated. But perhaps we can say that it would be unfair to the community, and its communal interest in perpetuating itself, for one of its members to demand that this practice, to which he owes his existence, should be stopped when it is advantageous to him to stop it.

This argument serves to introduce, by analogy, the second contribution made to theodicy by the fact that we owe our existence to evils. Suppose, as I think the theist should believe, that our existence will be a great good to us on the whole (except perhaps by our own fault). We have no reason to think that any evils that happen to us are unprecedented; others have suffered evils of similar magnitude before us. If one of us bears an unequal burden of evil, so did many of our ancestors. We have reason to be glad, for our own sakes, that God has not generally followed a policy of not permitting such evils, for we would never have existed if he had.

So it hardly seems unfair to us that he has not followed that policy in general. But neither does it seem to be a demand of fairness that God should end the policy that has benefited us, and cease pursuing whatever goals he has been pursuing in the way he has been pursuing them, once it becomes convenient for our generation that he should change. This is a reason for thinking, not only that we are not wronged by prior evils that were necessary for our coming to be, but also that God is not unfair to us in letting evils befall us in our own lifetime.

I would not claim that this argument provides a reply to all possible accusations against God's justice, but only against those whose burden is that he causes or permits people to suffer, in unequal measure, evils that are not individually advantageous on balance to them or to other creatures that already exist at the time of the evil. If God is accused, for example, of breaking a promise, or of judging unjustly, those charges must be dealt with in some other way.

It is also important to the argument that the evils be necessary for an end that is good and of which the benefits already received by those who suffer the evils are in some way instances. If the end were not good, or if the benefits already received were accidental consequences or mere means in relation to it, the argument would lose much or all of its force. For instance, if your life was accidentally saved by the workings of a policy that prevented you from traveling on a flight that crashed, that has no tendency to rebut charges that continuing the policy is unfair to you. But the creation of persons such as we are is presumably among the ends for whose sake God lets evils happen. And since a perfectly good being would not cause or permit evils for no point at all, theists should surely believe that the reason why God causes or permits them is that his permitting them is necessary (in a broadly logical sense) for goods that are sufficiently great.

(3) We may get some light on what theodicy should say about those goods by returning to the question of the kind of society to which we should hope our actions will lead in the further future. Many will say, of course, that it ought to be *the best* society, as measured by the total or average of happiness or by some other criterion. But it seems to me that this is not in general obligatory, and that we would not necessarily manifest any moral deficiency in striving for a kind of future society that is good but not the best we could achieve. I would quite strongly prefer the preservation of the human race, for example, to its ultimate replacement by a more excellent species, and think none the worse of myself for the preference. Similarly I think it may be a good thing, and no sign of imperfection, for someone to favor the preservation and internal de-

velopment of a particular civilization (e.g., Chinese or Western) or national culture (e.g., Welsh) though he knows that such a continuation will occupy space and resources from which something even more excellent could grow instead. A good person accepts significant costs—and sometimes, where he has a right to, imposes them on others—for the sake of what he loves, and not only for the sake of what is best.

Another example is the love of political or civil liberties, in defense of which one may rightly be willing to die, and to cause some hardships to other people—perhaps even to kill an unjust aggressor. (Even nonviolent resistance normally imposes costs on the foe.) In this one need not accept the extremely questionable assumption that people will be happier in a free than in a totalitarian society. And one also need not believe that the liberties one defends are objectively better than the ends (perhaps ecological and communitarian ends) that might be more adequately served in a less free society. It is enough that the type of society for which one strives is good, and worth loving.

The application to God is obvious, and provides occasion for a thumbnail sketch of a general approach to theodicy in which our owing our existence to evils takes its place. I have argued elsewhere (Adams, 1972 [see chapter 4 in this volume]) that God could be perfectly good and still have created a world less excellent than the best that was possible for him. Here it can be added that he could be perfectly good and cause or permit *evils* that are necessary for good ends that he loves, even if those goods are not the best states of affairs obtainable by him.

That there are such goods for which God's causing or permitting the evils that happen was necessary, I think the theist must believe. But if he is wise, he will not claim to know in detail what they are, or to see enough of the history of the world, and of each individual life, to see the point of everything God does or allows. It is part of the task of theodicy, nonetheless, to say something about the sort of goods for which God's causing or permitting evils might be necessary. Among the familiar examples that may have some part to play are moral responsibility before God; the exercise of fortitude, compassion, and forgiveness; and occasions for self-sacrifice and triumph over temptation. I am suggesting, in effect, that the existence of creatures such as we are, with the characteristic, subtle, and sometimes bittersweet values and beauties of human life, may also be a good of the relevant sort that is loved by God.

It is not enough, however, in vindicating the goodness of an action, even assuming good motives, to show that it was necessary for a good end. As a non-consequentialist in ethics, I would add that it is not enough even if the good end is the best total state of affairs that can be obtained.

It may still be morally objectionable on grounds of injustice or unkindness to one or more individual persons. Accordingly, it is an additional part of theodicy's task to vindicate God's goodness *to* individuals; and it is chiefly to this part that contributions are made by the fact that we would not be ourselves without many and great evils.

III. Self-identity and Gratitude

A third contribution was promised. It has to do with whether God has been not merely fair, but good to us, in letting evils befall us after we began to exist. Because our identities are established by our beginnings, it cannot plausibly be claimed that any such evils were metaphysically necessary for our existence. But something similar is true. There are evils that happen to people, without which they could, strictly speaking, have existed, but which shape their lives so profoundly that wishing the evils had not occurred would be morally very close to wishing that somebody else had existed instead of those particular people.

The story of Helen Keller (1880–1968) is familiar. Rendered blind and deaf by a fever at the age of nineteen months, she endured great misery until she was taught sign language by touch when she was almost seven. From then on she surmounted the formidable obstacles in her path with remarkable success. She learned to speak several languages, graduated from a distinguished college, and became (deservedly) a celebrity. Though certainly not untouched by pain and sorrow, she seems to have lived a happy and satisfying life.

Would it have been reasonable for Helen Keller, as an adult, to wish, for her own sake, that she had never been blind or deaf? I think not. Let us suppose that she would have had an even better and happier life if her sight and hearing had been spared (though that is not obviously true). But whatever its excellences, that life would not have had one day in it that would have been very like any day of her actual life after the age of nineteen months. Her actual life—in its emotional as well as its sensory qualities, in its skills and projects, and doubtless in much of her person-ality and character—was built around the fact of her blindness and deaf-ness. That other, happier life would have contained few of the particular joys and sorrows, trials and triumphs—in short very little of the concrete content—that she cared about in her actual life. Her never having been blind or deaf would have been very like her never having existed. Why should she wish for that, given that she had reason to be glad she existed?

What we are attached to in ourselves, in a reasonable self-concern, is not just our bare metaphysical identity, but also projects, friendships, and at least some of the most important features of our personal history and character. If our lives are good, we have the same sort of reason to be glad we have had them rather than lives that would have been even better but too thoroughly different, as we have to be glad that we exist and not better and happier people instead of us.

If a possible life contains so little of the concrete content that I care about in my actual life that it should not matter to me that it could, metaphysically, have been mine, let us say that it bears no *self-interest relation* to my actual life. This relation varies with time in two ways.

(1) The earlier a possible life branches off from one's actual life, up to some point in adulthood, the weaker the self-interest relation between them. Possible lives that diverge sharply from Helen Keller's actual life at the age of nineteen months bear no self-interest relation at all to her actual life, with which they share only a period that she hardly remembered. But possible lives that branch off in adolescence or adulthood have enough in common with one's actual life that they are bound to bear some self-interest relation to it.

(2) The strength of the self-interest relation between one's actual life and another life one could have lived is apt to diminish with time. Indeed it would be more accurate to speak of possible lives bearing a strong or weak or no self-interest relation, not to one's actual life without qualification, but to *one's actual life up to a certain time*. You may still think, for example, that the life you had planned or hoped for before an evil befell you ten years ago would have been better than your actual life. Yet you may be so attached to actual projects, friendships, and experiences that would not have been part of that other life that you would *not* now wish to have had it instead of your actual life. There is some self-interest relation between the other life and your actual life up to the present, but it may not be strong enough to give you sufficient reason now to prefer the one you judge to be better. Ten years ago, however, the life you hoped for bore the strongest possible self-interest relation to your actual life up to then, and you had no reason not to prefer it to the life you have now actually had.

This complicates the question whether it is better for *you* that this or that evil happened. It may be preferable for your sake from your present point of view, but not from the point of view you had before it happened. I think the retrospective point of view is not irrelevant to God's goodness. Knowing more about the future than we do, perhaps he can rightly love in advance things that we can love only in retrospect. And provided your actual life is worth living, I do not think he can have wronged you by

not giving you an even better life, if the latter bears no self-interest relation at all to your actual life up to any time at which you would be
capable of considering the question. Still, it is in general what is preferable before the action that is most relevant to the moral perfection of
an agent.

There is another aspect of the problem of evil, however, to which the
retrospective point of view is particularly relevant. In theistic religion we
are supposed to be grateful to God for our lives. But even if we believe
he has acted with perfect goodness, our gratitude may be eclipsed by
bitterness as we wish that we had not suffered various evils. This is commonly regarded as a merely psychological or pastoral version of the problem of evil, but there is a problem for rationality here. What reason have
we not to wish bitterly that we had been given better lives? No doubt the
bitterness is undesirable, but is it also inappropriate or groundless? It is,
if our actual lives are good and bear a weak enough self-interest relation
to the lives we might wish we'd had. For in that case we have reason to
prefer our actual lives. Bitter resentment might be answered by vindicating God's moral perfection, but reasons against bitter wishes must bear
on the preferability of the alternatives.

The retrospective preferability of our actual lives to even better ones
is based, as we have seen, on our attachment to actual projects, friendships, experiences, and other features of our actual lives. Alas, not everyone is able now to love his life in this way. But it is clear that love for
projects, experiences, and friendships that one is engaged in is highly
correlated with happiness. So to the extent the theist believes we shall all
be happy in the end, he may well believe we shall all have reason to
prefer our actual lives to others we could have had.

IV. The Problem of Evil for Atheists

The fact that we owe our existence to evils gives rise to a problem of
evil, not only for theists, but for anyone who loves an actual human individual—himself or anyone else. How is our love for actual human
selves to be reconciled with moral repudiation of the evils that crowd the
pages of history? Are we to wish that neither we nor the evils had existed?

On the one hand, it would be wrong, and terribly callous, for gratitude
at the fact of our own existence to blot out entirely from our lives the
sentiments of sorrow, outrage, and remorse. I have not meant to be defending such a result. Indeed theodicy should probably see our emotional
as well as practical opposition to evils as an important element in the
good for whose sake God lets evils happen.

On the other hand, the destruction of gladness about the existence of human individuals would also be disastrous. Love would be destroyed with it, or at least degraded. If I am not glad at all that you exist, I may feel sorry for you, or be kind to you, or desire you, but my attitude toward you can be at best only a borderline case of love.

Ambivalence is called for, then. But how shall the balance be struck? Shall gladness predominate, or sadness? Theists aspire to a stance in which particular regrets find a place within a more encompassing, and prevailing, gratitude for human lives. And I imagine that all who love would prefer not to wish on the whole that the individuals they love had never existed. We must face, however, the question whether too great a price has been paid for the existence of those human individuals that have come into being. I do not believe we are in a position to answer this question conclusively by research into human history. At any rate the answer that it is worth it all can only be given by faith—and I think it must probably be an eschatological faith.

References

Adams, Robert Merrihew. 1972. "Must God Create the Best?" *Philosophical Review* 81:317–32 [chapter 4 in this volume].

Kripke, Saul A. 1972. "Naming and Necessity." In *Semantics of Natural Language,* ed. Donald Davidson and Gilbert Harman, 253–355, 763–69. Dordrecht: Reidel.

Leibniz, Gottfried Wilhelm. 1967. *Confessio Philosophi.* Edited with German translation and commentary by Otto Saame. Frankfurt: Vittorio Klostermann.

———. 1948. *Textes inédits.* Edited by Gaston Grua. Paris: Presses Universitaires de France.

Parfit, Derek. 1984. *Reasons and Persons.* Oxford: Clarendon Press.

6

Middle Knowledge and the Problem of Evil

If President Kennedy had not been shot, would he have bombed North Vietnam? God only knows. Or does he? Does even he know what Kennedy would have done?

There is a little known but interesting literature on the general issue exemplified by this question. In the 1580s a fierce controversy erupted between the Jesuits and the Dominicans about the relation between God's grace and human free will. The Jesuits held, among other things, that many human actions are free in the sense that their agents are not logically or causally determined to do them. ("Free" will always be used in this sense in the present essay.) How then does God maintain control over human history? Not by causally determining human actions, as the Dominicans seemed to believe,[1] but by causing circumstances in which he knew that we would *freely* act in accordance with his plans. This answer was developed with great ingenuity by Luis de Molina, and defended by other Jesuit theologians, notably by Francisco Suarez. Their theory includes the thesis that God knows with certainty what every possible free creature would freely do in every situation in which that creature could possibly find himself. Such knowledge was called "middle knowledge" by the Jesuits, because they thought it had a middle status between other kinds of knowledge—between God's knowledge of the merely possible and his knowledge of the actual; or between his knowledge of necessary

I am indebted to several, including David Kaplan, and especially David Lewis and Alvin Plantinga, for discussion and for comments on an earlier version of this paper, which was read to an American Philosophical Association symposium. An abstract of the earlier version, "Middle Knowledge," appeared in *The Journal of Philosophy,* 70 (1973), pp. 552–4. Work on the present version was supported by the National Endowment for the Humanities.

truths, which all follow from the divine nature, and his knowledge of his own will and everything that is causally determined by his will.[2]

This paper is about two questions. The first is whether middle knowledge is possible, even for God. I shall argue that it is not, on the ground that conditional propositions of the sort that are supposed to be known by middle knowledge cannot be true. I will examine (in section II) the attempts of Molina and Suarez to explain how God can have middle knowledge; and then (in section III) the account recently offered by Alvin Plantinga, who has reinvented the theory of middle knowledge. Two objections to my position will be discussed in section IV.

The idea of middle knowledge emerges in recent philosophical discussion chiefly because of its relevance to the second question that I shall discuss, which is whether God could have made free creatures who would always have freely done right. More precisely: Could God have brought it about that he had creatures who made free choices, but none of whom ever made wrong choices? The relevance of this question to the problem of evil is obvious and well known. If he could have, why didn't he? If he couldn't have, that's a good enough reason why he didn't. He could not have done it by causally determining the choices of creatures, for then their choices and acts would not have been free in the relevant sense. But it might seem that if God has middle knowledge, he could have secured creatures sinless but free by just creating those that he knew would not sin if allowed to act freely. In section V, therefore, we shall see what light the discussion of middle knowledge may shed on the question whether God could have arranged to have free creatures who were all sinless.

But first of all (in section I), I will try to explain why there seems to me to be a problem about the possibility of middle knowledge.

I

In the twenty-third chapter of the first book of Samuel it is written that after David had rescued the Jewish city of Keilah from the Philistines, and settled his men there, Saul made plans to besiege Keilah in order to capture David. When David heard of Saul's plans, he consulted God by means of an ephod, which apparently was an instrument of divination that yielded a yes-or-no answer to questions. David asked, "Will Saul come down, as thy servant has heard?" The Lord answered affirmatively. Then David asked, "Will the men of Keilah surrender me and my men into the hand of Saul?" And the Lord replied, "They will surrender you." Thereupon David evacuated his men from Keilah, and hid out in the hills, with the result that Saul did not have the opportunity to besiege him in Keilah, and the men of Keilah did not have occasion to betray him to Saul (I Samuel 23:1–14, RSV).

This passage was a favorite proof text for the Jesuit theologians. They took it to prove that God knew the following two propositions to be true:

(1) If David stayed in Keilah, Saul would besiege the city.
(2) If David stayed in Keilah and Saul besieged the city, the men of Keilah would surrender David to Saul.

This is a case of middle knowledge; for it is assumed that all the actions mentioned in (1) and (2) would have been *free,* in the relevant sense, if they had occurred.

If we suppose that God is omniscient, we cannot consistently doubt that he had this middle knowledge unless we doubt that (1) and (2) were true. Therefore, as Suarez says, "the whole controversy comes back to this, that we should see whether those conditionals have a knowable determinate truth."[3]

But I do doubt that propositions (1) and (2) ever were, or ever will be, true.[4] This is not because I am inclined to assert the truth of their opposites,

(3) If David stayed in Keilah, Saul would *not* besiege the city.
(4) If David stayed in Keilah and Saul besieged the city, the men of Keilah would *not* surrender David to Saul.

Suarez would say that (1) and (3), and (2) and (4), respectively, are pairs of contradictories, and therefore that one member of each pair must be true. He thus affirms what has been called the law of Conditional Excluded Middle. But this is a mistake. To obtain the contradictory of a conditional proposition it is not enough to negate the consequent; one must negate the whole conditional, as was pointed out by Suarez's Dominican opponent, Diego Alvarez.[5] It is true that in everyday speech we might deny (1) by asserting (3), as we may deny a proposition by asserting any belief we hold that is obviously enough inconsistent with it. But we might also deny both of them by asserting, "If David stayed in Keilah, Saul might or might not besiege the city." I believe the case of what Saul would or might have done if David stayed in Keilah provides a plausible counterexample to the proposed law of Conditional Excluded Middle; and philosophers have found even more convincing counterexamples.[6]

I do not understand what it would be for any of propositions (1)–(4) to be true, given that the actions in question would have been free, and that David did not stay in Keilah. I will explain my incomprehension.

First we must note that middle knowledge is not simple *fore*knowledge. The answers that David got from the ephod—"He will come down," and "They will surrender you"—are not understood by the theologians as categorical predictions. If they were categorical predictions, they would be false. Most philosophers (including Suarez but not Molina) have supposed that categorical predictions, even about contingent events, can be true by corresponding to the actual occurrence of the event that they predict. But propositions (1) and (2) are not true in this way. For there never was nor will be an actual besieging of Keilah by Saul, nor an actual betrayal of David to Saul by the men of Keilah, to which those propositions might correspond.[7]

Some other grounds that might be suggested for the truth of (1) and (2) are ruled out by the assumption that the actions of Saul and the men of Keilah are and would be free in the relevant sense. The suggestion that Saul's besieging Keilah follows by *logical* necessity from David's staying there is implausible in any case.[8] It would be more plausible to suggest that Saul's besieging Keilah follows by *causal* necessity from David's staying there, together with a number of other features of the situation which in fact obtained. But both of these suggestions are inconsistent with the assumption that Saul's action would have been free.

Since necessitation is incompatible with the relevant sort of free will, we might seek nonnecessitating grounds for the truth of (1) and (2) in the actual intentions, desires, and character of Saul and the Keilahites. It does appear from the Biblical narrative that Saul actually intended to besiege David in Keilah if he could. Perhaps proposition (1) is true by virtue of its correspondence with Saul's intention. One might also suppose that (2) was true by virtue of correspondence with the desires and character of the leading men of Keilah, if not their fully formed intentions. Maybe they were cowardly, untrustworthy, and ungrateful. And I take it that neither the Jesuits nor Plantinga would say that Saul's intentions, or the desires and character of the Keilahites, necessitated their actions or interfered in any way with their freedom of will.

But the basis thus offered for the truth of (1) and (2) is inadequate precisely because it is not necessitating. A free agent may act out of character, or change his intentions, or fail to act on them. Therefore the propositions which may be true by virtue of correspondence with the intentions, desires and character of Saul and the men of Keilah are not (1) and (2) but

(5) If David stayed in Keilah, Saul would *probably* besiege the city.
(6) If David stayed in Keilah and Saul besieged the city, the men of Keilah would *probably* surrender David to Saul.

(5) and (6) are enough for David to act on, if he is prudent; but they will not satisfy the partisans of middle knowledge. It is part of their theory that God knows infallibly what definitely would happen, and not just what would probably happen or what free creatures would be likely to do.[9]

II

I trust that it is clear by this point that there is reason to doubt the possibility of middle knowledge.[10] Those who believe it possible have some explaining to do.

In Molina's explanation the superiority of God's cognitive powers bears the heaviest burden. He holds "that the certainty of that middle knowledge comes from the depth and unlimited perfection of the divine intellect, by which [God] knows certainly what is in itself uncertain."[11] This came to be known as the theory of "supercomprehension." According to it God's intellect so immensely surpasses, in its perfection, all created free wills, that it "supercomprehends" them—that is, it understands more about them than would be necessary merely to comprehend them.[12] But as Suarez pointed out in rejecting the theory of supercomprehension, to comprehend something is already to understand about it everything that is there to be understood, and it is absurd to suppose that anyone, even God, could understand more than that.[13] Molina seems to want to say that what free creatures would do under various possible conditions is not there, objectively, to be known, but that God's mind is so perfect that he knows it anyway. But that is impossible. The problem to be solved is how the relevant subjunctive conditionals can be true, and nothing that may be said about the excellence of God's cognitive powers contributes anything to the solution of that problem.

Suarez offers what seems to me the least clearly unsatisfactory type of explanation for the alleged possibility of middle knowledge. He appeals, in effect, to a primitive understanding, which needs no analysis, of what it is for the relevant subjunctive conditionals to be true. Consider a possible free creature, c, who may not ever exist, and a possible free action, a, which c may freely do or refrain from doing in a possible situation s. We are to consider c, not as actually existing, but as having "possible being" in the cause (God) that is able to produce c. So considered, according to Suarez, c has a property (a *habitudo*, as Suarez puts it) which is either the property of being a possible agent who would in s freely do a, or the property of being a possible agent who would in s freely refrain from doing a. c has one of these properties, although there is nothing either internal or external to c, except the property itself, which would make or determine c to have one of these properties rather than the other. God has middle knowledge of what c would do in s, because God knows which of the two properties c has.[14]

Many philosophers would object to Suarez's ontology of merely possible entities, but perhaps one could develop a similar account of the relevant conditionals without such an ontology. God's *idea* of c, for example, is presumably an *existing* subject of properties. And one might ascribe to it, as a primitive property, the property of being an idea which, if it were satisfied by anything in s, would be satisfied by an agent that freely did a in s. This would have the disadvantage, however, of implying that whether c would do a in s depends, not on a property of c, but on a property of God's idea of c. That consequence might seem to compromise c's freedom of will.

My principal objection to Suarez's defense of the possibility of middle knowledge is not based on ontological considerations, however. I do not think I have any conception, primitive or otherwise, of the sort of *habitudo* or property that Suarez ascribes to possible agents with respect to their acts under possible conditions. Nor do I think that I have any other primitive understanding of what it would be for the relevant subjunctive conditionals to be true. My reason for saying that Suarez's defense is of the least clearly unsatisfactory type is that it is very difficult to refute someone who claims to have a primitive understanding which I seem not to have.

III

In his several published discussions of the "free will defense" to the problem of evil, Alvin Plantinga has assumed, in effect, that God can have middle knowledge; and in the most recent of these discussions he has defended this assumption.[15] Following Robert Stalnaker and David Lewis, Plantinga adopts what he calls "the possible worlds explanation of counterfactuals."[16] For proposition (1) to be true, according to Plantinga's theory, is for the following to be the case:

> (7) The actual world is more similar to some possible world in which David stays in Keilah and Saul besieges the city than to any possible world in which David stays in Keilah and Saul does not besiege the city.

There are two important reasons for denying that this analysis establishes the possibility of middle knowledge.

(A) To the extent that it is plausible, the possible worlds explanation does not really give us a new solution to our problem about the truth of the crucial conditionals. It merely offers us a new and up-to-date form for the expression of attempted solutions that we may already have considered and rejected. (In fairness it should be said that Plantinga does not claim otherwise.) Two points must be made here.

(i) If the explanation is to be plausible, the kinds of similarity among possible worlds that are allowed to be relevant to the truth and falsity of counterfactual conditionals must mirror the considerations that would in any case determine our judgment of their truth and falsity. Some similarities cannot plausibly be allowed any relevance at all. Among the possible worlds in which David stays in Keilah, for example, I suspect the most similar to the actual world is one in which Saul does not besiege Keilah, and in which the subsequent history of David, Saul, and of Israel and Judah goes very much as it did in the actual world. Perhaps in such a world Saul has a slightly different character, or acts out of character in a way that he does not in the actual world; but I doubt that that is as great a dissimilarity as the dissimilarity between a world in which there is a siege of Keilah by Saul (and perhaps a killing of David by Saul) and a world in which there is not. I certainly would not conclude, however, that therefore Saul would not have besieged Keilah if David had stayed in the city.[17] That a world in which Saul besieges Keilah is in that respect unlike the actual world, is irrelevant to the question what Saul would have done if David stayed in Keilah. Some similarities between the actual world and other possible worlds are relevant to that question—for example, similarities and dissimilarities in causal laws and in people's characters. But we have already considered and rejected the idea of founding the truth of our crucial conditionals on causal laws or on people's characters.

(ii) Even the similarities that are allowed to be relevant to the truth of counterfactuals must not be given more decisiveness than we would otherwise accord to the considerations that they mirror. A world in which David stays in Keilah and Saul besieges the city is perhaps more similar to the actual world in respect of Saul's character than a world in which David stays in Keilah and Saul does not besiege the city. But we had better not conclude that therefore the former is more similar to the actual world than the latter for purposes of the possible worlds explanation, if we mean to adhere to the explanation. For this conclusion would give us more reason to reject the analysis in terms of similarity of possible worlds than to abandon our previous judgment that Saul *might* have acted out of character and so would only *probably*, not definitely, have laid siege to Keilah if David had stayed in the city. The issue here is a general one, and important. We have a well-entrenched belief that under many counterfactual conditions many a person *might* have acted out of character, although he probably would not have. If the possible worlds explanation is to be plausible, it must not give such decisiveness to similarities of character and behavior as to be inconsistent with this belief.

(B) On the possible worlds theory, moreover, the truth of the crucial conditionals cannot be settled soon enough to be of use to God. The chief importance of middle knowledge, for Plantinga as well as Molina and Suarez, is that God is supposed to be guided by it in making decisions about the creation and providential governance of the world. And as Molina and Suarez insist, if God is to make such use of it, his middle knowledge must be prior, if not temporally, at least in the order of explanation (*prius ratione,* as Suarez puts it), to his decisions about what creatures to create.[18] For similar reasons the truth of the conditional propositions which are the object of middle knowledge must not depend on God's creative decisions. Ignoring angels (fallen or unfallen) for the sake of argument, let us suppose that Adam and Eve were the first free creatures that God made. We are to think of God as choosing from among many alternatives; among them were creating Adam and Eve, creating other free creatures instead of them, and making no free creatures at all. According to the theory of middle knowledge, God's decisions to make some free creatures, and Adam and Eve in particular, are to be explained in part by the truth of

(8) If God created Adam and Eve, there would be more moral good than moral evil in the history of the world.[19]

This explanation would be viciously circular if the truth of (8) were later in the order of explanation than the decisions it is supposed to help explain.

Here we are dealing with a type of subjunctive conditionals that we may call *deliberative conditionals.* They ought not, in strictness, to be called *counterfactual.* For in asserting one of them one does not commit oneself to the falsity of its antecedent. That is because a deliberative conditional is asserted (or entertained) in a context of deliberation about whether to (try to) make its antecedent true or false. In asserting such a conditional one commits oneself rather to the view that its truth is independent of the truth or falsity of its antecedent.

There is a problem, which so far as I know has not been discussed in the literature, about applying to deliberative conditionals, as Plantinga does, the possible worlds explanation of counterfactuals.[20] Consider a deliberative conditional,

(9) If I did *x,* *y* would happen.

Is (9) true? According to the possible worlds explanation, that depends on whether the actual world is more similar to some world in which I do x and y happens than to any world in which I do x and y does not happen. That in turn seems to depend on which world is the actual world. And which world is the actual world? That depends in part on whether I do x. Thus the truth of (9) seems to depend on the truth or falsity of its antecedent. Similarly the truth of (8) will depend on whether God creates Adam and Eve.

I think it may be possible for a possible worlds theory of deliberative conditionals to overcome this difficulty in general, but not in such a way as to rescue the doctrine of middle knowledge. There is, I presume, a large class, K, of possible worlds that are more similar to some world in which I do x and y happens than to any world in which I do x and y does not happen. According to the possible worlds theory the truth of (9) depends on the actual world being some member of K, but not on *which* member of K it is. In asserting (9) in the context of deliberation I commit myself, in effect, to the view that the actual world is a member of K and that its membership in K does not depend on which I choose of the alternatives among which I am deliberating. This view may well be correct (if, for instance, x and y are linked by a strict causal law).

Similarly there is a class, K^*, of possible worlds that are more similar to some world in which God creates Adam and Eve and there is more moral good than moral evil in the history of the world than to any world in which God creates Adam and Eve and there is not more moral good than moral evil in the history of the world. The truth of (8) depends on the actual world being some member of K^*, according to the possible worlds theory. But how can the actual world's membership in K^* have been settled earlier in the order of explanation than God's decision whether to create Adam and Eve, or some other free creatures, or none? Here we face all the old difficulties about middle knowledge, and the possible worlds theory does nothing to help us answer this question. At most it explains why (8) is true, *given* that some member of K^* is actual.

Furthermore there is reason to believe that the actual world's membership in K^* cannot have been settled earlier in the order of explanation than God's decision. Let us say that one of God's alternatives is *represented in K^** if and only if there is some world in K^* in which he chooses that alternative. If any of the alternatives among which God was choosing is not represented in K^*, then the actual world's membership in K^* depends on his rejecting that alternative, and therefore cannot be prior in the order of explanation to his decision. But I think at least one of God's alternatives is indeed unrepresented in K^*. For one alternative was to make no free creatures at all, and I do not see how a world in which there are no free creatures at all could be a member of K^*. Since it is free actions that are morally good and morally evil,[21] no possible world, w, will be a member of K^* unless there is some feature of w by virtue of which a difference in the free actions of free creatures in some worlds u and v would be a reason for counting u as more similar than v to w (in relevant respects). And any such feature of w must surely involve the existence in w of free creatures. If there are no free creatures at all in w, what would make w more like a world in which most free creaturely decisions are good ones than like a world in which most free creaturely decisions are bad ones?[22] I conclude that the actual world's membership in K^* cannot be earlier in the order of explanation than God's decision to make some free creatures. Therefore the truth of (8), on the possible worlds analysis, cannot be prior in the order of explanation to that decision.

Perhaps it will be objected to me that the partisans of middle knowledge need not claim that the truth of (8) precedes God's creative choices in the order of explanation. It is enough for their explanations if God *believed* (8) prior to making the choices. My reply is that if God acted on a belief in (8) before it was settled that (8) is true, then the fact (if it is a fact) that there is more moral good than moral evil in the history of the world is due to God's good luck rather than his wisdom, whereas the chief motivation of the theological theory of middle knowledge has been the desire to maintain that such happy results of God's dealings with created freedom are due to his wisdom, and that he had no need at all of luck.

IV

Of the philosophical objections that may be raised against my critique of the theory of middle knowledge, two seem to me the most important.

(A) I have relied on the claim that in the circumstances assumed in our example about David and Saul at Keilah, what is true by virtue of Saul's intentions and character is not

(1) If David stayed in Keilah, Saul would besiege the city,

but

(5) If David stayed in Keilah, Saul would *probably* besiege the city.

Suarez has an interesting objection to this claim. He argues, in effect, that (5) can only mean that (1) is probably true, and that in accepting (5) one commits oneself, albeit with some trepidation, to the truth of (1).[23] Certainly it would be pragmatically inconsistent to assert that (1) is probably true and deny (as I do) that there is any way in which (1) can be true.

In proposing (5) as an alternative to (1), however, I do not understand it as a claim that (1), or any other proposition, *is* probable. It is rather a claim that

(10) Saul will besiege Keilah.

would be probable, given facts that would (definitely, not just probably) obtain if David stayed in Keilah. While "probably" is an epistemological term, moreover, it is used in (5) primarily to characterize dispositions or tendencies toward the truth of (10) that there would be if David stayed in Keilah. (5) does not imply that anyone would *know* the facts that would probabilify (10), but only that they would *obtain,* if David stayed in Keilah.

This view is consistent with treatment that (5) might receive under either of the two major types of theory of counterfactuals distinguished by Lewis. According to a *metalinguistic* theory, as Lewis puts it, "a counterfactual is true, or assertable, if and only if its antecedent, together with suitable further premises, implies its consequent."[24] Holding a theory of this type, we might say that (5) is true if and only if (10) would be probable on total evidence constituted by the antecedent of (5), together with suitable further premises. The suitable further premises in this case would be partly about Saul's intentions and character. Lewis has proposed for the *possible worlds* theory an essentially similar treatment of counterfactuals that involve probability in the way that (5) does.[25]

(B) Probably the most serious grounds for misgivings about my argument may be found in cases in which we seem to have confidence in what looks like a piece of middle knowledge. Suarez appeals to such confidence on the part of ordinary speakers,[26] and Plantinga endeavors to provide us with convincing examples of it.

In one of Plantinga's fictitious examples Curley Smith, a mayor of Boston, has accepted a bribe of $35,000 to drop his opposition to a proposed freeway route. In this case is the following true?

(11) Smith would still have accepted a bribe to drop his opposition, if the bribe had been $36,000.

Plantinga thinks "the answer seems fairly clear: indeed [Smith] would have" accepted the larger bribe,[27] and I agree.

But what makes (11) true? Let us note that it belongs to the class of subjunctive conditionals with antecedents assumed to be false and consequents assumed to be true, which have been called *semifactuals*. What makes (11) true, I think, is that its consequent is true and the truth of its antecedent would not have prevented, or made less likely, the event that makes the consequent true. My view here is in accord with Nelson Goodman's claim that "in practice full counterfactuals affirm, while semifactuals deny, that a certain connection obtains between antecedent and consequent."[28] My account of what makes (11) true does not suggest a way in which (1) and (2) could be true, since they do not have true consequents to help make them true.

Furthermore, if my account is right, it was presumably not settled that (11) is true before (in the order of explanation) it was settled that Smith was going to be offered, and accept, $35,000, since his actual acceptance is part of what makes (11) true. I see no reason, therefore, to suppose that God could have known of the truth of (11) early enough in the order of explanation to make use of it as he is supposed to make use of middle knowledge.

Another type of case, not presented by Plantinga, perplexes me more. There does not normally seem to be any uncertainty at all about what a butcher, for example, would have done if I had asked him to sell me a pound of ground beef, although we suppose he would have had free will in the matter. We say he would certainly have sold me the meat, if he had it to sell. What makes us regard it as certain? Chiefly his character, habits, desires, and intentions, and the absence of countervailing dispositions. (He would have had no motive to refuse me.)

There are three alternative views one might take of this case. One might say that if I had asked the butcher to sell me the meat, (i) he would only probably have sold it to me, though we normally ignore the minute but real chance there would have been that he would refuse; *or* (ii) he would certainly have sold me the meat, because he would have been causally determined to do so by his character and dispositions; *or* (iii) his character and dispositions would not have causally determined his action, but they render it absolutely certain that he would have complied with my request.

I have rested an important part of my argument on the assumption that what a person's character and dispositions do not causally determine, they do not render absolutely certain. Alternative (iii) is inconsistent with this assumption. It still seems to me, however, that my assumption is sound and alternative (iii) is more implausible than (i) or (ii), although I must admit that I am not altogether content with either of them. For what is the nature of the rendering certain in alternative (iii), if it is not causal determination? On some views—Humean views—of the nature of probability and causality, alternative (iii) is plainly impossible; and I do not know of any theory that would render it intelligble.

V

Could God have arranged to have creatures who would perform free actions but only right ones? Let us consider the question first on the assumption that God has middle knowledge. In that case, we might think, he could have obtained sinless free creatures simply by making only those that he knew would always freely do right in those situations in which he would permit them to act freely.[29] Plantinga's response to this argument, a response which he develops with much greater elegance than I have space to reproduce here, is that God could not do this unless there are some possible free creatures who would in fact behave so well, and that perhaps none would. Plantinga proposes the hypothesis that all possible free creatures (or their essences) have *trans-world depravity*. Roughly speaking, a possible free creature (or its essence) has trans-world depravity, in Plantinga's sense, if and only if that creature *would* do some wrong if God created it and permitted it to act freely, no matter what else God did. If the hypothesis of universal trans-world depravity is true, God must have known it is true, if he had middle knowledge, and must therefore have known that some evil was the inescapable price of created freedom.

Plantinga does not claim that the hypothesis is true, or even that it is plausible.[30] He argues only that it is logically possible, because he is using it to defend the view that it is logically possible that both God and evil exist. I do not doubt that the latter is logically possible; but religious thought must seek an account of the relations between God and evil that is credible, as well as logically possible.

It is worth asking, therefore, whether the hypothesis of universal transworld depravity is plausible, on the assumptions about truth of conditionals that Plantinga shares with the Jesuit theologians. I think Molina and Suarez would deny that any possible free creature (or any free creature's essence) has trans-world depravity; and they could support their denial with persuasive arguments. Suarez holds that "it is alien to the common doctrine . . . and to the divine perfection and omnipotence, and is therefore of itself incredible enough, to say that God cannot predetermine [*praedefinire*] an honorable free act, in particular and with all [its] circumstances, by His absolute and effective will, the freedom of the created will still being preserved."[31] God uses his middle knowledge to make such predeterminations effective, choosing conditions and helps of grace that he knows will elicit a favorable response, and avoiding those under which he knows that the creature would not act according to the divine purpose. This presupposes, of course, that for every possible honorable free act of every possible free creature, in any possible outward circumstances, there are some incentives or helps of grace that God could supply, to which the creature would respond favorably though he could have responded unfavorably. But this is a very plausible presupposition if we assume, as Suarez does, that the theory of middle knowledge is correct, and that there is an infinite variety of natural and supernatural ways in which God can work on us inwardly, assisting our reasoning, affecting our feelings and perhaps our beliefs and desires, without causally determining our response.[32]

And if it is plausible to suppose that for every possible *particular* occasion of action there are possible divine operations that would elicit a favorable free response, is it not also plausible to suppose that for many possible free creatures, and even for whole worlds full of them, there are possible series of divine operations to which those creatures would respond by *always* freely doing right, never doing wrong? Molina held that both Jesus and Mary were preserved from all sin throughout their whole lives by God supplying them with gifts and aids that he knew would always elicit a favorable free response from them.[33] Presumably he could have done the same for others.

If the hypothesis of universal trans-world depravity is implausible, it might seem that I offer theodicy a better alternative. I deny the possibility of middle knowledge, because I deny that the relevant subjunctive conditionals are true. In particular, I deny that the following is true:

(12) If God had acted differently in certain ways, he would have had creatures who made free choices, but none of whom ever made wrong choices.

In other words, I deny that God could have made free creatures who *would* always have freely done right. The supposition that he could have done so is burdened with all the difficulties about truth of conditionals that afflict the theory of middle knowledge. Since (12) is not true, a reproach against God cannot rightly be based on its truth. And God cannot know that (12) is true, and cannot rightly be blamed for not using such knowledge.

My views about the truth of conditionals, however, do not tend to show that the following could not be true:

(13) If God had acted differently in certain ways, he would *probably* have had creatures who made free choices, but none of whom ever made wrong choices.

(14) If God had acted differently in certain ways, he would *probably* have had better behaved free creatures, on the whole, than he actually has.

In fact (13) seems to me rather implausible. Without middle knowledge God must take real risks if he makes free creatures (thousands, millions, or trillions of risks, if each free creature makes thousands of morally significant free choices). No matter how shrewdly God acted in running so many risks, his winning on *every* risk would not be antecedently probable. But I think (14) is very plausible. These judgments suggest that the necessity of permitting some evil in order to have free will in creatures may play a part in a theodicy but cannot bear the whole weight of it, even if the possibility of middle knowledge is rejected.

Notes

1. An acutely argued Dominican contribution to the debate is Diego (Didacus) Alvarez, O.P., *De auxiliis divinae gratiae et humani arbitrii viribus, et libertate, ac legitima eius cum efficacia eorundem auxiliorum concordia* (Rome, 1590); see especially the seventh disputation.

2. I believe Molina originated the term "middle knowledge" (*scientia media*). I have given a very simplified account of his reasons for thinking it appropriate. See his *Liberi arbitrii cum gratiae donis, divina praescientia, providentia, praedestinatione et reprobatione concordia* [hereafter abbreviated, *Concordia*], ed. John Rabeneck (Oña and Madrid, 1953), qu. 14, art. 13, disp. 52, n. 9–10, and disp. 53, memb. 1, n. 6, and memb. 4, n. 4 (pp. 339f., 360, 394).

3. Suarez, *De gratia*, prol. 2, c. 7, n. 1, in his *Opera omnia* (Paris, 1856–78), vol. 7, p. 85. (All my page references to *De gratia* will be to this edition and volume.)

*4. This formulation leaves open the question whether such conditionals (for which David Vriend has suggested to me the apt name "counterfactuals of freedom") are false or rather lack truth value. As some readers have taken me to be suggesting the latter view, I wish to state clearly my preference for the simpler opinion that they are false.

5. Alvarez, op. cit., bk. 2, disp. 7, n. 30 (p. 74). See Suarez, *De gratia*, prol. 2, c. 7, n. 24 (p. 95).

6. David Lewis, *Counterfactuals* (Oxford, 1973), p. 79f.; John H. Pollock, "Four Kinds of Conditionals," *American Philosophical Quarterly*, 12 (1975), p. 53. The law of Conditional Excluded Middle was defended by Robert C. Stalnaker, in "A Theory of Conditionals," *American Philosophical Quarterly Monograph Series*, no. 2, *Studies in Logical Theory*, ed. Nicholas Rescher (Oxford, 1968), p. 106f.

7. Suarez saw this point pretty clearly; see his "De scientia Dei futurorum contingentium" [hereafter abbreviated, DSDFC], bk. 2, c. 5, n. 6 (*Opera omnia*, vol. 11, p. 357).

8. Suarez makes a similar point: DSDFC, bk. 2, c. 5, n. 11 (p. 358).

9. See Suarez, DSDFC, bk. 2, c. 1, n. 1–2, and c. 5, n. 9 (pp. 343f., 357f.).

*10. Another difficulty for the theory of middle knowledge is posed by this question: What would cause those counterfactuals of freedom that are true to be true? According to the theory they are contingent propositions, but their truth value is independent of God's will. And since their truth value is also supposed to be independent of the existence of the created agents they are about, it can hardly be determined by any actual exercise of the wills of those agents. I have further developed this objection to the theory of middle knowledge in "Plantinga on the Problem of Evil," my contribution to the "Profiles" volume, *Alvin Plantinga*, ed. James E. Tomberlin and Peter van Inwagen (Dordrecht: Reidel, 1985), p. 232.

11. Molina, *Concordia*, qu. 14, art. 13, disp. 53, memb. 3, n. 10 (p. 389f.).

12. Ibid., qu. 14, art. 13, disp. 52, n. 11, 17 (pp. 341, 345).

13. Suarez, DSDFC, bk. 2, c. 7, n. 6 (p. 366f.).

14. I believe this is what Suarez's views come to, as they are found in *De gratia*, prol. 2, c. 7, n. 21, 24, 25 (pp. 94–6).

15. The assumption passed unquestioned in Alvin Plantinga's *God and Other Minds* (Ithaca, 1967), ch. 6. In his *The Nature of Necessity* (Oxford, 1974), ch. 9, and less fully in "Which Worlds Could God Have Created?" *The Journal of Philosophy*, 70 (1973), pp. 539–52, it is defended. At the same time Plantinga has attempted (successfully, I think) to free a part of his larger argument from dependence on the assumption (*The Nature of Necessity*, op. cit., pp. 182–4). Plantinga has not used the term "middle knowledge," although it seems to me very apt for the expression of his views.

16. *The Nature of Necessity*, op. cit., p. 178. See also Stalnaker, op. cit., and Lewis, op, cit. In the present paper I shall disregard complications having to do with conditionals whose antecedents are impossible, as all the conditionals that will concern us have possible antecedents.

17. Similar problems are discussed by Plantinga, *The Nature of Necessity*, op. cit., pp. 174–9, and Lewis, *Counterfactuals*, op. cit., pp. 72–7, 91–5.

18. See especially Suarez, DSDFC, bk. 2, c. 4, n. 6, and c. 6, n. 3, 6 (pp. 355, 361, 363).

19. I have simplified here, particularly in the antecedent. God is supposed to have known that there would be more moral good than moral evil in the world if he executed a long series of actions, beginning with the creation of Adam and Eve. Many of these actions would be occasioned in part by responses he supposedly knew creatures would freely make to earlier actions in the series.

20. Stalnaker would apply it to deliberative conditionals too. Lewis might not; see his *Counterfactuals*, op. cit., p. 4.

21. Plantinga insists on this point (*The Nature of Necessity*, op. cit., p. 166f.).

*22. Plantinga has responded to this argument (in his "Replies to My Colleagues," p. 378 in the "Profiles" volume cited in note 10) as follows: "One thing that helps determine the similarity of a world W to a world W^* is the degree to which *W* and *W** share their counterfactuals." This view is supported, Plantinga argues, by the importance of similarity of causal laws to the relevant similarity between worlds. But then, he infers, "a world *W* in which there are no free creatures at all can be more similar to one in which there are free creatures who make more right than wrong choices; all that's needed is that the relevant counterfactuals be true in *W*. Of course," he adds, "this means we can't look to similarity, among possible worlds, as *explaining* counterfactuality, or as *founding* or *grounding* it." Rather, Plantinga proposes to accept the possible worlds account of counterfactuals only as stating a nonexplanatory equivalence that is useful for grasping the structure of issues about counterfactuals.

I want to make two points about this response of Plantinga's.

(i) He is appealing, in effect, to the possibility of treating counterfactuals of freedom as primitive in relation to similarities among possible worlds. The idea that the truth of counterfactuals of freedom is a primitive fact, not explainable in terms of something more fundamental, seems quite implausible to me. But it is not a formally inconsistent idea, and is very difficult to refute. (This is essentially the answer that I offered to Suarez in section II.) My argument in section III therefore cannot fairly be regarded as refuting a version of the theory of middle knowledge that is prepared to accept the truth of counterfactuals of freedom as a primitive fact.

(ii) The argument is not intended to do that, however. Its purpose is defensive rather than offensive. It is meant to show that the possibility of middle knowledge cannot be established by an explanatory version of the possible worlds analysis of counterfactuals (a version which I am not inclined to accept); and I still think it does show that. The argument it is intended to rebut or forestall claims that the truth of a counterfactual of freedom can be established (and explained) by establishing the relevant similarity relation among possible worlds.

23. Suarez, DSDFC, bk. 2, c. 5, n. 9 (p. 357f.). I am simplifying here, but I think not in such a way as to make this argument less plausible.

24. Lewis, *Counterfactuals,* op. cit., p. 65.

25. David Lewis, "Counterfactuals and Comparative Probability," *Journal of Philosophical Logic,* 2 (1973), p. 437f.

26. Suarez, DSDFC, bk. 2, c. 5, n. 8 (p. 357).

27. Plantinga. *The Nature of Necessity,* op. cit., p. 177.

28. Nelson Goodman, *Fact, Fiction, and Forecast* (London, 1954), p. 15.

29. This argument is crisply stated by Nelson Pike, "Plantinga on the Free Will Defense: A Reply," *The Journal of Philosophy,* 63 (1966), p. 93f. "Will" replaces "would" in Pike's formulation, but it is clearly middle knowledge that is involved.

30. Plantinga, *The Nature of Necessity,* op. cit., compare p. 165 with p. 189.

31. Suarez, DSDFC, bk. 2, c. 4, n. 4 (p. 354).

32. Cf. ibid., bk. 2, c. 4, n. 5 (p. 355).

33. Molina, *Concordia,* qu. 14, art. 13, disp. 53, memb. 4, n. 15–24 (pp. 399–405).

PART THREE

GOD AND ETHICS

7

A Modified Divine Command Theory of Ethical Wrongness

I

It is widely held that all those theories are indefensible which attempt to explain in terms of the will or commands of God what it is for an act to be ethically right or wrong. In this paper I shall state such a theory, which I believe to be defensible; and I shall try to defend it against what seem to me to be the most important and interesting objections to it. I call my theory a *modified* divine command theory because in it I renounce certain claims that are commonly made in divine command analyses of ethical terms. (I should add that it is *my* theory only in that I shall state it, and that I believe it is defensible—not that I am sure it is correct.) I present it as a theory of ethical *wrongness* partly for convenience. It could also be presented as a theory of the nature of ethical obligatoriness or of ethical permittedness. Indeed, I will have occasion to make some remarks about the concept of ethical permittedness. But as we shall see (in section IV) I am not prepared to claim that the theory can be extended to all ethical terms; and it is therefore important that it not be presented as a theory about ethical terms in general.

It will be helpful to begin with the statement of a simple, *unmodified* divine command theory of ethical wrongness. This is the theory that ethical wrongness *consists in* being contrary to God's commands, or that the word 'wrong' in ethical contexts *means* 'contrary to God's commands'. It implies that the following two statement forms are logically equivalent.

(1) It is wrong (for A) to do X.
(2) It is contrary to God's commands (for A) to do X.

I am indebted to many who have read, or heard, and discussed versions of this essay, and particularly to Richard Brandt, William Frankena, John Reeder, and Stephen Stich, for helpful criticisms.

Of course that is not all that the theory implies. It also implies that (2) is conceptually prior to (1), so that the meaning of (1) is to be explained in terms of (2), and not the other way around. It might prove fairly difficult to state or explain in what that conceptual priority consists, but I shall not go into that here. I do not wish ultimately to defend the theory in its unmodified form, and I think I have stated it fully enough for my present purposes.

I have stated it as a theory about the meaning of the word 'wrong' in ethical contexts. The most obvious objection to the theory is that the word 'wrong' is used in ethical contexts by many people who cannot mean by it what the theory says they must mean, since they do not believe that there exists a God. This objection seems to me sufficient to refute the theory if it is presented as an analysis of what *everybody* means by 'wrong' in ethical contexts. The theory cannot reasonably be offered except as a theory about what the word 'wrong' means as used by *some but not all* people in ethical contexts. Let us say that the theory offers an analysis of the meaning of 'wrong' in Judeo-Christian religious ethical discourse. This restriction of scope will apply to my modified divine command theory too. This restriction obviously gives rise to a possible objection. Isn't it more plausible to suppose that Judeo-Christian believers use 'wrong' with the same meaning as other people do? This problem will be discussed in section VI.

In section II, I will discuss what seems to me the most important objection to the unmodified divine command theory, and suggest how the theory can be modified to meet it. Section III will be devoted to a brief but fairly comprehensive account of the use of 'wrong' in Judeo-Christian ethical discourse, from the point of view of the modified divine command theory. The theory will be further elaborated in dealing with objections in sections IV to VI. In a seventh and final section, I will note some problems arising from unresolved issues in the general theory of analysis and meaning, and briefly discuss their bearing on the modified divine command theory.

II

The following seems to me to be the gravest objection to the divine command theory of ethical wrongness, in the form in which I have stated it. Suppose God should command me to make it my chief end in life to inflict suffering on other human beings, for no other reason than that he commanded it. (For convenience I shall abbreviate this hypothesis to 'Suppose God should command cruelty for its own sake'.) Will it seriously be claimed that in that case it would be wrong for me not to practice cruelty for its own sake? I see three possible answers to this question.

(1) It might be claimed that it is logically impossible for God to command cruelty for its own sake. In that case, of course, we need not worry about whether it would be wrong to disobey if he did command it. It is senseless to agonize about what one should do in a logically impossible situation. This solution to the problem seems unlikely to be available to the divine command theorist, however. For why would he hold that it is logically impossible for God to command cruelty for its own sake? Some theologians (for instance, Thomas Aquinas) have believed (a) that what is right and wrong is independent of God's will, *and* (b) that God always does right by the necessity of his nature. Such theologians, if they believe that it would be wrong for God to command cruelty for its own sake, have reason to believe that it is logically impossible for him to do so. But the divine command theorist, who does not agree that what is right and wrong is independent of God's will, does not seem to have such a reason to deny that it is logically possible for God to command cruelty for its own sake.

(2) Let us assume that it is logically possible for God to command cruelty for its own sake. In that case the divine command theory seems to imply that it would be wrong not to practice cruelty for its own sake. There have been at least a few adherents of divine command ethics who have been prepared to accept this consequence. William Ockham held that those acts which we call "theft," "adultery," and "hatred of God" would be meritorious if God had commanded them.[1] He would surely have said the same about what I have been calling the practice of "cruelty for its own sake."

This position is one which I suspect most of us are likely to find somewhat shocking, even repulsive. We should therefore be particularly careful not to misunderstand it. We need not imagine that Ockham disciplined himself to be ready to practice cruelty for its own sake if God should command it. It was doubtless an article of faith for him that God is unalterably opposed to any such practice. The mere logical possibility that theft, adultery, and cruelty might have been commanded by God (and therefore meritorious) doubtless did not represent in Ockham's view any real possibility.

(3) Nonetheless, the view that if God commanded cruelty for its own sake it would be wrong not to practice it seems unacceptable to me; and I think many, perhaps most, other Jewish and Christian believers would find it unacceptable too. I must make clear the sense in which I find it unsatisfactory. It is not that I find an internal inconsistency in it. And I

would not deny that it may reflect, accurately enough, the way in which some believers use the word 'wrong'. I might as well frankly avow that I am looking for a divine command theory which at least might possibly be a correct account of how *I* use the word 'wrong'. I do not use the word 'wrong' in such a way that I would say that it would be wrong not to practice cruelty if God commanded it, and I am sure that many other believers agree with me on this point.

But now have I not rejected the divine command theory? I have assumed that it would be logically possible for God to command cruelty for its own sake. And I have rejected the view that if God commanded cruelty for its own sake, it would be wrong not to obey. It seems to follow that I am committed to the view that in certain logically possible circumstances it would not be wrong to disobey God. This position seems to be inconsistent with the theory that 'wrong' means 'contrary to God's commands'.

I want to argue, however, that it is still open to me to accept a modified form of the divine command theory of ethical wrongness. According to the modified divine command theory, when I say, 'It is wrong to do X', (at least part of) what I *mean* is that it is contrary to God's commands to do X. 'It is wrong to do X' *implies* 'It is contrary to God's commands to do X'. But 'It is contrary to God's commands to do X' implies 'It is wrong to do X' only if certain conditions are assumed—namely, only if it is assumed that God has the character which I believe him to have, of loving his human creatures. If God were really to command us to make cruelty our goal, then he would not have that character of loving us, and I would not say it would be wrong to disobey him.

But do I say that it would be wrong to obey him in such a case? This is the point at which I am in danger of abandoning the divine command theory completely. I do abandon it completely if I say both of the following things.

(A) It would be wrong to obey God if he commanded cruelty for its own sake.

(B) In (A), 'wrong' is used in what is for me its normal ethical sense.

If I assert both (A) and (B), it is clear that I cannot consistently maintain that 'wrong' in its normal ethical sense for me means or implies 'contrary to God's commands'.

But from the fact that I deny that it would be wrong to disobey God if He commanded cruelty for its own sake, it does not follow that I must accept (A) and (B). Of course someone might claim that obedience and disobedience would both be ethically permitted in such a case; but that is not the view that I am suggesting. If I adopt the modified divine command theory as an analysis of my present concept of ethical wrongness (and if I adopt a similar analysis of my concept of ethical permittedness), I will not hold either that it would be wrong to disobey, or that it would be ethically permitted to disobey, or that it would be wrong to obey, or that it would be ethically permitted to obey, if God commanded cruelty for its own sake. For I will say that my concept of ethical wrongness (and my concept of ethical permittedness) would "break down" if I really believed that God commanded cruelty for its own sake. Or to put the matter somewhat more prosaically, I will say that my concepts of ethical wrongness and permittedness could not serve the functions they now serve, because using those concepts I could not call any action ethically wrong or ethically permitted, if I believed that God's will was so unloving. This position can be explained or developed in either of two ways, each of which has its advantages.

I could say that by 'X is ethically wrong' I mean 'X is contrary to the commands of a *loving* God' (i.e., 'There is a *loving* God and X is contrary to his commands') and by 'X is ethically permitted' I mean 'X is in accord with the commands of a *loving* God' (i.e., 'There is a *loving* God and X is not contrary to his commands'). On this analysis we can reason as follows. If there is only one God and he commands cruelty for its own sake, then presumably there is not a *loving* God. If there is not a loving God then neither 'X is ethically wrong' nor 'X is ethically permitted' is true of any X. Using my present concepts of ethical wrongness and permittedness, therefore, I could not (consistently) call any action ethically wrong or permitted if I believed that God commanded cruelty for its own sake. This way of developing the modified divine command theory is the simpler and neater of the two, and that might reasonably lead one to choose it for the construction of a theological ethical theory. On the other hand, I think it is also simpler and neater than ordinary religious ethical discourse, in which (for example) it may be felt that the statement that a certain act is wrong is *about* the will or commands of God in a way in which it is not about his love.

In this essay I shall prefer a second, rather similar, but somewhat untidier, understanding of the modified divine command theory, because I think it may lead us into some insights about the complexities of actual religious ethical discourse. According to this second version of the theory, the statement that something is ethically wrong (or permitted) says something about the will or commands of God, but not about his love. Every such statement, however, *presupposes* that certain conditions for the applicability of the believer's concepts of ethical right and wrong are satisfied. Among these conditions is that God does not command cruelty for its own sake—or, more generally, that God loves his human creatures. It need not be assumed that God's love is the only such condition.

The modified divine command theorist can say that the possibility of God commanding cruelty for its own sake is not provided for in the Judeo-Christian religious ethical system as he understands it. The possibility is not provided for, in the sense that the concepts of right and wrong have not been developed in such a way that actions could be correctly said to be right or wrong if God were believed to command cruelty for its own sake. The modified divine command theorist agrees that it is logically possible[2] that God should command cruelty for its own sake; but he holds that it is unthinkable that God should do so. To have *faith* in God is not just to believe that he exists, but also to trust in his love for mankind. The believer's concepts of ethical wrongness and permittedness are developed within the framework of his (or the religious community's) religious life, and therefore within the framework of the assumption that God loves us. The concept of the will or commands of God has a certain function in the believer's life, and the use of the words 'right' (in the sense of 'ethically permitted') and 'wrong' is tied to that function of that concept. But one of the reasons why the concept of the will of God can function as it does is that the love which God is believed to have toward men arouses in the believer certain attitudes of love toward God and devotion to his will. If the believer thinks about the unthinkable but logically possible situation in which God commands cruelty for its own sake, he finds that in relation to that kind of command of God he cannot take up the same attitude, and that the concept of the will or commands of God could not then have the same function in his life. For this reason he will not say that it would be wrong to disobey God, or right to obey him, in that situation. At the same time he will not say that it would be wrong to obey God in that situation, because he is accustomed to use the word 'wrong' to say that something is contrary to the will of God, and it does not seem to him to be the right word to use to express his own personal revulsion toward an act against which there would be no divine authority. Similarly, he will not say that it would be "right" in the sense of 'ethically permitted', to disobey God's command of cruelty; for that does not seem to him to be the right way to express his own personal attitude toward an act which would not be in accord with a divine authority. In this way the believer's concepts of ethical rightness and wrongness would break down in the situation in which he believed that God commanded cruelty for its own sake; that is, they would not function as they now do, because he would not be prepared to use them to say that any action was right or wrong.

III

It is clear that according to this modified divine command theory, the meaning of the word 'wrong' in Judeo-Christian ethical discourse must be understood in terms of a complex of relations which believers' use of the word has, not only to their beliefs about God's commands, but also to their attitudes toward certain types of action. I think it will help us to understand the theory better if we can give a brief but fairly comprehensive description of the most important features of the Judeo-Christian ethical use of 'wrong', from the point of view of the modified divine command theory. That is what I shall try to do in this section.

(1) 'Wrong' and 'contrary to God's commands' at least contextually imply each other in Judeo-Christian ethical discourse. 'It is wrong to do X' will be assented to by the sincere Jewish or Christian believer if and only if he assents to 'It is contrary to God's commands to do X'. This is a fact sufficiently well known that the known believer who says the one commits himself publicly to the other.

Indeed 'wrong' and such expressions as 'against the will of God' seem to be used interchangeably in religious ethical discourse. If a believer asks his pastor, "Do you think it's always against the will of God to use contraceptives?" and the pastor replies, "I don't see anything wrong with the use of contraceptives in many cases," the pastor has answered the same question the inquirer asked.

(2) In ethical contexts, the statement that a certain action is wrong normally expresses certain volitional and emotional attitudes toward that action. In particular it normally expresses an intention, or at least an inclination, not to perform the action, and/or dispositions to feel guilty if one has performed it, to discourage others from performing it, and to react with anger, sorrow, or diminished respect toward others if they have performed it. I think this is true of Judeo-Christian ethical discourse as well as of other ethical discourse.

The interchangeability of 'wrong' and 'against the will of God' applies in full force here. It seems to make no difference to the expressive function of an ethical statement in a Judeo-Christian context which of these expressions is used. So far as I can see, the feelings and dispositions normally expressed by 'It is wrong to commit suicide' in a Judeo-Christian context are exactly the same as those normally expressed by 'It is against God's will to commit suicide', or by 'Suicide is a violation of the commandments of God'.

I am speaking of attitudes *normally* expressed by statements that it is wrong to do a certain thing, or that it would be against God's will or commands to do that thing. I am not claiming that such attitudes are *always* expressed by statements of those sorts. Neither am I now suggesting any analysis of the *meaning* of the statements in terms of the attitudes they normally express. The relation between the meaning of the statements and the attitudes expressed is a matter about which I shall have somewhat more to say, later in this section and in section VI. At this point I am simply observing that in fact statements of the forms 'It is wrong to do X', 'It is against God's will to do X', 'X is a violation of the commandments of God', normally do express certain attitudes, and that in Judeo-Christian ethical discourse they all typically express the same attitudes.

Of course these attitudes can be specified only within certain very wide limits of normality. The experience of guilt, for instance, or the feelings that one has about conduct of others of which one disapproves, vary greatly from one individual to another, and in the same individual from one occasion to another.

(3) In a Judeo-Christian context, moreover, the attitudes expressed by a statement that something is wrong are normally quite strongly affected and colored by specifically religious feelings and interests. They are apt to be motivated in various degrees by, and mixed in various proportions with, love, devotion, and loyalty toward God, and/or fear of God. Ethical wrongdoing is seen and experienced as *sin,* as rupture of personal or communal relationship with God. The normal feelings and experience of guilt for Judeo-Christian believers surely cannot be separated from beliefs, and ritual and devotional practices, having to do with God's judgment and forgiveness.

In all sin there is offense against a person (God), even when there is no offense against any other human person—for instance, if I have a vice which harms me but does not importantly harm any other human being. Therefore in the Judeo-Christian tradition reactions which are appropriate when one has offended another person are felt to be appropriate reactions to any ethical fault, regardless of whether another human being has been offended. I think this affects rather importantly the emotional connections of the word 'wrong' in Judeo-Christian discourse.

(4) When a Judeo-Christian believer is trying to decide, in an ethical way, whether it would be wrong for him to do a certain thing, he typically thinks of himself as trying to determine whether it would be against God's will for him to do it. His deliberations may turn on the interpretation of certain religiously authoritative texts. They may be partly carried out in the form of prayer. It is quite possible, however, that his deliberations will take forms more familiar to the nonbeliever. Possibly his theology will encourage him to give some weight to his own intuitions and feelings

about the matter, and those of other people. Such encouragement might be provided, for instance, by a doctrine of the leading of the Holy Spirit. Probably the believer will accept certain very general ethical principles as expressing commandments of God, and most of these may be principles which many nonbelievers would also accept (for instance, that it is always, or with very few exceptions, wrong to kill another human being). The believer's deliberation might consist entirely of reasoning from such general principles. But he would still regard it as an attempt to discover God's will on the matter.

(5) Typically, the Judeo-Christian believer is a nonnaturalist objectivist about ethical wrongness. When he says that something is (ethically) wrong, he means to be stating what he believes to be a fact of a certain sort—what I shall call a "nonnatural objective fact." Such a fact is objective in the sense that whether it obtains or not does not depend on whether any human being thinks it does. It is harder to give a satisfactory explanation of what I mean by 'nonnatural' here. Let us say that a nonnatural fact is one which does not consist simply in any fact or complex of facts which can be stated entirely in the languages of physics, chemistry, biology, and human psychology. That way of putting it obviously raises questions which it leaves unanswered, but I hope it may be clear enough for present purposes.

That ethical facts are objective and nonnatural has been believed by many people, including some famous philosophers—for instance, Plato and G. E. Moore. The term 'nonnaturalism' is sometimes used rather narrowly, to refer to a position held by Moore, and positions closely resembling it. Clearly, I am using 'nonnaturalist' in a broader sense here.

Given that the facts of wrongness asserted in Judeo-Christian ethics are nonnatural in the sense explained above, and that they accordingly do not consist entirely in facts of physics, chemistry, biology, and human psychology, the question arises, in what they do consist. According to the divine command theory (even the modified divine command theory), insofar as they are nonnatural and objective, they consist in facts about the will or commands of God. I think this is really the central point in a divine command theory of ethical wrongness. This is the point at which the divine command theory is distinguished from alternative theological theories of ethical wrongness, such as the theory that facts of ethical rightness and wrongness are objective, nonnatural facts about ideas or essences subsisting eternally in God's understanding, not subject to his will but guiding it.

The divine command account of the nonnatural fact-stating function of Judeo-Christian ethical discourse has at least one advantage over its competitors. It is clear, I think, that in stating that X is wrong a believer normally commits himself to the view that X is contrary to the will or commands of God. And the fact (if it is a fact) that X is contrary to the will or commands of God is surely a nonnatural objective fact. But it is not nearly so clear that in saying that X is wrong, the believer normally commits himself to belief in any *other* nonnatural objective fact. (The preceding sentence presupposes the rejection of the Moorean view that the fact that X is wrong[3] is an objective nonnatural fact which cannot and should not be analyzed in terms of other facts, natural or nonnatural.)

(6) The modified divine command theorist cannot consistently claim that 'wrong' and 'contrary to God's commands' have exactly the same meaning for him. For he admits that there is a logically possible situation which he would describe by saying, 'God commands cruelty for its own sake', but not by saying, 'It would be wrong not to practice cruelty for its own sake'. If there were not at least some little difference between the meanings with which he actually, normally uses the expressions 'wrong' and 'contrary to God's commands', there would be no reason for them to differ in their applicability or inapplicability to the far-out unthinkable case. We may now be in a position to improve somewhat our understanding of what the modified divine command theorist can suppose that difference in meaning to be, and of why he supposes that the believer is unwilling to say that disobedience to a divine command of cruelty for its own sake would be wrong.

We have seen that the expressions 'It is wrong' and 'It is contrary to God's commands' or 'It is against the will of God' have virtually the same uses in religious ethical discourse, and the same functions in the religious ethical life. No doubt they differ slightly in the situations in which they are most likely to be used and the emotional overtones they are most apt to carry. But in all situations experienced or expected by the believer as a believer they at least contextually imply each other, and normally express the same or extremely similar emotional and volitional attitudes.

There is also a difference in meaning, however: a difference which is normally of no practical importance. All three of the following are aspects of the normal use of 'It is wrong' in the life and conversation of believers. (a) It is used to state what are believed to be facts about the will or commands of God. (b) It is used in formulating decisions and arguments about what to do (i.e., not just in deciding what one *ought* to do, but in deciding *what to do*). (c) It expresses certain emotional and volitional attitudes toward the action under discussion. 'It is wrong' is commonly used to do all three of those things at once.

The same is true of 'It is contrary to God's commands' and 'It is against the will of God'. They are commonly used by believers to do the same three things, and to do them at once. But because of their grammatical form and their formal relationships with other straightforwardly descriptive expressions about God, they are taken to be, first and last, descriptive expressions about God and his relation to whatever actions are under discussion. They can therefore be used to state what are supposed to be facts about God, even when one's emotional and decision-making attitude toward those supposed facts is quite contrary to the attitudes normally expressed by the words 'against the will of God'.

In the case of 'It is wrong', however, it is not clear that one of its functions, or one of the aspects of its normal use, is to be preferred in case of conflict with the others. I am not willing to say, 'It would be wrong not to do X', when both my own attitude and the attitude of most other people toward the doing of X under the indicated circumstances is one of unqualified revulsion. On the other hand, neither am I willing to say, 'It would be wrong to do X', when I would merely be expressing my own personal revulsion (and perhaps that of other people as well) but nothing that I could regard as clothed in the majesty of a divine authority. The believer's concept of ethical wrongness therefore breaks down if one tries to apply it to the unthinkable case in which God commands cruelty for its own sake.

None of this seems to me inconsistent with the claim that part of what the believer normally means in saying 'X is wrong' is that X is contrary to God's will or commands.

IV

The modified divine command theory clearly conceives of believers as valuing some things independently of their relation to God's commands. If the believer will not say that it would be wrong not to practice cruelty for its own sake if God commanded it, that is because he values kindness, and has a revulsion for cruelty, in a way that is at least to some extent independent of his belief that God commands kindness and forbids cruelty. This point may be made the basis of both philosophical and theological objections to the modified divine command theory, but I think the objections can be answered.

The philosophical objection is, roughly, that if there are some things I value independently of their relation to God's commands, then my value concepts cannot rightly be analyzed in terms of God's commands. According to the modified divine command theory, the acceptability of divine command ethics depends in part on the believer's independent positive valuation of the sorts of things that God is believed to command. But then, the philosophical critic objects, the believer must have a prior, nontheological conception of ethical right and wrong, in terms of which he judges God's commandments to be acceptable—and to admit that the believer has a prior, nontheological conception of ethical right and wrong is to abandon the divine command theory.

The weakness of this philosophical objection is that it fails to note the distinctions that can be drawn among various value concepts. From the fact that the believer values some things independently of his beliefs about God's commands, the objector concludes, illegitimately, that the believer must have a conception of ethical right and wrong that is independent of his beliefs about God's commands. This inference is illegitimate because there can be valuations which do not imply or presuppose a judgment of ethical right or wrong. For instance, I may simply like something, or want something, or feel a revulsion at something.

What the modified divine command theorist will hold, then, is that the believer values some things independently of their relation to God's commands, but that these valuations are not judgments of ethical right and wrong and do not of themselves imply judgments of ethical right and wrong. He will maintain, on the other hand, that such independent valuations are involved in, or even necessary for, judgments of ethical right and wrong which also involve beliefs about God's will or commands. The adherent of a divine command ethics will normally be able to give reasons for his adherence. Such reasons might include: "Because I am grateful to God for his love"; "Because I find it the most satisfying form of ethical life"; "Because there's got to be an objective moral law if life isn't to fall to pieces, and I can't understand what it would be if not the will of God."[4] As we have already noted, the modified divine command theorist also has reasons why he would not accept a divine command ethics in certain logically possible situations which he believes not to be actual. All of these reasons seem to me to involve valuations that are independent of divine command ethics. The person who has such reasons wants certain things—happiness, certain satisfactions—for himself and others; he hates cruelty and loves kindness; he has perhaps a certain unique and "numinous" awe of God. And these are not attitudes which he has simply because of his beliefs about God's commands.[5] They are not attitudes, however, which presuppose judgments of moral right and wrong.

It is sometimes objected to divine command theories of moral obligation, or of ethical rightness and wrongness, that one must have some reason for obeying God's commands or for adopting a divine command ethics, and that therefore a nontheological concept of moral obligation or of ethical rightness and wrongness must be presupposed, in order that one may judge that one ought to obey God's commands.[6] This objection is groundless. For one can certainly have reasons for doing something which do not involve believing one morally ought to do it or believing it would be ethically wrong not to do it.

I grant that in giving reasons for his attitudes toward God's commands the believer will probably use or presuppose concepts which, in the context, it is reasonable to count as nontheological value concepts (e.g., concepts of satisfactoriness and repulsiveness). Perhaps some of them might count as moral concepts. But all that the defender of a divine command theory of ethical wrongness has to maintain is that the concept of ethical wrongness which occurs in the ethical thought and discourse of believers is not one of the concepts which are used or presupposed in this way. Divine command theorists, including the modified divine command theorist, need not maintain that *all* value concepts, or even all moral concepts, must be understood in terms of God's commands.

In fact some well-known philosophers have held forms of divine command theory which quite explicitly presuppose some nontheological value concepts. Locke, for instance, says in his *Essay,*

> Good and evil . . . are nothing but pleasure or pain, or that which occasions or procures pleasure or pain to us. *Morally good and evil,* then, is only the conformity or disagreement of our voluntary actions to some law, whereby good or evil is drawn on us from the will and power of the law-maker . . . (*Essay,* II, xxviii, 5)[7].

Locke goes on to distinguish three laws, or types of law, by reference to which actions are commonly judged as to moral good and evil: "(1) The *divine* law. (2) The *civil* law. (3) The law of *opinion* or *reputation,* if I may so call it" (*Essay,* II, xxviii, 7). Of these three Locke says that the third is "the common *measure of virtue and vice*" (*Essay,* II, xxviii, 11). In Locke's opinion the terms 'virtue' and 'vice' are particularly closely attached to the praise and blame of society. But the terms 'duty' and 'sin' are connected with the commandments of God. About the divine law Locke says,

> This is the only true touchstone of *moral rectitude;* and by comparing them to this law, it is that men judge of the most considerable *moral good* or *evil* of their actions: that is, whether, as *duties or sins,* they are like to procure them happiness or misery from the hands of the ALMIGHTY (*Essay,* II, xxviii, 8).

The structure of Locke's analysis is clear enough. By 'good' and 'evil' we *mean* (nontheologically enough) pleasurable and painful. By 'morally good' and 'morally evil' we *mean* that the actions so described agree or disagree with some law under which the agent stands to be rewarded or punished. By 'duty' and 'sin', which denote the most important sort of moral good and evil, we *mean* (theologically now) actions which are apt to cause the agent good or evil (in the nontheological sense) because they agree or disagree with the law of God. I take it that the divine command theory advocated by Peter Geach,[8] and hinted at by G. E. M. Anscombe,[9] is similar in structure, though not in all details, to Locke's.

The modified divine command theory that I have in mind does not rely as heavily as Locke's theory does on God's power to reward and punish, nor do I wish to assume Locke's analysis of 'good' and 'evil'. The point I want to make by discussing Locke here is just that there are many different value concepts and it is clearly possible to give one or more of them a theological analysis while giving others a nontheological analysis. And I do assume that the modified divine command theorist will give a nontheological analysis of some value concepts although he gives a theological analysis of the concept of ethical wrongness. For instance, he may give a nontheological analysis, perhaps a naturalistic one or a noncognitivist one, of the meaning of 'satisfactory' and 'repulsive', as he uses them in some contexts. He may even regard as *moral* concepts some value concepts of which he gives a nontheological analysis.

For it is not essential to a divine command theory of ethical wrongness to maintain that all valuing, or all value concepts, or even all moral concepts, depend on beliefs about God's commands. What is essential to such a theory is to maintain that when a believer says something is (ethically) *wrong,* at least part of what he means is that the action in question is contrary to God's will or commands. Another way of putting the matter is this. What depends on beliefs about God and his will is not all of the religious person's value concepts, nor in general his ability to value things, but only his ability to appraise actions (and possible actions) in terms of their relation to a superhuman, nonnaturally objective, law. Indeed, it is obvious that Judeo-Christian ethics presupposes concepts that have at least ethical overtones and that are not essentially theological but have their background in human social relations and political institutions—such as the concepts of promise, kindness, law, and command. What the specifically theological doctrines introduce into Judeo-Christian ethics, according to the divine command theory, is the belief in a law that is superior to all human laws.

This version of the divine command theory may seem *theologically* objectionable to some believers. One of the reasons, surely, why divine command theories of ethics have appealed to some theologians is that such theories seem especially congruous with the religious demand that God be the object of our highest allegiance. If our supreme commitment in life is to doing what is right just because it is right, and if what is right is right just because God wills or commands it, then surely our highest allegiance is to God. But the modified divine command theory seems not to have this advantage. For the modified divine command theorist is forced to admit, as we have seen, that he has reasons for his adherence to a divine command ethics, and that his having these reasons implies that there are some things which he values independently of his beliefs about God's commands. It is therefore not correct to say of him that he is committed to doing the will of God *just* because it is the will of God; he is committed to doing it partly because of other things which he values independently. Indeed it appears that there are certain logically possible situations in which his present attitudes would not commit him to obey God's commands (for instance, if God commanded cruelty for its own sake). This may even suggest that he values some things, not just independently of God's commands, but more than God's commands.

We have here a real problem in religious ethical motivation. The Judeo-Christian believer is supposed to make God the supreme focus of his loyalties; that is clear. One possible interpretation of this fact is the following. Obedience to whatever God may command is (or at least ought to be) the one thing that the believer values for its own sake and more than anything and everything else. Anything else that he values, he values (or ought to) only to a lesser degree and as a means to obedience to God. This conception of religious ethical motivation is obviously favorable to an *un*modified divine command theory of ethical wrongness.

But I think it is not a realistic conception. Loyalty to God, for instance, is very often explained, by believers themselves, as motivated by gratitude for benefits conferred. And I think it is clear in most cases that the gratitude presupposes that the benefits are valued, at least to some extent, independently of loyalty to God. Similarly, I do not think that most devout Judeo-Christian believers would say that it would be wrong to disobey God if he commanded cruelty for its own sake. And if I am right about that I think it shows that their positive valuation of (emotional/volitional pro-attitude toward) doing *whatever* God may command is not clearly greater than their independent negative valuation of cruelty.

In analyzing ethical motivation in general, as well as Judeo-Christian ethical motivation in particular, it is probably a mistake to suppose that there is (or can be expected to be) one only thing that is valued supremely and for its own sake, with nothing else being valued independently of it. The motivation for a person's ethical orientation in life is normally much more complex than that, and involves a plurality of emotional and volitional attitudes of different sorts which are at least partly independent of each other. At any rate, I think the modified divine command theorist is bound to say that that is true of his ethical motivation.

In what sense, then, can the modified divine command theorist maintain that God is the supreme focus of his loyalties? I suggest the following interpretation of the single-hearted loyalty to God which is demanded in Judeo-Christian religion. In this interpretation the crucial idea is *not* that some one thing is valued for its own sake and more than anything else, and nothing else valued independently of it. It is freely admitted that the religious person will have a plurality of motives for his ethical position, and that these will be at least partly independent of each other. It is admitted further that a desire to obey the commands of God (*whatever* they may be) may not be the strongest of these motives. What will be claimed is that certain beliefs about God enable the believer to integrate or focus his motives in a loyalty to God and his commands. Some of these beliefs are about what God commands or wills (contingently: that is, although he could logically have commanded or willed something else instead).

Some of the motives in question might be called egoistic; they include desires for satisfactions for oneself—which God is believed to have given or to be going to give. Other motives may be desires for satisfaction for other people—these may be called altruistic. Still other motives might not be desires for anyone's satisfaction, but might be valuations of certain kinds of action for their own sakes—these might be called idealistic. I do not think my argument depends heavily on this particular classification, but it seems plausible that all of these types, and perhaps others as well, might be distinguished among the motives for a religious person's ethical position. Obviously such motives might pull one in different directions, conflicting with one another. But in Judeo-Christian ethics beliefs about what God does in fact will (although he could have willed otherwise) are supposed to enable one to *fuse* these motives, so to speak, into one's devotion to God and his will, so that they all pull together. Doubtless the believer will still have some motives which conflict with his loyalty to God. But the religious ideal is that these should all be merely momentary desires and impulses, and kept under control. They ought not to be allowed to influence voluntary action. The deeper, more stable, and controlling desires, intentions, and psychic energies are supposed to be fused in devotion to God. As I interpret it, however, it need not be inconsistent with the Judeo-Christian ethical and religious ideal that this fusion of motives, this integration of moral energies, depends on belief in certain propositions which are taken to be contingent truths about God.

Lest it be thought that I am proposing unprecedented theological positions, or simply altering Judeo-Christian religious beliefs to suit my theories, I will call to my aid on this point a theologian known for his insistence on the sovereignty of God. Karl Barth seems to me to hold a divine command theory of ethics. But when he raises the question of why we should obey God, he rejects with scorn the suggestion that God's *power* provides the basis for his claim on us. "By deciding for God [man] has definitely decided not to be obedient to power as power."[10] God's claim on us is based rather on his grace. "God calls us and orders us and claims us by being gracious to us in Jesus Christ."[11] I do not mean to suggest that Barth would agree with everything I have said about motivation, or that he offers a lucid account of a divine command theory. But he does agree with the position I have proposed on this point, that the believer's loyalty is not to be construed as a loyalty to God *as* all-powerful, nor to God *whatever* he might conceivably have willed. It is a loyalty to God *as* having a certain attitude toward us, a certain will for us, which God was free not to have, but to which, in Barth's view, he has committed himself irrevocably in Jesus Christ. The believer's devotion is not to merely possible commands of God as such, but to God's actual (and gracious) will.

V

The ascription of moral qualities to God is commonly thought to cause problems for divine command theories of ethics. It is doubted that God, as an agent, can properly be called 'good' in the moral sense if he is not subject to a moral law that is not of his own making. For if he is morally good, mustn't he do what is right *because* it is right? And how can he do that, if what's right is right because he wills it? Or it may be charged that divine command theories trivialize the claim that God is good. If 'X is (morally) good' means roughly 'X does what God wills', then 'God is (morally) good' means only that God does what he wills—which is surely much less than people are normally taken to mean when they say that God is (morally) good. In this section I will suggest an answer to these objections.

Surely no analysis of Judeo-Christian ethical discourse can be regarded as adequate which does not provide for a sense in which the believer can seriously assert that God is good. Indeed an adequate analysis should provide a plausible account of what believers do in fact mean when they say, 'God is good'. I believe that a divine command theory of ethical (rightness and) wrongness can include such an account. I will try to indicate its chief features.

(1) In saying 'God is good' one is normally expressing a favorable emotional attitude toward God. I shall not try to determine whether or not this is part of the meaning of 'God is good'; but it is normally, perhaps almost always, at least one of the things one is doing if one says that God is good. If we were to try to be more precise about the type of favorable emotional attitude normally expressed by 'God is good', I suspect we would find that the attitude expressed is most commonly one of *gratitude*.

(2) This leads to a second point, which is that when God is called 'good' it is very often meant that he is *good to us,* or *good to* the speaker. 'Good' is sometimes virtually a synonym for 'kind'. And for the modified divine command theorist it is not a trivial truth that God is kind. In saying that God is good in the sense of 'kind', one presupposes, of course, that there are some things which the beneficiaries of God's goodness value. We need not discuss here whether the beneficiaries must value them independently of their beliefs about God's will. For the modified divine command theorist does admit that there are some things which believers value independently of their beliefs about God's commands. Nothing that the modified divine command theorist says about the meaning of ('right' and) 'wrong' implies that it is a trivial truth that God bestows on his creatures things that they value.

(3) I would not suggest that the descriptive force of 'good' as applied to God is exhausted by the notion of kindness. 'God is good' must be taken in many contexts as ascribing to God, rather generally, qualities of character which the believing speaker regards as virtues in human beings. Among such qualities might be faithfulness, ethical consistency, a forgiving disposition, and, in general, various aspects of love, as well as kindness. Not that there is some definite list of qualities, the ascription of which to God is clearly implied by the claim that God is good. But saying that God is good normally commits one to the position that God has some important set of qualities which one regards as virtues in human beings.

(4) It will not be thought that God has *all* the qualities which are virtues in human beings. Some such qualities are logically inapplicable to a being such as God is supposed to be. For example, aside from certain complications arising from the doctrine of the incarnation, it would be logically inappropriate to speak of God as controlling his sexual desires. (He doesn't have any.) And given some widely held conceptions of God and his relation to the world, it would hardly make sense to speak of him as *cou-*

rageous. For if he is impassible and has predetermined absolutely every-thing that happens, he has no risks to face and cannot endure (because he cannot suffer) pain or displeasure.[12]

Believers in God's goodness also typically think he lacks some human virtues which would *not* be logically inapplicable to a being like him. A virtuous man, for instance, does not intentionally cause the death of other human beings, except under exceptional circumstances. But God has in-tentionally brought it about that all men die. There are agonizing forms of the problem of evil; but I think that for most Judeo-Christian believers (especially those who believe in life after death), this is not one of them. They believe that God's making men mortal and his commanding them not to kill each other, fit together in a larger pattern of harmonious pur-poses. How then can one distinguish between human virtues which God must have if he is good and human virtues which God may lack and still be good? This is an interesting and important question, but I will not attempt here to formulate a precise or adequate criterion for making the distinction. I fear it would require a lengthy digression from the issues with which we are principally concerned.

(5) If we accept a divine command theory of ethical rightness and wrongness, I think we shall have to say that *dutifulness* is a human virtue which, like sexual chastity, is logically inapplicable to God. God cannot either do or fail to do his duty, since he does not have a duty—at least not in the most important sense in which human beings have a duty. For he is not subject to a moral law not of his own making. Dutifulness is one virtuous disposition which men can have that God cannot have. But there are other virtuous dispositions which God can have as well as men. Love, for instance. It hardly makes sense to say that God does what he does *because* it is right. But it does not follow that God cannot have any reason for doing what he does. It does not even follow that he cannot have reasons of a type on which it would be morally virtuous for a man to act. For example, he might do something because he knew it would make his creatures happier.

(6) The modified divine command theorist must deny that in calling God 'good' one presupposes a standard of moral rightness and wrongness superior to the will of God, by reference to which it is determined whether God's character is virtuous or not. And I think he can consistently deny that. He can say that morally virtuous and vicious qualities of character are those which agree and conflict, respectively, with God's commands, and that it is their agreement or disagreement with God's commands that makes them virtuous or vicious. But the believer normally thinks he has at least a general idea of what qualities of character are in fact virtuous and vicious (approved and disapproved by God). Having such an idea,

he can apply the word 'good' descriptively to God, meaning that (with some exceptions, as I have noted) God has the qualities which the believer regards as virtues, such as faithfulness and kindness.

I will sum up by contrasting what the believer can mean when he says, 'Moses is good', with what he can mean when he says, 'God is good', according to the modified divine command theory. When the believer says, 'Moses is good', (a) he normally is expressing a favorable emotional attitude toward Moses (normally, though perhaps not always— sometimes a person's moral goodness displeases us). (b) He normally implies that Moses possesses a large proportion of those qualities of character which are recognized in the religious-ethical community as virtues, and few if any of those which are regarded as vices. (c) He normally implies that the qualities of Moses' character on the basis of which he describes Moses as good are qualities approved by God.

When the believer says, 'God is good', (a) he normally is expressing a favorable emotional attitude toward God, and I think exceptions on this point would be rarer than in the case of statements that a man is good. (b) He normally is ascribing to God certain qualities of character. He may mean primarily that God is kind or benevolent, that he is *good* to human beings or certain ones of them. Or he may mean that God possesses (with some exceptions) those qualities of character which are regarded as virtues in the religious-ethical community. (c) Whereas in saying, 'Moses is good', the believer was stating or implying that the qualities of character which he was ascribing to Moses conform to a standard of ethical rightness which is independent of the will of Moses, he is not stating or implying that the qualities of character which he ascribes to God conform to a standard of ethical rightness which is independent of the will of God.

VI

As I noted at the outset, the divine command theory of ethical wrongness, even in its modified form, has the consequence that believers and nonbelievers use the word 'wrong' with different meanings in ethical contexts, since it will hardly be thought that nonbelievers mean by 'wrong' what the theory says believers mean by it. This consequence gives rise to an objection. For the phenomena of common moral discourse between believers and nonbelievers suggest that they mean the same thing by 'wrong' in ethical contexts. In the present section I shall try to explain how the modified divine command theorist can account for the facts of common ethical discourse.

I will first indicate what I think the troublesome facts are. Judeo-Christian believers enter into ethical discussions with people whose religious or antireligious beliefs they do not know. It seems to be possible to conduct quite a lot of ethical discourse, with apparent understanding, without knowing one's partner's views on religious issues. Believers also discuss ethical questions with persons who are known to them to be nonbelievers. They agree with such persons, disagree with them, and try to persuade them, about what acts are morally wrong. (Or at least it is normally *said,* by the participants and others, that they agree and disagree about such issues.) Believers ascribe, to people who are known not to believe in God, beliefs that certain acts are morally wrong. Yet surely believers do not suppose that nonbelievers, in calling acts wrong, mean that they are contrary to the will or commandments of God. Under these circumstances how can the believer really mean 'contrary to the will or commandments of God' when he says 'wrong'? If he agrees and disagrees with nonbelievers about what is wrong, if he ascribes to them beliefs that certain acts are wrong, must he not be using 'wrong' in a nontheological sense?

What I shall argue is that in some ordinary (and I fear imprecise) sense of 'mean', what believers and nonbelievers mean by 'wrong' in ethical contexts may well be partly the same and partly different. There are agreements between believers and nonbelievers which make common moral discourse between them possible. But these agreements do not show that the two groups mean exactly the same thing by 'wrong'. They do not show that 'contrary to God's will or commands' is not part of what believers mean by 'wrong'.

Let us consider first the agreements which make possible common moral discourse between believers and nonbelievers.

(1) One important agreement, which is so obvious as to be easily overlooked, is that they use many of the same ethical terms—'wrong', 'right', 'ought', 'duty', and others. And they may utter many of the same ethical sentences, such as 'Racial discrimination is morally wrong'. In determining what people believe we rely very heavily on what they say (when they seem to be speaking sincerely)—and that means, in large part, on the words that they use and the sentences they utter. If I know that somebody says, with apparent sincerity, 'Racial discrimination is morally wrong', I will normally ascribe to him the belief that racial discrimination is morally wrong, even if I also know that he does not mean *exactly* the same thing as I do by 'racial discrimination' or 'morally wrong'. Of course if I know he means something *completely* different, I would not ascribe the belief to him without explicit qualification.

I would not claim that believers and nonbelievers use *all* the same ethical terms. 'Sin', 'law of God', and 'Christian', for instance, occur as ethical terms in the discourse of many believers, but would be much less likely to occur in the same way in nonbelievers' discourse.

(2) The shared ethical terms have the same basic grammatical status for believers as for nonbelievers, and at least many of the same logical connections with other expressions. Everyone agrees, for instance, in treating 'wrong' as an adjective and 'Racial discrimination is morally wrong' as a declarative sentence. '(All) racial discrimination is morally wrong' would be treated by all parties as expressing an A-type (universal affirmative) proposition, from which consequences can be drawn by syllogistic reasoning or the predicate calculus. All agree that if X is morally wrong, then it isn't morally right and refraining from X is morally obligatory. Such grammatical and formal agreements are important to common moral discourse.

(3) There is a great deal of agreement, among believers and nonbelievers, as to what types of action they call 'wrong' in an ethical sense and I think that that agreement is one of the things that make common moral discourse possible.[13] It is certainly not complete agreement. Obviously there is a lot of ethical disagreement in the world. Much of it cuts right across religious lines, but not all of it does. There are things which are typically called 'wrong' by members of some religious groups, and not by others. Nonetheless there are types of action which everyone or almost everyone would call morally wrong, such as torturing someone to death because he accidentally broke a small window in your house. Moreover any two people (including any one believer and one nonbeliever) are likely to find some actions they both call wrong that not everyone does. I imagine that most ethical discussion takes place among people whose area of agreement in what they call wrong is relatively large.

There is probably much less agreement about the most basic issues in moral theory than there is about many ethical issues of less generality. There is much more unanimity in what people (sincerely) say in answer to such questions as 'Was what Hitler did to the Jews wrong'? or 'Is it normally wrong to disobey the laws of one's country'? than in what they (sincerely) say in answer to such questions as 'Is it always right to do the act which will have the best results'? or 'Is pleasure the only thing that is good for its own sake'? The issue between adherents and nonadherents of divine command ethics is typical of basic issues in ethical and metaethical theory in this respect.

(4) The emotional and volitional attitudes normally expressed by the statement that something is 'wrong' are similar in believers and nonbelievers. They are not exactly the same; the attitudes typically expressed

by the believer's statement that something is 'wrong' are importantly related to his religious practice and beliefs about God, and this doubtless makes them different in some ways from the attitudes expressed by nonbelievers uttering the same sentence. But the attitudes are certainly similar, and that is important for the possibility of common moral discourse.

(5) Perhaps even more important is the related fact that the social functions of a statement that something is (morally) 'wrong' are similar for believers and nonbelievers. To say that something someone else is known to have done is 'wrong' is commonly to attack him. If you say that something you are known to have done is 'wrong', you abandon certain types of defense. To say that a public policy is 'wrong' is normally to register oneself as opposed to it, and is sometimes a signal that one is willing to be supportive of common action to change it. These social functions of moral discourse are extremely important. It is perhaps not surprising that we are inclined to say that two people agree with each other when they both utter the same sentence and thereby indicate their readiness to take the same side in a conflict.

Let us sum up these observations about the conditions which make common moral discourse between believers and nonbelievers possible. (1) They use many of the same ethical terms, such as 'wrong'. (2) They treat those terms as having the same basic grammatical and logical status, and many of the same logical connections with other expressions. (3) They agree to a large extent about what types of action are to be called 'wrong'. To call an action 'wrong' is, among other things, to classify it with certain other actions, and there is considerable agreement between believers and nonbelievers as to what actions those are. (4) The emotional and volitional attitudes which believers and nonbelievers normally express in saying that something is 'wrong' are similar, and (5) saying that something is 'wrong' has much the same social functions for believers and nonbelievers.

So far as I can see, none of this is inconsistent with the modified divine command theory of ethical wrongness. According to that theory there are several things which are true of the believer's use of 'wrong' which cannot plausibly be supposed to be true of the nonbeliever's. In saying 'X is wrong', the believer commits himself (subjectively, at least, and publicly if he is known to be a believer) to the claim that X is contrary to God's will or commandments. The believer will not say that anything would be wrong, under any possible circumstances, if it were not contrary to God's will or commandments. In many contexts he uses the term 'wrong' interchangeably with 'against the will of God' or 'against the commandments of God'. The heart of the modified divine command theory, I have suggested, is the claim that when the believer says, 'X is wrong', one thing he means to be doing is stating a nonnatural objective fact about X, and the nonnatural objective fact he means to be stating is that X is contrary to the will or commandments of God. This claim may be true even though the uses of 'wrong' by believers and nonbelievers are similar in all five of the ways pointed out above.

Suppose these contentions of the modified divine command theory are correct. (I think they are very plausible as claims about the ethical discourse of at least some religious believers.) In that case believers and nonbelievers surely do not mean exactly the same thing by 'X is wrong' in ethical contexts. But neither is it plausible to suppose that they mean entirely different things, given the phenomena of common moral discourse. We must suppose, then, that their meaning is partly the same and partly different. 'Contrary to God's will or commands' must be taken as expressing only part of the meaning with which the believer uses 'wrong'. Some of the similarities between believers' and nonbelievers' use of 'wrong' must also be taken as expressing parts of the meaning with which the believer uses 'wrong'. This view of the matter agrees with the account of the modified divine command theory in section III, where I pointed out that the modified divine command theorist cannot mean exactly the same thing by 'wrong' that he means by 'contrary to God's commands'.

We have here a situation which commonly arises when some people hold, and others do not hold, a given theory about the nature of something which everyone talks about. The chemist, who believes that water is a compound of hydrogen and oxygen, and the man who knows nothing of chemistry, surely do not use the word 'water' in entirely different senses, but neither is it very plausible to suppose that they use it with exactly the same meaning. I am inclined to say that in some fairly ordinary sense of 'mean', a phenomenalist, and a philosopher who holds some conflicting theory about what it is for a physical object to exist, do not mean exactly the same thing by 'There is a bottle of milk in the refrigerator'. But they certainly do not mean entirely different things, and they can agree that there is a bottle of milk in the refrigerator.

VII

These remarks bring us face to face with some important issues in the general theory of analysis and meaning. What are the criteria for determining whether two utterers of the same expression mean exactly the same thing by it, or something partly different, or something entirely different? What is the relation between philosophical analyses, and philosophical theories about the natures of things, on the one hand, and the meanings of terms in ordinary discourse on the other hand? I have permitted myself the liberty of speaking as if these issues did not exist. But their existence is notorious, and I certainly cannot resolve them in this essay. Indeed, I do not have resolutions to offer.

In view of these uncertainties in the theory of meaning, it is worth noting that much of what the modified divine command theorist wants to say can be said without making claims about the *meaning* of ethical terms. He wants to say, for instance, that believers' claims that certain acts are wrong normally express certain attitudes toward those acts, whether or not that is part of their meaning; that an act is wrong if and only if it is contrary to God's will or commands (assuming God loves us); that nonetheless, if God commanded cruelty for its own sake, neither obedience nor disobedience would be ethically wrong or ethically permitted; that if an act is contrary to God's will or commands that is a nonnatural objective fact about it; and that that is the only nonnatural objective fact which obtains if and only if the act is wrong. These are among the most important claims of the modified divine command theory—perhaps they include the very most important. But in the form in which I have just stated them, they are not claims about the *meaning* of ethical terms.

I do not mean to reject the claims about the meanings of terms in religious ethical discourse which I have included in the modified divine command theory. In the absence of general solutions to general problems in the theory of meaning, we may perhaps say what seems to us intuitively plausible in particular cases. That is presumably what the modified divine command theorist is doing when he claims that 'contrary to the will or commands of God' is part of the meaning of '(ethically) wrong' for many Judeo-Christian believers. And I think it is fair to say that if we have found unresolved problems about meaning in the modified divine command theory, they are problems much more about what we mean in general by 'meaning' than about what Judeo-Christian believers mean by 'wrong'.

Notes

1. Guillelmus de Occam, *Super 4 libros sententiarum,* bk. II, qu. 19, O, in vol. IV of his *Opera plurima* (Lyon, 1494–6; réimpression en fac-similé, Farnborough, Hants., England: Gregg Press, 1962). I am not claiming that Ockham held a divine command theory of exactly the same sort that I have been discussing.

2. Perhaps he will even think it is causally possible, but I do not regard any view on that issue as an integral part of the theory. The question whether it is causally possible for God to act 'out of character' is a difficult one, which we need not go into here.

3. Moore took goodness and badness as primitive, rather than rightness and wrongness; but that need not concern us here.

4. The mention of moral law in the last of these reasons may presuppose the ability to *mention* concepts of moral right and wrong, which may or may not be theological and which may or may not be concepts one uses oneself to make judgments of right and wrong. So far as I can see, it does not *presuppose* the *use* of such concepts to make judgments of right and wrong, or one's adoption of them for such use, which is the crucial point here.

5. The independence ascribed to these attitudes is not a *genetic* independence. It may be that the person would not have come to have some of them had it not been for his religious beliefs. The point is that he has come to hold them in such a way that his holding them does not now depend entirely on his beliefs about God's commands.

6. I take A. C. Ewing to be offering an objection of this type on p. 112 of his book *Ethics* (London: English Univs. Press, 1953).

7. I quote from John Yolton's edition of *An Essay Concerning Human Understanding*, 2 vols. (London and New York: Everyman's Library, 1967).

8. In *God and the Soul* (London: Routledge, 1969), ch. 9.

9. In "Modern Moral Philosophy," *Philosophy*, 33 (1958), pp. 1–19.

10. Karl Barth, *Church Dogmatics*, vol. II, pt. 2, trans. G. W. Bromiley and others (Edinburgh: T. & T. Clark, 1957), p. 553.

11. Ibid., p. 560.

12. The argument here is similar to one which is used for another purpose by Ninian Smart in "Omnipotence, Evil, and Superman," *Philosophy*, 36 (1961), reprinted in Nelson Pike, ed., *God and Evil* (Englewood Cliffs, N.J.: Prentice-Hall, 1964), pp. 103–12.

I do not mean to endorse the doctrines of divine impassibility and theological determinism.

13. Cf. Ludwig Wittgenstein, *Philosophical Investigations*, 2d ed. (Oxford: Blackwell, 1958), pt. I, sec. 242: "If language is to be a means of communication there must be agreement not only in definitions but also (queer as this may sound) in judgments." In contemporary society I think it may well be the case that because there is not agreement in ethical definitions, common ethical discourse requires a measure of agreement in ethical judgments. (I do not mean to comment here more broadly on the truth or falsity of Wittgenstein's statement as a statement about the conditions of linguistic communication in general.)

8

Autonomy and Theological Ethics

Some theists believe that the moral rightness and wrongness of actions consists in agreement and disagreement, respectively, with God's commands. And even theists who do not hold this metaethical view do generally believe that all right action is commanded by God and should be done in obedience to him. I wish to respond here to one of the commonest objections to this belief: that it is incompatible with a proper regard for the virtue of autonomy.[1]

It has become something of an axiom in modern ethical theory that we ought to be autonomous in our moral actions. The senses in which this axiom is understood are surprisingly varied; and the reasons for which it is accepted, when it is not part of a Kantian or noncognitivist metaethics, are often obscure. I will discuss two reasons that may be given for thinking that we ought to be autonomous in a sense that is incompatible with regarding all our moral action as obedience to any commander.

One reason has to do with *responsibility*. As a recent critic of divine command ethics puts it,

> There is no room in morality for commands, whether they are the father's, the schoolmaster's or the priest's. There is still no room for them when they are God's commands. A moral agent is only in very special circumstances permitted to shelter behind the excuse, 'I was ordered to do it'. In morality we are responsible even for those actions which are responses to commands. We are responsible for obeying a command. Some commands given by some people ought not to be obeyed. It would be wicked to obey them.[2]

An earlier version of this paper formed part of a presentation at a meeting of the American Philosophical Association, at which Philip L. Quinn was my co-symposiast. For a different approach to these issues, see his interesting article on 'Religious Obedience and Moral Autonomy' in *Religious Studies*, 11 (1975), pp. 265–81.

The adherent of divine command ethics is sometimes compared to a soldier or official of the Nazi government of Germany in the Second World War who claims that he cannot be blamed for anything he did if he did it in obedience to orders. In both cases, it may be charged, there is an abdication of moral responsibility. The comparison is distasteful, but may be helpful in understanding the issues that are raised here.

Let us consider two hypothetical Nazi concentration camp guards who took part in the killing of hundreds of innocent and unresisting prisoners. We may call them the Conscientiously Obedient Nazi and the Cynical Nazi. The Conscientiously Obedient Nazi has always believed that he was doing the right thing, because he identifies his moral duty with his institutional duty to obey his superiors, and he killed in obedience to orders. It is somewhat misleading to say that he has abdicated his moral responsibility. He holds himself morally responsible to do his duty as he sees it, which is always to obey orders. We think he has an erroneous view of what his moral duty is. Indeed we think it is so horribly erroneous that we do not set much value on his conscientiousness. But it is as true of him as it is of anyone, that he holds himself responsible to do his moral duty.

The Cynical Nazi, on the other hand, has always thought that it was wrong for him to participate in killing the prisoners. But he thinks he ought to be excused for any serious blame, because his disobedience would have resulted in his own death and would not have saved any of the prisoners. He may be said to have abdicated his moral responsibility; he refuses to hold himself seriously responsible for what he did.

In so far as the conscientious adherent of divine command ethics is like either of these malefactors, he is clearly more like the Conscientiously Obedient Nazi than the Cynical Nazi. He holds himself responsible to do his ethical duty, which is to live in accordance with God's commands.

But perhaps what I have just said reflects a one-sided interpretation of the charge of abdicating responsibility. The Conscientiously Obedient Nazi does hold himself morally responsible for what he does, but he narrows the scope of his responsibility. He holds himself responsible only to obey orders. The first responsibility which a child receives from its parents is normally responsibility to follow very simple and direct instructions: for example, not to go in the street under any circumstances. As the child matures, it is ready to receive more responsibility. We speak of someone receiving or accepting *more* responsibility in proportion as fulfilling the responsibility involves making decisions that are more than just decisions to obey.

Of course divine command ethics can allow very large areas of discretion, and hence very large responsibility, if the divine commands are for the most part as general as 'Love your neighbor as yourself' and 'If possible, so far as it depends on you, live in peace with everyone'.[3] Still, it may be objected, in such an ethics there is a specific responsibility that is abdicated to the Divine Commander: namely, the responsibility of determining whether it is indeed right to love one's neighbor as oneself. This objection seems to me confused. What is it that we are told we ought to determine for ourselves? Whether God ought to have commanded neighbor-love? Surely that is his responsibility (so to speak) and not ours. Whether neighbor-love would have been right if God had not commanded it? That would seem to be a question of no immediate practical relevance for those who believe that God has commanded neighbor-love. Are we responsible, then, to determine whether neighbor-love is right, given that God commands it? But the adherent of divine command ethics does determine that for himself; he just does so on the basis of his belief that everything God commands is right. You may regard him as mistaken, but why irresponsible?

I suspect, however, that the discussion of responsibility does not get to the bottom of the matter. The second argument for autonomy has to do with *motives*. Let us compare the Conscientiously Obedient Nazi with three other characters: the Autonomous Nazi, the Conscientiously Obedient Relief Worker, and the Autonomous Relief Worker.

The Autonomous Nazi is a concentration camp guard who treats the prisoners just as the Conscientiously Obedient and Cynical Nazis treat them. But he kills prisoners, not merely from obedience or fear, as they do, but from a deep emotional and intellectual commitment to the aims and principles of Nazism. He would disobey orders if they seemed to him to betray the Nazi cause. Do we think better of him for his autonomy? I certainly don't. I would call him fanatical as well as autonomous, and think worse of him than of the Conscientiously Obedient Nazi.

Our relief workers are employed in a warehouse that handles shipments of food. Both of them try to ensure that the food actually goes to people who desperately need it, and does not end up in the hands of corrupt officials. The Conscientiously Obedient Relief Worker does this only because he has been instructed by his employers to do it, and believes unquestioningly that that morally obliges him to do it. The Autonomous Relief Worker directs the food to the poor, not just because he has been instructed to do so, but primarily because he cares about the needs of the poor. He would disobey instructions if they seemed to him to betray the humanitarian cause. I do think better of him than of the Conscientiously Obedient Relief Worker.

The chief difference between the autonomous and the conscientiously obedient person in these examples is that the latter does what he does just in order to be obedient, whereas the autonomous person does what he does at least partly for its own sake or for the sake of its consequences. Evildoing is worse, and well-doing is better, if done for its own sake and not just from obedience. This suggests another reason why one might think that divine command ethics leaves less room than it ought to for autonomy. It is presumably only in well-doing that it is morally good to obey God's commands. But in well-doing one will do even better if one acts out of love for the good to be accomplished, and not just for obedience' sake. It is better to avoid lies because one loves truthfulness, to deal fairly because one loves fairness, and to give to charity because one cares about people's needs, than to do those things just because one has been commanded, even by God, to do them. So perhaps the introduction of divine commands in ethics threatens to debase our motivation in well-doing.

Here it may be helpful to borrow the term 'theonomous' from Paul Tillich. According to Tillich,

> Autonomy asserts that man . . . is his own law. Heteronomy asserts that man . . . must be subjected to a law, strange and superior to him. Theonomy asserts that the superior law is at the same time, the innermost law of man himself, rooted in the divine ground which is man's own ground.[4]

Let us say that a person is *theonomous* to the extent that the following is true of him: He regards his moral principles as given him by God, and adheres to them partly out of love or loyalty to God, but he also prizes them for their own sakes, so that they are the principles he *would* give himself if he were giving himself a moral law. The theonomous agent, in so far as he is right, acts morally because he loves God, but also because he loves what God loves. He has the motivational goods both of obedience and of autonomy.

There is much in theological ethics that favors theonomy rather than pure heteronomy. We are told that God commands us to love our neighbors as ourselves. But we do not love them at all unless we care about them at least partly for their own sakes. The believer aspires to be filled with God's Spirit. But God presumably loves truthfulness, fairness, kindness, mercy, and other good qualities for their own sakes, and not just because he has commanded them. And one who is filled with God's Spirit ought to love them in some measure as God loves them. Suppose that God loves us and also loves those qualities. Should we expect him to want us to be truthful, fair, kind, merciful, and so forth heteronomously, solely because he has commanded us to behave that way? Should we not rather expect God to prefer us to be theonomous—loyal to him, but also acting out of love for the things that he loves?

Theonomy conforms with a normative principle of obedience to God. It is also compatible with some forms of divine command metaethics. For the theonomous person may love his moral principles for their own sake, but believe that they owe their status as moral principles wholly or partly to their divine sponsorship.

Notes

1. I believe this constitutes the most important objection to divine command metaethics that I have not discussed in "A Modified Divine Command Theory of Ethical Wrongness," in Gene Outka and John P. Reeder, Jr., eds., *Religion and Morality* (Garden City, NJ: Doubleday, 1973), pp. 318–47 [chapter 7 in the present volume].

2. Graeme de Graaff, "God and Morality," in Ian T. Ramsey, ed., *Christian Ethics and Contemporary Philosophy* (London: SCM Press, 1966), p. 34.

3. Leviticus 19:18 and Romans 12:18.

4. Paul Tillich, *The Protestant Era,* abridged edition, trans. J. L. Adams (Chicago: University of Chicago Press, 1960), p. 56f.

9

Divine Command Metaethics
Modified Again

In a recent issue of *The Journal of Religious Ethics,* Jeffrey Stout (1978) has written about an earlier paper of mine (Adams, 1973: chap. 7 in this volume) urging development and modification of the very point on which, as it happens, my own metaethical views have changed most. My thoughts have been moving in a rather different direction from his, however.[1] For that reason, and because of his paper's interesting and perceptive linkage of metaethical issues with the most fundamental questions in the theory of meaning, I would like to respond to him.

I. My Old Position

My modified divine command theory was proposed as a partial analysis of the *meaning* of '(ethically) wrong'. Recognizing that it would be most implausible as an analysis of the sense in which the expression is used by many speakers (for instance, by atheists), I proposed the theory only as an analysis of the meaning of 'wrong' in the discourse of some Jewish and Christian believers. In the theory that I now prefer, as we shall see, the identification of wrongness with contrariety to God's commands is neither presented as a meaning analysis nor relativized to a group of believers. According to the old theory, however, it is part of the meaning of '(ethically) wrong' for at least some believers that

(1) (for any action X) X is ethically wrong if and only if X is contrary to God's commands,

but also that

(2) 'X is wrong' normally expresses opposition or certain other negative attitudes toward X.

The meaning of 'wrong' seems to be overdetermined by (1) and (2). Conflicts could arise. Suppose God commanded me to practice cruelty for its own sake. (More precisely, suppose he commanded me to make it my chief end in life to inflict suffering on other human beings, for no other reason than that he commanded it.) I cannot summon up the relevant sort of opposition or negative attitude toward disobedience to such a command, and I will not say that it would be wrong to disobey it.

Such conflicts within the religious ethical belief system are prevented by various background beliefs, which are *presupposed* by (1). Particularly important is the belief that

> (3) God is loving, and therefore does not and will not command such things as (e.g.) the practice of cruelty for its own sake.

But (3) is contingent. It is allowed by the theory to be logically possible for God to command cruelty for its own sake, although the believer is confident he will not do such a thing. Were the believer to come to think (3) false, however, I suggested that his concept of ethical wrongness would "break down." It would not function as it now does, because he would not be prepared to use it to say that any action is wrong (Adams, 1973:100–102).

Because of the interplay and tension of the various considerations involved in it, this picture of the meaning of '(ethically) wrong' is (as I acknowledged) somewhat "untidy." But its untidiness should not obscure the fact that I meant it quite definitely to follow from the theory that the following are necessary truths:

> (4) If X is wrong, then X is contrary to the commands of God.
> (5) If X is obligatory, then X is required by the commands of God.
> (6) If X is ethically permitted, then X is permitted by the commands of God.
> (7) If there is not a *loving* God, then nothing is ethically wrong or obligatory or permitted.

These four theses are still taken to be necessary truths in my present divine command theory.

II. Stout's Holism

According to the theory of my earlier paper, as we have seen, what believers mean by 'wrong' depends, in some sense, on their belief about the truth or falsity of (3), which is admitted to be a synthetic and contingent matter of fact. To that extent I may be seen as having moved toward a breach in the wall that in earlier analytical philosophy separated analytical propositions, true by virtue of meanings alone, from synthetic propositions. Stout urges me to follow that path to what he calls 'holism'.

He suggests that the meaning of an expression is given by its role in "the evidence-inference-action game," which is a system of relations among "observational situations," inferences, "beliefs, desires, intentions," and actions, as well as sentences used in thought or speech (Stout, 1978:5–6). The expression derives its meaning from its relation to the system as a whole. The idea that the meaning is given by one or a few analytically true sentences, and/or by a well defined set of observations that would conclusively verify or falsify certain crucial sentences containing the expression, is discarded. For Stout seems to accept the view that if one has an experience that seems to conflict with something else one believes, there will be no belief that absolutely must be given up (none that will be falsified with absolute conclusiveness) and none of one's beliefs is so certain *a priori* that it can be immune from possible revision in the light of experience. One's system of beliefs constantly needs revisions to bring it or keep it in harmony with experience, but there is no set of purely *a priori* or analytic beliefs which cannot be revised.

This is not to say that all beliefs are equally revisable. Stout (1978:7–9) holds that there are "lawlike sentences" that "play a special role" in the evidence-inference-action language game, and that are particularly "deeply entrenched." Though not immune from revision, they are less likely than other sentences to be revised in most situations. They determine what is possible in the game, "relative to the entire scheme as it stands."

They are especially "important in determining conceptual role" (Stout, 1978:7). It seems to follow that the beliefs they express contribute more than other beliefs to determining the meaning of an expression, but not that they alone determine meanings. Every belief plays some part (perhaps too small to be noticeable) in the determination of meanings. "Holism . . . draws no sharp distinction between changes in meaning and changes in belief" (Stout, 1978:11).

The most important impetus for such holism has come from Quine— and specifically from the suspicion, defended in his famous 1951 essay, "Two Dogmas of Empiricism" (Quine, 1963:20–46), that

> (8) The analytic/synthetic distinction cannot be made sense of in such a way as to allow for there being any analytic truths.

This suspicion does indeed strike, as Quine suggested, at one of the central dogmas of earlier twentieth-century empiricism. But Quinean holism has commonly left standing another typical assumption of that school of thought, about the relation between necessity and analyticity. By 'broadly logical necessity' we shall mean logical (or absolute or metaphysical, as opposed to epistemic and causal) necessity, in a sense that embraces more than just validity relative to some system of formal logic. The empiricist assumption commonly retained by holists is that

(9) Broadly logical necessity can be understood only as analyticity.

From (8) and (9) it clearly follows that

(10) It cannot intelligibly be supposed that there are any broadly logically necessary truths.

Both Quine and Stout seem to suspect, at least, that (10) is true, and to doubt the intelligibility of broadly logical modality in general (Quine, 1966:169; Stout, 1978:8f.).

Stout quite rightly leaves it an open question how far my 1973 paper was based on such a holistic view. The answer, I think, is "Not very far." Such departure from traditional empiricist assumptions about meaning as appeared in that paper was probably more of Wittgensteinian than of Quinean inspiration; and if my present approach is less Wittgensteinian, it is not more Quinean. I have never accepted (8) or (10), and have long doubted (9). I now reject (9), as will be explained at some length below.

But I admire Stout's ingenious development of my metaethical claims in terms of his holism. On the basis of his views about the special role of "those lawlike sentences deemed virtually unconditionally assertible by the linguistic community at large," Stout says that

it makes sense, according to holism, that the meaning of "wrong" in "Judeo-Christian ethical discourse" will be determined in large part by the role of this word in the following conditional: "For any x, if x is contrary to God's commands, then x is ethically wrong." And we may assume that this lawlike sentence is in fact widely accepted and deeply entrenched in "Judeo-Christian" epistemic communities. It is deemed virtually indubitable by believers (Stout, 1978:9).

Deeply entrenched as it is, this conditional is still subject in principle to revision, and would be abandoned (as Stout seems to agree) if it came to be believed that God commanded cruelty for its own sake. According to Stout's holism, "implication will *always* be relative to background assumptions. . . . Since it is possible that some of these background assumptions will be called into question by surprising events, it is also possible that familiar implications will someday fail to hold" (Stout, 1978:9f.).

Stout doubts, however, "that the meaning of 'ethically wrong' [for believers] would in fact break down quite so drastically" as I had predicted in such an "epistemological crisis."

> The meaning of "ethically wrong" in Adams' discourse is determined not only by its role in deeply entrenched conditionals about God's commands, but also by its role in a host of other lawlike sentences, equally entrenched, which make no reference to God at all. Were this not the case, it would be unclear why Adams would be thrown for such a loop by a command of cruelty for its own sake.

These other entrenched sentences contribute to determining the meaning of 'ethically wrong'. "And they provide critical leverage in the event that God commands the unthinkable" (Stout, 1978:10). This criticism is perceptive and substantially correct; and I am no longer prepared to claim that my concept of ethical wrongness would break down in such an event.

But one of my sources of dissatisfaction with Stout's development of my position also emerges here. Many of my metaethical theses are rendered in his interpretation as claims about the *entrenchment* of "lawlike sentences," which seems to be the best approximation he thinks we can have to analyticity and broadly logical necessity. I take it that entrenchment is, at least in large part, an index of how strongly the relevant individual or community is disposed to resist additional epistemological pressures to abandon a belief; Stout speaks of a "deeply entrenched" sentence as "deemed virtually indubitable by believers" (Stout, 1978:9). On reflection, however, I think my central metaethical claims should not be about entrenchment in this sense. It was and is my view that the principle, 'Any action is ethically wrong if and only if it is contrary to the commands of a loving God', is a necessary truth, whereas 'Any action is ethically wrong if it is undertaken for the sake of cruelty alone' is not. Yet I certainly agree with Stout's suggestion that the latter principle is at least as entrenched in my belief system as the former. Indeed, I think that divine command metaethics can as correctly be adopted by a believer or community whose theistic faith is quite shaky as by one that believes unquestioningly. But the principles that are treated as necessary in divine command metaethics, such as (4), may be much less entrenched for the doubting believer than many normative ethical principles, both general and specific, that should be contingent according to a divine command theory. I hasten to add that these considerations probably tell not only against Stout's interpretation, but also against the interpretation of my central claims as meaning analyses that I offered in my 1973 paper.

In the end, Stout thinks, the thoroughgoing holist has "no reason for speaking of *conceptual analysis* or of *meanings* at all." He welcomes "the passing of philosophy as a discipline devoted to conceptual analysis and the grasping of natures or essences," and proposes to replace "descriptive metaethics" with the history of ethics (Stout, 178:15f.). Historical understanding can certainly illuminate philosophical problems, but Stout does not explain in any detail what he expects the historian to do for ethics. His insistence on the possibility of reasoned testing and revision of all beliefs, including ethical beliefs, would hardly be consistent with the sort of historicism according to which the scope of *wissenschaftliche,* academically respectable religious and ethical studies includes the description and causal explanation of religious and ethical beliefs, but excludes issues about the truth or acceptability of such beliefs. But the reasoned study of the latter issues is the task of the philosopher rather than the historian, even if it cannot be accomplished by analysis of meanings. I would welcome the passing of the idea of philosophy as defined by a method of conceptual analysis. But that is not the passing of philosophy, and it leaves the philosopher with a task of grasping natures or essences (among other things).

III. The Separation of Necessity and Natures from Analyticity and Concepts

An important group of recent papers (especially Donnellan, 1966 and 1972; Kripke, 1972; and Putnam, 1975:196–290)[2] has made a persuasive case for a view that there are necessary truths that are neither analytic nor knowable *a priori*. Among these are truths about the nature of many properties. And I am now inclined to believe that the truth about the nature of ethical wrongness is of this sort.

A case of individual identity or nonidentity provides a first example of a truth that is necessary but empirical. In the Gospels according to Mark (2:14) and Luke (5:27–9) there is a story about a tax collector named 'Levi', who left his business to follow Jesus. There is a tradition, supported by the relevant texts in Matthew (9:9 and 10:3), that this man was the Matthew who appears in the lists of the twelve apostles. This belief is naturally expressed by saying that Levi was Matthew, or that Levi and Matthew were the same man. But perhaps they were not; none of us really knows.

Suppose they were in fact two different men. That is a truth that is in principle knowable, but only empirically knowable. It is certainly not an analytic truth, which could be discovered by analyzing our concepts of Levi and Matthew. But there is a compelling argument for believing it to be a necessary truth if it is true at all. For suppose it were a contingent truth. Then the actual world, w_1, would be one in which Matthew the apostle and Levi the tax collector are not identical, but a world, w_2, in which they would be identical would also be possible. Since identity is a transitive relation, however, and since Levi in w_1, is identical with Levi in w_2, and Levi in w_2 is identical with Matthew in w_2, and Matthew in w_2 with Matthew in w_1, it follows that Levi in w_1 is identical with Matthew in w_1. Thus the hypothesis that the nonidentity of Matthew and Levi is contingent leads to a contradiction. This argument is not completely uncontroversial in its assumptions about trans-world identity, but it seems to me to be correct. A similar argument can be given for holding that if Levi and Matthew were in fact identical, that is a necessary truth, although it is not *a priori*.

It should be emphasized that 'possible' is not being used in its *epistemic* sense here. Both worlds in which Matthew and Levi are identical and worlds in which they are distinct are epistemically possible; that is, either sort may be actual for all we know. But whichever sort is actual, the other sort lacks broadly logical possibility, or "metaphysical possibility" as it is often called by those who hold the views I am exploring here.

Another interesting feature of this example is that there is a property which our understanding of the meaning of 'Matthew' and 'Levi' in this context tells us Matthew and Levi must have had if they (or he) existed, but which is a property that they (or he) possessed contingently. By 'Matthew' we mean the individual who stands in a certain historical relation (not yet spelled out in a very detailed way by philosophers of language) to the use of 'Matthew' (on certain occasions known to us) as a name of a man believed to have been one of the disciples of Jesus. It is epistemically possible that Matthew was named 'Levi' and not 'Matthew', or that he was not one of the twelve apostles but got counted as one by mistake. But no one who does not stand in an appropriate historical relation to the relevant uses of 'Matthew' counts as Matthew; that is what is settled by the meaning with which we use 'Matthew'. Standing in this relation to these uses of 'Matthew' is surely a contingent property of Matthew, however. Matthew could have existed in a world in which he was never called 'Matthew' during or after his life, or in a world in which Jesus never had any disciples and the relevant uses of 'Matthew' never occurred.

Similar considerations apply to theories about the natures of properties, or of kinds of things. Hilary Putnam uses the theory that the nature of water is to be H_2O as an example in arguing that such theories, if true, are commonly necessary truths but not *a priori* (see also Kripke, 1972:314–

31). (As it happens, this example was given a somewhat different treatment, hereby superseded, in Adams, 1973:120.)

Suppose a vessel from outer space landed, carrying a group of intelligent creatures that brought with them, and drank, a transparent, colorless, odorless, tasteless liquid that dissolved sugar and salt and other things that normally dissolve in water. Even if we nonchemists could not distinguish it from water, we might intelligibly (and prudently) ask whether this substance really is water. Our question would be answered, in the negative, by a laboratory analysis showing that the beverage from outer space was not H_2O but a different liquid whose long and complicated chemical formula may be abbreviated as *XYZ* (see Putnam, 1975:223).

Why is it right to say that this *XYZ* would not be water? I take it to be Putnam's view that it is not an analytic truth that water is H_2O. What is true analytically, by virtue of what every competent user of the word 'water' must know about its meaning, is rather that if most of the stuff that we (our linguistic community) have been calling 'water' is of a single nature, water is liquid that is of the same nature as *that*.

This view enables Putnam to maintain against Quine that substantial change and development in scientific theories is possible without change in meaning (although he agrees with Quine "that meaning change and theory change cannot be sharply separated," and that *some* possible changes in scientific theory would change the meaning of crucial terms [see Putnam, 1975:255f.]). "Thus, the fact that an English speaker in 1750 might have called *XYZ* 'water', while he or his successors would not have called *XYZ* water in 1800 or 1850 does not mean that the 'meaning' of 'water' changed for the average speaker in the interval" (Putnam, 1975:225). This claim is plausible. Had the visitors from outer space arrived with their clear, tasteless liquid in England in 1750, the English of that time might wisely have wondered whether the stuff was really water, even if it satisfied all the tests they yet knew for being water. And the correct answer to *their* question too would have been negative, if the liquid was *XYZ* and not H_2O.

Although it is not an *a priori* but an empirical truth that water is H_2O, Putnam thinks it is metaphysically necessary. Suppose there is a possible world, w_3, in which there is no H_2O but *XYZ* fills the ecological and cultural role that belongs to H_2O in the actual world. *XYZ* looks, tastes, etc. like H_2O, and is even called 'water' by English speakers in w_3. In such a case, Putnam (1975:231) maintains, the *XYZ* in w_3 is *not* water, for in order to be water a liquid in *any* possible world must be the same liquid (must have the same nature, I would say) as the stuff that we actually call 'water', which is H_2O. We may say, on this view, that the property of being water *is* the property of being H_2O, so that nothing could have the one property without having the other, or lack one without lacking the other.

It should also be noted that on this view the property ascribed to water by the description that expresses the *concept* of water, or what every competent user of 'water' knows, is not a property that belongs to water necessarily. The description is 'liquid of the same nature as most of the stuff that we have been calling "water."' But it is only contingent that water is called 'water'. Water could perfectly well have existed if no one had given it a name at all, or if the English had called it 'yoof'.

This view of the relation between the nature of water and the meaning of 'water' seems to me plausible. And if we think it is correct, that will enhance the plausibility of an analogous treatment of the nature of right and wrong. But even if Putnam's claims about 'water' are mistaken, we certainly *could* use an expression as he says we use 'water'; and it would be worth considering whether 'right' and 'wrong' are used in something like that way.

IV. The Nature of Wrongness and the Meaning of 'Wrong'

I do not think that every competent user of 'wrong' in its ethical sense must know what the nature of wrongness is. The word is used—with the same meaning, I would now say—by people who have different views, or none at all, about the nature of wrongness. As I remarked in my earlier paper, "There is probably much less agreement about the most basic issues in moral theory than there is about many ethical issues of less generality" (Adams, 1973:118). That people can use an expression to signify an ethical property, knowing it is a property they seek (or shun, as the case may be), but not knowing what its nature is, was realized by Plato when he characterized the good as

> That which every soul pursues, doing everything for the sake of it, divining that it is something, but perplexed and unable to grasp adequately what it is or to have such a stable belief as about other things (*Republic* 505D–E).

What every competent user of 'wrong' must know about wrongness is, first of all, that wrongness is a property of actions (perhaps also of intentions and of various attitudes, but certainly of actions), and second, that people are generally opposed to actions they regard as wrong, and count wrongness as a reason (often a conclusive reason) for opposing an action. In addition I think the competent user must have some opinions about what actions have this property, and some fairly settled dispositions as to what he will count as reasons for and against regarding an action as wrong. There is an important measure of agreement among competent users in these opinions and dispositions—not complete agreement, nor universal agreement on some points and disagreement on others, but overlapping agreements of one person with another on some points and with still others on other points. "To call an action 'wrong' is, among other things, to classify it with certain other actions," as having a common property, "and there is considerable agreement . . . as to what actions those are" (Adams, 1973:119). Torturing children for fun is one of them, in virtually everyone's opinion.

Analysis of the concept or understanding with which the word 'wrong' is used is not sufficient to determine what wrongness is. What it can tell us about the nature of wrongness, I think, is that wrongness will be the property of actions (if there is one) that best fills the role assigned to wrongness by the concept. My theory is that contrariety to the commands of a loving God is that property; but we will come to that in section V. Meanwhile I will try to say something about what is involved in being the property that *best* fills the relevant role, though I do not claim to be giving an adequate set of individually necessary and jointly sufficient conditions.

(i) We normally speak of actions being right and wrong as of facts that obtain objectively, independently of whether we think they do. 'Wrong' has the syntax of an ordinary predicate, and we worry that we may be mistaken in our ethical judgments. This feature of ethical concepts gives emotivism and prescriptivism in metaethics much of their initial implausibility. If possible, therefore, the property to be identified with ethical wrongness should be one that actions have or lack objectively.

(ii) The property that is wrongness should belong to those types of action that are thought to be wrong—or at least it should belong to an important central group of them. It would be unreasonable to expect a theory of the nature of wrongness to yield results that agree perfectly with pretheoretical opinion. One of the purposes a metaethical theory may serve is to give guidance in revising one's particular ethical opinions. But there is a limit to how far those opinions may be revised without changing the subject entirely, and we are bound to take it as a major test of the acceptability of a theory of the nature of wrongness that it should in some sense account for the wrongness of a major portion of the types of action we have believed to be wrong.

(iii) Wrongness should be a property that not only belongs to the most important types of action that are thought to be wrong, but also plays a causal role (or a role as object of perception) in their coming to be regarded as wrong. It should not be connected in a merely fortuitous way with our classification of actions as wrong and not wrong.[3]

(iv) Understanding the nature of wrongness should give one more rather than less reason to oppose wrong actions as such. Even if it were discovered (as it surely will not be) that there is a certain sensory pleasure produced by all and only wrong actions, it would be absurd to say that wrongness *is* the property of producing that pleasure. For the property of producing such a pleasure, in itself, gives us no reason whatever to oppose an action that has the property.

(v) The best theory about the nature of wrongness should satisfy other intuitions about wrongness as far as possible. One intuition that is rather widely held and is relevant to theological metaethics is that rightness and wrongness are determined by a law or standard that has a sanctity that is greater than that of any merely human will or institution.

We are left, on this view, with a concept of wrongness that has both objective and subjective aspects. The best theory of the nature of wrongness, I think, will be one that identifies wrongness with some property that actions have or lack objectively. But we do not have a fully objective procedure for determining which theory of the nature of wrongness is the best, and therefore which property is wrongness.

For example, the property that is wrongness should belong to the most important types of action that are believed to be wrong. But the concept possessed by every competent user of 'wrong' does not dictate exactly which types of action those are. A sufficiently eccentric classification of types of actions as right or wrong would not fit the concept. But there is still room for much difference of opinion. In testing theories of the nature of wrongness by their implications about what types of action are wrong, I will be guided by my own classification of types of action as right and wrong, and by my own sense of which parts of the classification are most important.

Similarly, in considering whether identifying wrongness with a given property, P, makes wrongness more or less of a reason for opposing an action, I will decide partly on the basis of how P weighs with me. And in general I think that this much is right about prescriptivist intuitions in metaethics: To identify a property with ethical wrongness is in part to assign it a certain complex role in my life (and, for my part, in the life of society); in deciding to do that I will (quite reasonably) be influenced by what attracts and repels me personally. But it does not follow that the theory I should choose is not one that identifies wrongness with a property that actions would have or lack regardless of how I felt about them.

V. A New Divine Command Theory

The account I have given of the concept of wrongness that every competent user of 'wrong' must have is consistent with many different theories about the nature of wrongness—for example, with the view that wrongness is the property of failing to maximize human happiness, and with a Marxist theory that wrongness is the property of being contrary to the objective interests of the progressive class or classes. But given typical Christian beliefs about God, it seems to me most plausible to identify wrongness with the property of being contrary to the commands of a loving God. (i) This is a property that actions have or lack objectively, regardless of whether we think they do. (I assume the theory can be filled out with a satisfactory account of what love consists in here.) (ii) The property of being contrary to the commands of a loving God is certainly believed by Christians to belong to all and only wrong actions. (iii) It also plays a causal role in our classification of actions as wrong, insofar as God has created our moral faculties to reflect his commands. (iv) Because of what is believed about God's actions, purposes, character, and power, he inspires such devotion and/or fear that contrariness to his commands is seen as a supremely weighty reason for opposing an action. Indeed, (v) God's commands constitute a law or standard that seems to believers to have a sanctity that is not possessed by any merely human will or institution.

My new divine command theory of the nature of ethical wrongness, then, is that ethical wrongness *is* (i.e., is identical with) the property of being contrary to the commands of a loving God. I regard this as a metaphysically necessary, but not an analytic or a priori truth. Because it is not a conceptual analysis, this claim is not relative to a religious subcommunity of the larger linguistic community. It purports to be the correct theory of the nature of the ethical wrongness that *everybody* (or almost everybody) is talking about.

Further explanation is in order, first about the notion of a divine *command,* and second about the *necessity* that is claimed here. On the first point I can only indicate here the character of the explanation that is needed, for it amounts to nothing less than a theory of revelation. Theists sometimes speak of wrong action as action contrary to the "will" of God, but that way of speaking ignores some important distinctions. One is the distinction between the absolute will of God (his "good pleasure") and his revealed will. Any Christian theology will grant that God in his good pleasure sometimes decides, for reasons that may be mysterious to us, not to do everything he could to prevent a wrong action. According to some theologies nothing at all can happen contrary to God's good pleasure. It is difficult, therefore, to suppose that all wrong actions are unqualifiedly contrary to God's will in the sense of his good pleasure. It is God's *revealed* will—not what he wants or plans to have happen, but what he has told us to do—that is thought to determine the rightness and wrongness of human actions. Roman Catholic theology has made a further distinction, within God's revealed will, between his commands, which it would be wrong not to follow, and "counsels (of perfection)," which it would be better to follow but not wrong not to follow. It is best, therefore, in our metaethical theory, to say that wrongness is contrariety to God's *commands,* and commands must have been issued, promulgated, or somehow revealed.

The notion of the issuance of a divine command requires a theory of revelation for its adequate development. The first such theory that comes to mind may be a biblical literalism that takes divine commands to be just what is written in the Bible as commanded by God. But there will also be Roman Catholic theories involving the *magisterium* of the Church, a Quaker theory about "the inner light," theories about "general revelation" through the moral feelings and intuitions of unbelievers as well as believers, and other theories as well. To develop these theories and choose among them is far too large a task for the present essay.

The thesis that wrongness is (identical with) contrariety to a loving God's commands must be *metaphysically necessary* if it is true. That is, it cannot be false in any possible world if it is true in the actual world. For if it were false in some possible world, then wrongness would be nonidentical with contrariety to God's commands in the actual world as well, by the transitivity of identity, just as Matthew and Levi must be nonidentical in all worlds if they are nonidentical in any.

This argument establishes the metaphysical necessity of property identities in general; and that leads me to identify wrongness with contrariety to the commands of a *loving* God, rather than simply with contrariety to the commands of God. Most theists believe that both of those properties are in fact possessed by all and only wrong actions. But if wrongness is simply contrariety to the commands of God, it is necessarily so, which implies that it would be wrong to disobey God even if he were so unloving as to command the practice of cruelty for its own sake. That consequence is unacceptable. I am not prepared to adopt the negative attitude toward possible disobedience in that situation that would be involved in identifying wrongness simply with contrariety to God's commands. The loving character of the God who issues them seems to me therefore to be a metaethically relevant feature of divine commands. (I assume that in deciding what property is wrongness, and therefore would be wrongness in all possible worlds, we are to rely on our own actual moral feelings and convictions, rather than on those that we or others would have in other possible worlds.)

If it is necessary that ethical wrongness is contrariety to a loving God's commands, it follows that no actions would be ethically wrong if there were not a loving God. This consequence will seem (at least initially) implausible to many, but I will try to dispel as much as I can of the air of paradox. It should be emphasized, first of all, that my theory does not imply what would ordinarily be meant by saying that no actions *are* ethically wrong if there *is* no loving God. If there is no loving God, then the theological part of my theory is false; but the more general part presented in section IV implies that in that case ethical wrongness is the property with which it is identified by the best remaining alternative theory.

Similarly, if there is in fact a loving God, and if ethical wrongness is the property of being contrary to the commands of a loving God, there is still, I suppose, a possible world, w_4, in which there would not be a loving God but there would be people to whom w_4 would seem much as the actual world seems to us, and who would use the world 'wrong' much as we use it. We may say that they would associate it with the same *concept* as we do,[4] although the property it would signify in their mouths is not wrongness. The actions they call 'wrong' would not be wrong; that is, they would not have the property that actually is wrongness (the property of being contrary to the commands of a loving God). But that is not to say that they would be mistaken whenever they predicated 'is wrong' of an action. For 'wrong' in their speech would signify the property (if any) that is assigned to it by the metaethical theory that would be the best in relation to an accurate knowledge of their situation in w_4. We can even say that they would believe, as we do, that cruelty is wrong, if by that we mean, not that the property they would ascribe to cruelty by calling it 'wrong' is the same as the property that we so ascribe, but that the subjective psychological state that they would express by the ascription is that same that we express.

Readers who think that I have not sufficiently dispelled the air of paradox may wish to consider a slightly different divine command theory, according to which it is a contingent truth that contrariety to God's commands constitutes the nature of wrongness. Instead of saying that wrongness is the property that in the actual world best fills a certain role, we could say that wrongness is the property of having whatever property best fills that role in whatever possible world is in question. On the latter view it would be reasonable to say that the property that best fills the role constitutes the nature of wrongness, but that the nature of wrongness may differ in different possible worlds. The theist could still hold that the nature of wrongness in the actual world is constituted by contrariety to the commands of God (or of a loving God—it does not make as much difference which we say, on this view, since the theist believes God is loving in the actual world anyway). But it might be constituted by other properties in some other possible worlds. This theory does not imply that no actions would be wrong if there were no loving God; and that may still seem to be an advantage. On the other hand I think there is also an air of paradox about the idea that wrongness may have different natures in different possible worlds; and if a loving God does issue commands, actual wrongness has a very different character from anything that could occur in a world without a loving God.

The difference between this alternative theory and the one I have endorsed should not be exaggerated. On both theories the nature of wrongness is actually constituted by contrariety to the commands of (a loving) God. And on both theories there may be other possible worlds in which other properties best fill the role by which contrariety to a loving God's commands is linked in the actual world to our concept of wrongness.

Notes

1. The metaethical position to be presented here was briefly indicated in Adams (1979). Though not all the arguments given there in favor of the theory are repeated here, the position is much more fully expounded in the present essay.

2. I have selected from these papers points that are relevant to my theory. I do not claim to give a comprehensive account of their aims and contents. I am also indebted here to David Kaplan and Bernard Kobes, for discussion and for the opportunity of reading unpublished papers of theirs.

*3. Cf. Putnam (1975:290): "I would apply a generally causal account of reference also to moral terms . . ." I do not know how similar the metaethical views at which Putnam hints are to those that are developed in section IV of the present paper.

I should add that I do not (and never did) mean here to apply to the property of wrongness every feature of a "causal theory of reference" that has been devised for proper names or "natural kinds." I have not even meant that wrongness *is* a natural kind. I think some readers may have assumed that I did mean that, and I should have guarded more carefully against the misinterpretation. What I have meant to claim is just that there are *some* analogies between the semantics and metaphysics of wrongness and those proposed by Putnam for natural kinds. Condition (ii) here, for example, corresponds to a requirement, in Putnam's theory, that the nature of water, if it can be clearly identified, must belong, for the most part, to the samples of liquid that we have been calling 'water'. But there are also *dis*analogies. For instance, the nature of wrongness may not be accessible to empirical science in the same way that the nature of water is, and my discussion reflects this fact.

4. I follow Putnam in this use of 'concept'. I have avoided committing myself as to whether English speakers in w_4 would use 'wrong' with the same *meaning* as we do. See Putnam, 1975:234.

References

Adams, Robert Merrihew. 1973. "A Modified Divine Command Theory of Ethical Wrongness." In *Religion and Morality,* ed. Gene Outka and John P. Reeder, Jr., 318–47. Garden City, N.Y.: Anchor [chapter 7 in this volume; page references are to the present reprinting].

————. 1979. "Moral Arguments for Theistic Belief." In *Rationality and Religious Belief,* ed. C. F. Delaney, 116–40. Notre Dame, Ind.: University of Notre Dame Press [chapter 10 in this volume].

Donnellan, Keith. 1966. "Reference and Definite Descriptions." *Philosophical Review* 75:281–304.

————. 1972. "Proper Names and Identifying Descriptions." In *The Semantics of Natural Languages,* ed. Donald Davidson and Gilbert Harman, 356–79. Dordrecht and Boston: Reidel.

Kripke, Saul A. 1972. "Naming and Necessity." In *The Semantics of Natural Languages,* ed. Donald Davidson and Gilbert Harman, 253–355, 763–69. Dordrecht and Boston: Reidel.

Putnam, Hilary. 1975. *Mind, Language and Reality: Philosophical Papers,* vol. 2. Cambridge: Cambridge University Press.

Quine, Willard Van Orman. 1963. *From a Logical Point of View: 9 Logico-Philosophical Essays.* 2d ed. New York and Evanston, Ill.: Harper Torchbooks.

————. 1966. *The Ways of Paradox and Other Essays.* New York: Random House.

Stout, Jeffrey L. 1978. "Metaethics and the Death of Meaning: Adams' Tantalizing Closing." *The Journal of Religious Ethics* 6:1–18.

10

Moral Arguments for Theistic Belief

Moral arguments were the type of theistic argument most characteristic of the nineteenth and early twentieth centuries. More recently they have become one of philosophy's abandoned farms. The fields are still fertile, but they have not been cultivated systematically since the latest methods came in. The rambling Victorian farmhouse has not been kept up as well as similar structures, and people have not been stripping the sentimental gingerbread off the porches to reveal the clean lines of argument. This paper is intended to contribute to the remedy of this neglect. It will deal with quite a number of arguments, because I think we can understand them better if we place them in relation to each other. This will not leave time to be as subtle, historically or philosophically, as I would like to be, but I hope I will be able to prove something more than my own taste for Victoriana.

I

Let us begin with one of the most obvious, though perhaps never the most fashionable, arguments on the farm: an Argument from the Nature of Right and Wrong. We believe quite firmly that certain things are morally right and others are morally wrong (for example, that it is wrong to torture another person to death just for fun). Questions may be raised about the nature of that which is believed in these beliefs: what does the rightness or wrongness of an act consist in? I believe that the most ad-

I have discussed the topics of this paper for several years in classes at the University of Michigan and UCLA, with students and colleagues to whom I am indebted in more ways than I can now remember. I am particularly grateful to Thomas E. Hill, Jr., Bernard Kobes, and Barry Miller for their comments on the penultimate draft.

equate answer is provided by a theory that entails the existence of God—specifically, by the theory that moral rightness and wrongness consist in agreement and disagreement, respectively, with the will or commands of a loving God. One of the most generally accepted reasons for believing in the existence of anything is that its existence is implied by the theory that seems to account most adequately for some subject matter. I take it, therefore, that my metaethical views provide me with a reason of some weight for believing in the existence of God.

Perhaps some will think it disreputably "tender-minded" to accept such a reason where the subject matter is moral. It may be suggested that the epistemological status of moral beliefs is so far inferior to that of physical beliefs, for example, that any moral belief found to entail the existence of an otherwise unknown object ought simply to be abandoned. But in spite of the general uneasiness about morality that pervades our culture, most of us do hold many moral beliefs with almost the highest degree of confidence. So long as we think it reasonable to argue at all from grounds that are not absolutely certain, there is no clear reason why such confident beliefs, in ethics as in other fields, should not be accepted as premises in arguing for the existence of anything that is required for the most satisfactory theory of their subject matter.[1]

The divine command theory of the nature of right and wrong combines two advantages not jointly possessed by any of its nontheological competitors. These advantages are sufficiently obvious that their nature can be indicated quite briefly to persons familiar with the metaethical debate, though they are also so controversial that it would take a book-length review of the contending theories to defend my claims. The first advantage of divine command metaethics is that it presents facts of moral rightness and wrongness as objective, nonnatural facts—objective in the sense that whether they obtain or not does not depend on whether any human being thinks they do, and nonnatural in the sense that they cannot be stated entirely in the language of physics, chemistry, biology, and human or animal psychology. For it is an objective but not a natural fact that God commands, permits, or forbids something. Intuitively this is an advantage. If we are tempted to say that there are only natural facts of right and wrong, or that there are no objective facts of right and wrong at all, it is chiefly because we have found so much obscurity in theories about objective, nonnatural ethical facts. We seem not to be acquainted with the simple, nonnatural ethical properties of the intuitionists, and we do not understand what a Platonic Form of the Good or the Just would be. The second advantage of divine command metaethics is that it is relatively intelligible. There are certainly difficulties in the notion of a divine command, but at least it provides us more clearly with matter for thought than the intuitionist and Platonic conceptions do.

We need not discuss here to what extent these advantages of the divine command theory may be possessed by other theological metaethical theories—for example, by views according to which moral principles do not depend on God's will for their validity, but on his understanding for their ontological status. Such theories, if one is inclined to accept them, can of course be made the basis of an argument for theism.[2]

What we cannot avoid discussing, and at greater length than the advantages, are the alleged disadvantages of divine command metaethics. The advantages may be easily recognized, but the disadvantages are generally thought to be decisive. I have argued elsewhere, in some detail, that they are not decisive.[3] Here let us concentrate on three objections that are particularly important for the present argument.

(1) In accordance with the conception of metaethics as analysis of the meanings of terms, a divine command theory is often construed as claiming that 'right' *means* commanded (or permitted) by God, and that 'wrong' *means* forbidden by God. This gives rise to the objection that people who do not believe that there exists a God to command or forbid still use the terms 'right' and 'wrong', and are said (even by theists) to believe that certain actions are right and others wrong. Surely those atheists do not mean by 'right' and 'wrong' what the divine command theory seems to say they must mean. Moreover, it may be objected that any argument for the existence of God from the premise that certain actions are right and others wrong will be viciously circular if that premise *means* that certain actions are commanded or permitted by God and others forbidden by God.

One might reply that it is not obviously impossible for someone to disbelieve something that is analytically implied by something else that he asserts. Nor is it impossible for the conclusion of a perfectly good, noncircular argument to be analytically implied by its premises. But issues about the nature of conceptual analysis, and of circularity in argument, can be avoided here. For in the present argument, a divine command theory need not be construed as saying that the existence of God is analytically implied by ascriptions of rightness and wrongness. It can be construed as proposing an answer to a question left open by the meaning of 'right' and 'wrong', rather than as a theory of the meaning of those terms.

The ordinary meanings of many terms that signify properties, such as 'hot' and 'electrically charged', do not contain enough information to answer all questions about the nature (or even in some cases the identity) of the properties signified. Analysis of the meaning of 'wrong' might show, for example, that 'Nuclear deterrence is wrong' ascribes to nuclear deterrence a property about which the speaker may be certain of very little except that it belongs, independently of his views, to many actions that he opposes, such as torturing people just for fun. The analysis of meaning need not completely determine the identity of this property, but it may still be argued that a divine command theory identifies it most adequately.

(2) The gravest objection to the more extreme forms of divine command theory is that they imply that if God commanded us, for example, to make it our chief end in life to inflict suffering on other human beings, for no other reason than that he commanded it, it would be *wrong* not to obey. Finding this conclusion unacceptable, I prefer a less extreme, or modified, divine command theory, which identifies the ethical property of wrongness with the property of being contrary to the commands of a *loving* God. Since a God who commanded us to practice cruelty for its own sake would not be a loving God, this modified divine command theory does not imply that it would be wrong to disobey such a command.

But the objector may continue his attack: "Suppose that God did not exist, or that he existed but did not love us. Even the modified divine command theory implies that in that case it would not be wrong to be cruel to other people. But surely it would be wrong."

The objector may have failed to distinguish sharply two claims he may want to make: that some acts *would* be wrong even if God *did* not exist, and that some acts *are* wrong even if God *does* not exist. I grant the latter. Even if divine command metaethics is the best theory of the nature of right and wrong, there are other theories which are more plausible than denying that cruelty is wrong. If God does not exist, my theory is false, but presumably the best alternative to it is true, and cruelty is still wrong.

But suppose there is in fact a God—indeed a loving God—and that the ethical property of wrongness is the property of being forbidden by a loving God. It follows that no actions would be wrong in a world in which no loving God existed, if 'wrong' designates rigidly (that is, in every possible world) the property that it actually designates.[4] For no actions would have that property in such a world. Even in a world without God, however, the best remaining alternative to divine command metaethics might be correct in the following way. In such a world there could be people very like us who would say truly, "Kindness is right," and "Cruelty is wrong." They would be speaking about kindness and cruelty, but not about rightness and wrongness. That is, they would not be speaking about the properties that *are* rightness and wrongness, though they might be speaking about properties (perhaps natural properties) that they would be *calling* 'rightness' and 'wrongness'. But they would be using the words 'right' and 'wrong' with the same *meaning* as we actually do. For the meaning of the words, I assume, leaves open some questions about the identity of the properties they designate.

Some divine command theorists could not consistently reply as I have suggested to the present objection. Their theory is about the meaning of 'right' and 'wrong', or they think all alternatives to it (except the complete denial of moral distinctions) are too absurd to play the role I have suggested for alternative theories. But there is another reply that is open to them. They can say that although wrongness is not a property that would be possessed by cruelty in a world without God, the possibility or idea of cruelty-in-a-world-without-God *does* possess, in the actual world (with God), a property that is close kin to wrongness: the property of being frowned on, or viewed with disfavor, by God. The experience of responding emotionally to fiction should convince us that it is possible to view with the strongest favor or disfavor events regarded as taking place in a world that would not, or might not, include one's own existence—and if possible for us, why not for God? If we are inclined to say that cruelty in a world without God would be wrong, that is surely because of an attitude of disfavor that we have in the actual world toward such a possibility. And if our attitude corresponds to an objective, nonnatural moral fact, why cannot that fact be one that obtains in the actual world, rather than in the supposed world without God?

(3) It may be objected that the advantages of the divine command theory can be obtained without an entailment of God's existence. For the rightness of an action might be said to consist in the fact that the action *would* agree with the commands of a loving God if one existed, *or* does so agree if a loving God exists. This modification transforms the divine command theory into a nonnaturalistic form of the ideal observer theory of the nature of right and wrong.[5] It has the advantage of identifying rightness and wrongness with properties that actions could have even if God does not exist. And of course it takes away the basis of my metaethical argument for theism.

The flaw in this theory is that it is difficult to see what is supposed to be the force of the counterfactual conditional that is centrally involved in it. If there is no loving God, what makes it the case if there were one, he would command this rather than that? Without an answer to this question, the crucial counterfactual lacks a clear sense (cf. chapter 6 in this volume). I can see only two possible answers: either that what any possible loving God would command is logically determined by the concept of a loving God, or that it is determined by a causal law. Neither answer seems likely to work without depriving the theory of some part of the advantages of divine command metaethics.

No doubt some conclusions about what he would not command follow *logically* or analytically from the concept of a loving God. He would not command us to practice cruelty for its own sake, for example. But in some cases, at least, in which we believe the act is wrong, it seems only contingent that a loving God does or would frown on increasing the happiness of other people by the painless and undetected killing of a person who wants to live but will almost certainly not live happily.[6] Very diverse preferences about what things are to be treated as personal rights seem compatible with love and certainly with deity. Of course, you could explicitly build all your moral principles into the definition of the kind of hypothetical divine commands that you take to make facts of right and wrong. But then the fact that your principles *would* be endorsed by the commands of such a God adds nothing to the principles themselves; whereas, endorsement by an *actual* divine command would add something, which is one of the advantages of divine command metaethics.

Nor is it plausible to suppose that there are *causal* laws that determine what would be commanded by a loving God, if there is no God. All causal laws, at bottom, are about actual things. There are no causal laws, though there could be legends, about the metabolism of chimeras or the susceptibility of centaurs to polio. There are physical laws about frictionless motions which never occur, but they are extrapolated from facts about actual motions. And we can hardly obtain a causal law about the commands of a possible loving God by extrapolating from causal laws governing the behavior of monkeys, chimpanzees, and human beings, as if every possible God would simply be a very superior primate. Any such extrapolation, moreover, would destroy the character of the theory of hypothetical divine commands as a theory of *nonnatural* facts.

Our discussion of the Argument from the Nature of Right and Wrong may be concluded with some reflections on the nature of the God in whose existence it gives us some reason to believe. (1) The appeal of the argument lies in the provision of an explanation of moral facts of whose truth we are already confident. It must therefore be taken as an argument for the existence of a God whose commands—and presumably, whose purposes and character as well—are in accord with our most confident judgments of right and wrong. I have suggested that he must be a loving God. (2) He must be an intelligent being, so that it makes sense to speak of his having a will and issuing commands. Maximum adequacy of a divine command theory surely requires that God be supposed to have enormous knowledge and understanding of ethically relevant facts, if not absolute omniscience. He should be a God "unto whom all hearts are open, all desires known, and from whom no secrets are hid." (3) The argument does not seem to imply very much about God's power, however—certainly not that he is omnipotent. (4) Nor is it obvious that the argument supports belief in the unity or uniqueness of God. Maybe the metaethical place of divine commands could be taken by the unanimous deliverances of a senate of deities, although that conception raises troublesome questions about the nature of the morality or quasi-morality that must govern the relations of the gods with each other.

II

The most influential moral arguments for theistic belief have been a family of arguments that may be called Kantian. They have a common center in the idea of a moral order of the universe and are arguments for belief in a God sufficiently powerful to establish and maintain such an order. The Kantian family has members on both sides of one of the most fundamental distinctions in this area: the distinction between *theoretical* and *practical* arguments. By "a theoretical moral argument for theistic belief" I mean an argument having an ethical premise and purporting to prove the *truth,* or enhance the *probability,* of theism. By "a practical argument for theistic belief" I mean an argument purporting only to give ethical or other practical reasons for *believing* that God exists. The practical argument may have no direct bearing at all on the truth or probability of the belief whose practical advantage it extols.

Arguments from the Nature of Right and Wrong are clearly theoretical moral arguments for theistic belief. Kant, without warning us of any such distinction, gives us sometimes a theoretical and sometimes a practical argument (in my sense of "theoretical" and "practical," not his). His theoretical argument goes roughly as follows:

(A) We ought (morally) to promote the realization of the highest good.
(B) What we ought to do must be possible for us to do.
(C) It is not possible for us to promote the realization of the highest good unless there exists a God who makes the realization possible.
(D) Therefore, there exists such a God.

Kant was not clear about the theoretical character of this argument, and stated as its conclusion that "it is morally necessary to *assume* the existence of God."[7] Its premises, however, plainly imply the more theoretical conclusion that God exists.

(C) needs explanation. Kant conceived of the highest good as composed of two elements. The first element, moral virtue, depends on the wills of moral agents and does not require divine intervention for its possibility. But the second element, the happiness of moral agents in strict proportion to their virtue, will not be realized unless there is a moral order of the universe. Such an order, Kant argues, cannot be expected of the laws of nature, without God.

Doubts may be raised whether Kant's conception of the highest good is ethically correct and whether there might not be some nontheistic basis for a perfect proportionment of happiness to virtue. But a more decisive objection has often been made to (A): In any reasonable morality we will be obligated to promote only the best attainable approximation of the highest good. For this reason Kant's theoretical moral argument for theism does not seem very promising to me.[8]

Elsewhere Kant argues quite differently. He even denies that a command to promote the highest good is contained in, or analytically derivable from, the moral law. He claims rather that we will be "hindered" from doing what the moral law commands us to do unless we can regard our actions as contributing to the realization of "a final end of all things" which we can also make a "final end for all our actions and abstentions." He argues that only the highest good can serve morally as such a final end and that we therefore have a compelling moral need to believe in the possibility of its realization.[9] This yields only a practical argument for theistic belief. Stripped of some of its more distinctively Kantian dress, it can be stated in terms of "demoralization," by which I mean a weakening or deterioration of moral motivation.

(E) It would be demoralizing not to believe there is a moral order of the universe, for then we would have to regard it as very likely that the history of the universe will not be good on the whole, no matter what we do.

(F) Demoralization is morally undesirable.

(G) Therefore, there is moral advantage in believing that there is a moral order of the universe.

(H) Theism provides the most adequate theory of a moral order of the universe.

(J) Therefore, there is a moral advantage in accepting theism.

What is a moral order of the universe? I shall not formulate any necessary condition. But let us say that the following is *logically sufficient* for the universe's having a moral order: (1) A good world-history requires something besides human virtue (it might, as Kant thought, require the happiness of the virtuous); but (2) the universe is such that morally good actions will probably contribute to a good world-history. (I use 'world' as a convenient synonym for 'universe'.)

Theism has several secular competitors as a theory of a moral order of the universe in this sense. The idea of scientific and cultural progress has provided liberal thinkers, and Marxism has provided socialists, with hopes of a good world-history without God. It would be rash to attempt to adjudicate this competition here. I shall therefore not comment further on the truth of (H) but concentrate on the argument from (E) and (F) to (G). It is, after all, of great interest in itself, religiously and in other ways, if morality gives us a reason to believe in a moral order of the universe.

Is (E) true? Would it indeed be demoralizing not to believe there is a moral order of the universe? The issue is in large part empirical. It is for sociologists and psychologists to investigate scientifically what are the effects of various beliefs on human motivation. And the motivational effects of religious belief form one of the central themes of the classics of speculative sociology.[10] But I have the impression there has not yet been very much "hard" empirical research casting light directly on the question whether (E) is true.

It may be particularly difficult to develop empirical research techniques subtle enough philosophically to produce results relevant to our present argument. One would have to specify which phenomena count as a weakening or deterioration of moral motivation. One would also have to distinguish the effects of belief in a moral world order from the effects of other religious beliefs, for (E) could be true even if, as some have held, the effects of actual religious beliefs have been predominantly bad from a moral point of view. The bad consequences might be due to doctrines which are separable from faith in a moral order of the universe.

Lacking scientifically established answers to the empirical aspects of our question, we may say, provisionally, what seems plausible to us. And (E) does seem quite plausible to me. Seeing our lives as contributing to a valued larger whole is one of the things that gives them a point in our own eyes. The morally good person cares about the goodness of what happens in the world and not just about the goodness of his own actions. If a right action can be seen as contributing to some great good, that increases the importance it has for him. Conversely, if he thinks that things will turn out badly no matter what he does, and especially if he thinks that (as often appears to be the case) the long-range effects of right action are about as likely to be bad as good,[11] that will diminish the emotional attraction that duty exerts on him.[12] Having to regard it as very likely that the history of the universe will not be good on the whole, no matter what one does, seems apt to induce a cynical sense of futility about the moral life, undermining one's moral resolve and one's interest in moral considerations. My judgment on this issue is subject to two qualifications, however.

(1) We cannot plausibly ascribe more than a demoralizing *tendency* to disbelief in a moral order of the universe. There are certainly people who do not believe in such an order, but show no signs of demoralization.

(2) It may be doubted how much most people are affected by beliefs or expectations about the history of the universe as a whole. Perhaps most of us could sustain with comparative equanimity the bleakest of pessimism about the twenty-third century if only we held brighter hopes for the nearer future of our own culture, country, or family, or even (God forgive us!) our own philosophy department. The belief that we can accomplish something significant and good for our own immediate collectivities may be quite enough to keep us going morally. On the other hand, belief in a larger-scale moral order of the universe might be an important bulwark against demoralization if all or most of one's more immediate hopes were being dashed. I doubt that there has ever been a time when moralists could afford to ignore questions about the motivational resources available in such desperate situations. Certainly it would be unimaginative to suppose that we live in such a time.

Some will object that those with the finest moral motivation can find all the inspiration they need in a tragic beauty of the moral life itself, even if they despair about the course of history. The most persuasive argument for this view is a presentation that succeeds in evoking moral emotion in connection with the thought of tragedy: Bertrand Russell's early essay "A Free Man's Worship"[13] is an eloquent example. But I remain somewhat skeptical. Regarded aesthetically, from the outside, tragedy may be sublimely beautiful; lived from the inside, over a long period of time, I fear it is only too likely to end in discouragement and bitterness, though no doubt there have been shining exceptions.

But the main objection to the present argument is an objection to all practical arguments. It is claimed that none of them give justifying reasons for believing anything at all. If there are any practical advantages that are worthy to sway us in accepting or rejecting a belief, the advantage of not being demoralized is surely one of them. But can it be right, and intellectually honest, to believe something, or try to believe it, for the sake of any practical advantage, however noble?

I believe it can. This favorable verdict on practical arguments for theoretical conclusions is particularly plausible in "cases where faith creates its own verification," as William James puts it,[14] or where your wish is at least more likely to come true if you believe it will. Suppose you are running for Congress and an unexpected misfortune has made it doubtful whether you still have a good chance of winning. Probably it will at least be clear that you are more likely to win if you continue to believe that your chances are good. Believing will keep up your spirits and your alertness, boost the morale of your campaign workers, and make other people more likely to take you seriously. In this case it seems to me eminently reasonable for you to cling, for the sake of practical advantage, to the belief that you have a good chance of winning.

Another type of belief for which practical arguments can seem particularly compelling is trust in a person. Suppose a close friend of mine is accused of a serious crime. I know him well and can hardly believe he would do such a thing. He insists he is innocent. But the evidence against him, though not conclusive, is very strong. So far as I can judge the total evidence (including my knowledge of his character) in a cool, detached way, I would have to say it is quite evenly balanced. I want to believe in his innocence, and there is reason to think that I ought, morally, to believe in it if I can. For he may well be innocent. If he is, he will have a deep psychological need for someone to believe him. If no one believes him, he will suffer unjustly a loneliness perhaps greater than the loneliness of guilt. And who will believe him if his close friends do not? Who will believe him if I do not? Of course I could try to *pretend* to believe him. If I do that I will certainly be less honest with him, and I doubt that I will be more honest with myself, than if I really cling to the belief that he is innocent. Moreover, the pretense is unlikely to satisfy his need to be believed. If he knows me well and sees me often, my insincerity will probably betray itself to him in some spontaneous reaction.

The legitimacy of practical arguments must obviously be subject to some restrictions. Two important restrictions were suggested by William James. (1) Practical arguments should be employed only on questions that "cannot . . . be decided on intellectual grounds."[15] There should be a plurality of alternatives that one finds intellectually plausible. (The option should be "living," as James would put it.) Faith ought not to be "believing what you know ain't so." It also ought not to short-circuit rational inquiry; we ought not to try to settle by practical argument an issue that we could settle by further investigation of evidence in the time available for settling it. (2) The question to be decided by practical argument should be urgent and of practical importance ("forced" and "momentous," James would say). If it can wait or is pragmatically inconsequential, we can afford to suspend judgment about it and it is healthier to do so.

To these I would add a third important restriction: It would be irrational to accept a belief on the ground that it gives you a *reason* for doing something that you want to do. To the extent that your belief is based on a desire to do x, it cannot add to your reasons for doing x. There will be a vicious practical circle in a practical argument for any belief unless it is judged that the belief would be advantageous even if it were no more probable than it seems to be in advance of the practical argument. It may be rational to be swayed by a practical argument, on the other hand, if one is not inventing a reason for doing something, but trying to sustain in oneself the emotional conditions for doing something one already has enough reason to want to do.

Suppose again that you are a congressional candidate trying, for practical reasons, to maintain in yourself the belief that you have a good chance to win. This is irrational if your aim is to get yourself to do things that you think it would be unreasonable to do if you were less confident. But it is not irrational if your primary aim is to foster in yourself the right spirit to do most effectively things you think it reasonable to do anyway. The rationality of your trying, for practical reasons, to believe depends in this case on the strength of your antecedent commitment to going all out to win the election.

Similarly I think that the rationality of trying for moral reasons to believe in a moral order of the universe depends in large measure on the antecedent strength of one's commitment to morality. If one is strongly committed, so that one wishes to be moral even if the world is not, and if one seeks, not reasons to be moral, but emotional undergirding for the moral life, then it may well be rational to be swayed by the practical argument for the belief.

It can also be intellectually honest, provided that one acknowledges to oneself the partly voluntary character and practical basis of one's belief. In speaking of honesty here, what I have in mind is that there is no self-deception going on, and that one is forming one's belief in accordance with principles that one approves and would commend in other cases.

But there are other intellectual virtues besides honesty.[16] It is an intellectual virtue to proportion the strength of one's belief to the strength of the evidence, in most cases.[17] On the other hand, it seems to be an intellectual virtue, and is surely not a vice, to think charitably of other people. And what is it to think charitably of others? It is, in part, to require less evidence to think well of them than to think ill of them, and thus, in some cases, not to proportion the strength of one's belief to the strength of the evidence. Yet thinking charitably of others is not a species of intellectual dishonesty. Neither is it invariably an intellectual vice to be swayed by practical arguments.

III

Both Kantian and Christian theism imply that true self-interest is in harmony with morality. Kant believed that in the long run one's happiness

will be strictly proportioned to one's virtue. And if that would be denied
by many Christian theologians for the sake of the doctrine of grace, they
would at least maintain that no one can enjoy the greatest happiness without a deep moral commitment and that every good person will be very
happy in the long run. They believe that the most important parts of a
good person's self-interest are eternally *safe,* no matter how much his
virtue or saintliness may lead him to sacrifice here below. The truth of
these beliefs is surely another logically sufficient condition of the universe's having a moral order. (I assume that virtue is not so richly its
own reward as to be sufficient in itself for happiness.)

There are both theoretical and practical arguments for theistic belief
which are first of all arguments for faith in a moral world order that
harmonizes self-interest with morality. As such, they belong to the Kantian type. For obvious reasons, let us call them "individualistic," by contrast with Kant's own, more "universalistic," arguments.

The practical arguments of this individualistic Kantian type depend on
the claim that it would be demoralizing not to believe in a harmony of
self-interest with virtue. Many religious and social thinkers, from Greek
antiquity to Freud,[18] have ascribed to the gods the function of invisible
policemen, reinforcing moral motivation with self-concern, through belief
in supernatural rewards and punishments. Disbelief in this cosmic con-
stabulary has been widely feared as a breach in the dike that holds back
our baser desires. It is doubtful, however, that the gods have been effective policemen. One of the few relatively "hard" empirical data in this
area is that criminal behavior is not negatively correlated with assent to
religious doctrines.[19]

For this reason I think we are likely to obtain a more plausible argument
for the moral advantage of belief in a harmony of self-interest with virtue
if we focus not on gross but on subtle demoralization—not on the avoid-
ance of crime but on the higher reaches of the moral life.[20] The conviction
that every good person will be very happy in the long run has often con-
tributed, in religious believers, to a cheerfulness and single-heartedness
of moral devotion that they probably would not have had without it. This
integration of motives may be regarded as morally advantageous even if
its loss does not lead to criminality.

I anticipate the objection that self-interest has no place in the highest
ethical motives, and that belief in the harmony of self-interest with morality therefore debases rather than elevates one's motivation. What could
be nobler than the virtuous sacrifice of what one regards as one's only
chance for great happiness? Yet such sacrifice is rendered impossible by
faith in the sure reward of virtue.

I have two replies:

(1) Self-interest remains a powerful motive in the best of us; a life of which that was not true would hardly be recognizable as human. It is not obvious that a hard-won victory over even the most enlightened self-interest is morally preferable to the integration of motives resulting from the belief that it will be well with the righteous in the long run. Those who hold that belief still have plenty of victories to win over shorter-sighted desires. And it is plausible to suppose—though I do not know that anyone has proved it—that we are *more likely* to attain to the goodness that is possible through an integration of motives, than to win a death struggle with our own deepest self-interest, since the latter is so hard.

(2) It is not only in our own case that we have to be concerned about the relation between self-interest and virtue. We influence the actions of other people and particularly of people we love. Morally, no doubt, we ought to influence them in the direction of always doing right (so far as it is appropriate to influence them deliberately at all). But as we care about their self-interest too, our encouragement of virtue in them is apt to be more wholehearted and therefore more effective, if we believe that they will be happy in the long run if they do right.[21] It is hard to see any ground for a charge of selfishness in this aspect of faith in the sure reward of virtue. It is not unambiguously noble (though it might be right) to encourage someone else—even someone you love—to make a great and permanent sacrifice of his true self-interest. We have no reason to regret the loss of opportunities to influence others so sadly.

I am more disturbed by another objection. I have said that it is irrational to accept a belief on the ground that it gives you a *reason* for doing something. Someone may, of course, seriously and reflectively want to live always as he morally ought, even if doing so really costs him his only chance at happiness. He may therefore already have reason enough to resist cowardice, weakness of will, and any grudging attitude toward his duty. And he may correctly judge that thinking of his happiness as assured in the long run (in a life after death, if necessary) would provide *emotional* strength against such temptations. Only in such a case may one reasonably be swayed by a practical argument for faith in a harmony of self-interest with virtue. But this faith—much more than faith in the possibility of a good world-history—seems perilously likely to be regarded as morally advantageous chiefly on the fraudulent ground that it gives one a reason for living virtuously, or perhaps takes away reasons for not living virtuously. Indeed, where it is our encouragement of *other* people's virtue that is at issue, it seems doubtful that we *ought* to seek comfort or fortitude in anything but reasons. There is no particular virtue in my *feeling* better about the sacrifices I encourage you to make.

This interest in reasons for being moral, which threatens to vitiate a practical argument, forms the basis of an interesting theoretical moral argument for a harmony of self-interest with morality.[22] It is widely thought that moral judgments have an action- and preference-guiding force that they could not have unless everyone had reason to follow them in his actions and preferences. But there has also been widespread dissatisfaction with arguments purporting to show that everyone does have reason always to be moral. It has even been suggested that this dissatisfaction ought to lead us to moderate the claims we have been accustomed to make for the force of the moral "ought."[23]

It is plausibly assumed, however, that virtually everyone has a deep and strong desire for his own happiness. So if happiness will in the long run be strictly proportioned to moral goodness, that explains how virtually everyone does have an important reason to want to be good. We may fairly count this as a theoretical advantage of Kantian theism, if we are intuitively inclined to believe that moral judgments have a force that implies that virtually everyone has reason to follow them.

This advantage of Kantian theism may be shared by other, perhaps more Christian theologies in which the connection between happiness and virtue is less strict, provided they imply (as I would expect them to) that everyone would be very happy, and more satisfied with his life, in the long run, if he lived always as he morally and religiously ought. The advantage is certainly shared by some nontheistic theories. The Buddhist doctrine of Karma is instanced by Sidgwick as a theory of "rewards inseparably attaching to right conduct . . . by the natural operation of an impersonal Law."[24] I think it is plausible, however, to suppose that if we are to have such a harmony of self-interest with duty, we must have recourse to the supernatural and presumably to an enormously powerful and knowledgeable virtuous agent.

I doubt that this line of argument can provide a really strong support for any sort of theism. For on the basis of intuitive appeal, the premise that moral judgments have a force that implies that virtually everyone has reason to follow them will not bear nearly as much weight as the conviction that some acts are morally right and others wrong, which served as a premise in my Argument from the Nature of Right and Wrong.

I have focused, as most philosophical discussion of the moral arguments has, on the connections of theism with the nature of right and wrong and with the idea of a moral order of the universe. I am keenly aware that they form only part of the total moral case for theistic belief. Theistic conceptions of guilt and forgiveness,[25] for example, or of God as a friend who witnesses, judges, appreciates, and can remember all of our actions, choices, and emotions, may well have theoretical and practical moral advantages at least as compelling as any that we have discussed.

IV

Perhaps moral arguments establish, at most, subsidiary advantages of belief in God's existence. They are more crucial to the case for his goodness. Causal arguments from the existence and qualities of the world may have some force to persuade us that there is a God, but they plainly have much less support to offer the proposition,

(K) If there is a God, he is morally very good.

(Here I define 'a God' as a creator and governor of the whole universe, supreme in understanding and knowledge as well as in power, so that (K) is not a tautology.)

There is a powerful moral argument for (K). Belief in the existence of an evil or amoral God would be morally intolerable. In view of his power, such belief would be apt to carry with it all the disadvantages, theoretical and practical, of disbelief in a moral order of the universe. But I am even more concerned about the consequences it would have in view of his knowledge and understanding. We are to think of a being who understands human life much better than we do—understands it well enough to create and control it. Among other things, he must surely understand our moral ideas and feelings. He understands everyone's point of view, and has a more objective, or at least a more complete and balanced view of human relationships than any of us can have. He has whatever self-control, stability, and integration of purpose are implied in his having produced a world as constant in its causal order as our own. And now we are to suppose that that being does not care to support with his will the moral principles that we believe are true. We are to suppose that he either opposes some of them, or does not care enough about some of them to act on them. I submit that if we really believed there is a God like that, who understands so much and yet disregards some or all of our moral principles, it would be extremely difficult for us to continue to regard those principles with the respect that we believe is due them. Since we believe that we ought to pay them that respect, this is a great moral disadvantage of the belief that there is an evil or amoral God.

I think the same disadvantage attends even the belief that there is a morally slack God, since moral slackness involves some disregard of moral principles. There might seem to be less danger in the belief that there is a morally weak God: perhaps one who can't resist the impulse to toy with us immorally, but who feels guilty about it. At least he would be seen as caring enough about moral principles to feel guilty. But he would not be seen as caring enough about them to control a childish impulse. And I think that our respect for the moral law will be undermined by any belief which implies that our moral sensibilities were created, and are thoroughly understood, by a being who does not find an absolutely controlling importance in the ends and principles of true morality.

I shall not offer here a definitive answer to the question, whether this moral argument for belief in God's goodness is theoretical or practical. There may be metaethical views—perhaps some ideal observer theory— which imply that nothing could be a true moral principle if there is a God who does not fully accept it. Such views, together with the thesis that there are true moral principles, would imply the truth of (K) and not merely the desirability of believing (K). That would produce a theoretical argument.

On the other hand, it might be claimed that moral principles would still be true, and the respect that is due them undiminished, if there were an evil or amoral God, but that it would be psychologically difficult or impossible for us to respect them as we ought if we believed them to be disregarded or lightly regarded by an all-knowing Creator. This claim implies that there is a morally important advantage in believing that if there is a God he is morally very good. I think that this practical argument for believing (K) is sound, if the theoretical argument is not.

In closing, I shall permit myself an argument *ad hominem*. The hypothesis that there is an amoral God is not open to the best known objection to theism, the argument from evil. Whatever may be said against the design argument for theism, it is at least far from obvious that the world was not designed. Yet hardly any philosopher takes seriously the hypothesis that it was designed by an amoral or evil being. Are there any good grounds for rejecting that hypothesis? Only moral grounds. One ought to reflect on that before asserting that moral arguments are out of place in these matters.

Notes

1. Cf. Henry Sidgwick, *The Methods of Ethics,* 7th ed. (New York: Dover, 1966), p. 509: "Those who hold that the edifice of physical science is really constructed of conclusions inferred from self-evident premises, may reasonably demand that any practical judgments claiming philosophic certainty should be based on an equally firm foundation. If on the other hand we find that in our supposed knowledge of the world of nature propositions are commonly taken to be universally true, which yet seem to rest on no other grounds than that we have

a strong disposition to accept them, and that they are indispensable to the systematic coherence of our beliefs,—it will be more difficult to reject a similarly supported assumption in ethics, without opening the door to universal scepticism." (Sidgwick is discussing the legitimacy of postulating, on ethical grounds, a coincidence of self-interest with duty.) Cf. also A. E. Taylor, *Does God Exist?* (London: Macmillan, 1945), p. 84f.

2. A theistic Argument from the Nature of Right and Wrong, proposed by Hastings Rashdall (*The Theory of Good and Evil* [Oxford: Clarendon Press, 1907], pp. 206–20) and taken up by W. R. Sorley (*Moral Values and the Idea of God* [Cambridge University Press, 1921], pp. 346–53) and A. E. Taylor (*Does God Exist?* p. 92f.), focuses on the question of ontological status rather than validity. It is not clear to me exactly what view those authors meant to take of the relation between God's will and moral truths.

3. Robert Merrihew Adams, "A Modified Divine Command Theory of Ethical Wrongness," in Gene Outka and John P. Reeder, Jr., eds., *Religion and Morality: A Collection of Essays* (Garden City, N.Y.: Doubleday Anchor, 1973), pp. 318–47 [chapter 7 in this volume]. I take a somewhat different view here, laying more emphasis on questions of property-identity, and less on questions of meaning, than in my earlier work. This more recent view is more fully developed in chapter 9 in this volume.

4. Here and in this discussion generally my debt to recent treatments, by Saul Kripke and others, of the relations between modality and property-identity is obvious.

5. A very similar modification is proposed by Richard B. Brandt in *Ethical Theory* (Englewood Cliffs, N.J.: Prentice-Hall, 1959), p. 73f. Brandt explicitly envisages a naturalistic version of the theory, however, thereby giving up, in my opinion, an important advantage of the divine command theory.

6. Perhaps it is necessary that if a loving God commanded killing in such circumstances, he would cause us to feel otherwise than we do about killing. But our belief is not "It is wrong for us to kill in these situations so long as we (and/ or people generally) feel as we do about it." We believe rather "Our feelings indicate to us a moral fact about such killing that is not a fact about our feelings."

7. Immanuel Kant, *Critique of Practical Reason,* trans. L. W. Beck (New York: Liberal Arts Press, 1956), p. 130 (p. 125 of the Prussian Academy edition).

8. C. D. Broad, in his review of A. E. Taylor's *The Faith of a Moralist* (*Mind,* 40 [1931], 364–75), neatly distills from Taylor a recognizable but interestingly different variant of Kant's theoretical argument. But that version still does not persuade me.

9. Immanuel Kant, *Religion within the Limits of Reason Alone,* trans. T. M. Greene and H. H. Hudson (New York: Harper, 1960), pp. 5–7. (The long footnote is particularly important.) In the *Critique of Practical Reason,* pp. 147–51 (142–6, Prussian Academy edition), Kant seems to me to be presenting his argument predominantly as practical, but less clearly so than in the later work. In

my reading of Kant I owe much to Allen Wood, *Kant's Moral Religion* (Ithaca, N.Y.: Cornell University Press, 1970).

10. One thinks of Comte, Durkheim, Weber, and Parsons.

11. Here I am indebted to R. M. Hare, "The Simple Believer," in Outka and Reeder, eds., pp. 412–4. Actually Hare proposes what I would call a theoretical moral argument. He seems to think that no set of moral principles could be right unless following them would generally turn out for the best (best from a moral point of view, that is). From this and from the belief that some (intuitively acceptable) set of moral principles is right, it follows that there is such a moral order of the universe that following some (intuitively acceptable) set of moral principles will generally turn out for the best. Of course many utilitarians would say that there is such a moral order in the universe with or without God. I am not so sure as Hare that it is a theoretical requirement that following moral principles must generally turn out for the best if the principles are correct, but his idea can at least be used in a practical argument.

12. It is not necessary to discuss here to what extent I am agreeing or disagreeing with Kant's views about the motives that a morally good person should have.

13. 1903, reprinted in Bertrand Russell, *Why I Am Not A Christian, and Other Essays on Religion and Related Subjects* (New York: Simon and Schuster, n.d.).

14. William James, "The Sentiment of Rationality," in his *The Will to Believe and Other Essays in Popular Philosophy* (New York: Dover Publications, 1956), p. 97.

15. William James, "The Will to Believe," ibid., p. 11. The terminology of "living," "forced," and "momentous options" comes from the same essay.

16. This paragraph was inspired by a similar remark on the variety of intellectual virtues by Nicholas Wolterstorff.

17. Cf. David Hume, *An Enquiry Concerning Human Understanding,* sec. X, pt. I, par. 4.

18. Sigmund Freud, *The Future of an Illusion,* trans. W. D. Robson-Scott, rev. James Strachey (Garden City, N.Y.: Doubleday Anchor, 1964). Freud thought (though he expressed uncertainty) that society could learn to get along without this function of religion. A vivid ancient Greek statement of this reason for prizing belief in gods is quoted by Wallace I. Matson, *The Existence of God* (Ithaca, N.Y.: Cornell University Press, 1965), p. 221f.

19. See Michael Argyle, *Religious Behaviour* (London: Routledge & Kegan Paul, 1958), pp. 96–9.

20. Cf. John Stuart Mill, *Utility of Religion,* ed., with Mill's *Nature,* by George Nakhnikian (New York: Liberal Arts Press, 1958), p. 62: "The value of religion as a supplement to human laws, a more cunning sort of police, an auxiliary to the thief-catcher and the hangman, is not that part of its claims which the more high-minded of its votaries are fondest of insisting on; and they would probably be as ready as anyone to admit that, if the nobler offices of religion in the soul could be dispensed with, a substitute might be found for so coarse and selfish a

social instrument as the fear of hell. In their view of the matter, the best of mankind absolutely require religion for the perfection of their own character, even though the coercion of the worst might possibly be accomplished without its aid."

21. Cf. the interesting argument on the relevance of faith in a moral order of the universe to child-rearing in Peter L. Berger, *A Rumor of Angels* (Garden City, N.Y.: Doubleday, 1969), pp. 66–71.

22. The attempt to discover or prove such a harmony has been one of the recurrent preoccupations of moral theory. Sidgwick thought it might be necessary to postulate "a connexion of Virtue and self-interest" in order to avoid "an ultimate and fundamental contradiction in our apparent intuitions of what is Reasonable in conduct" (*The Methods of Ethics*, p. 508). This led him into what may fairly be described as a flirtation with a moral argument for faith in a moral world order if not in God. He believed that our intuitions endorse both the principle that one ought always to do what will maximize one's own happiness and the principle that one ought always to do what will maximize the happiness of all. But these principles cannot both be true unless there is a moral order of the universe by virtue of which the act that maximizes universal happiness always maximizes the agent's happiness too. I think Sidgwick's reasoning claims too much obligatoriness for the egoistic principle. But the inspiration for the argument I present in the text came originally from him and from William K. Frankena, "Sidgwick and the Dualism of Practical Reason," *The Monist*, 58 (1974), 449–67.

23. I take Philippa Foot to be suggesting this in "Morality as a System of Hypothetical Imperatives," *Philosophical Review*, 81 (1972), pp. 305–16.

24. *The Methods of Ethics*, p. 507n.

25. A theistic argument from the nature of guilt has been offered by A. E. Taylor, *The Faith of a Moralist*, vol. I (London: Macmillan, 1930), pp. 206–10. Cf. also H. P. Owen, *The Moral Argument for Christian Theism* (London: George Allen & Unwin, 1965), pp. 57–59.

11

Saints

One of the merits of Susan Wolf's fascinating and disturbing essay on "Moral Saints"[1] is that it brings out very sharply a fundamental problem in modern moral philosophy. On the one hand, we want to say that morality is of supreme value, always taking precedence over other grounds of choice, and that what is morally best must be absolutely best. On the other hand, if we consider what it would be like really to live in accordance with that complete priority of the moral, the ideal of life that emerges is apt to seem dismally grey and unattractive, as Wolf persuasively argues. I want to present a diagnosis of the problem that differs from Wolf's. Replies to Wolf might be offered on behalf of the utilitarian and Kantian moral theories that she discusses, but of them I shall have little to say. My concern here is to see that sainthood, not Kant or utilitarianism, receives its due.

I. What Are Saints Like?

The first thing to be said is that there *are* saints—people like St. Francis of Assisi and Gandhi and Mother Teresa—and they are quite different from what Wolf thinks a moral saint would be. In the end I will conclude that they are not exactly *moral* saints in Wolf's sense. But she writes about some of them as if they were, and discussions of moral sainthood surely owe to the real saints much of their grip on our attention. So it will be to the point to contrast the actuality of sainthood with Wolf's picture of the moral saint.

I wish to thank the Center of Theological Inquiry, for fellowship support during the writing of this paper; and Marilyn McCord Adams, for helpful comments on an earlier version.

Wolf argues that moral saints will be "unattractive" (p. 426) because they will be lacking in individuality and in the "ability to enjoy the enjoyable in life" (p. 424), and will be so "very, very nice" and inoffensive that they "will have to be dull-witted or humorless or bland" (p. 422). But the real saints are not like that. It is easier to think of St. Francis as eccentric than as lacking in individuality. And saints are not bland. Many have been offended at them for being very, very truthful instead of very, very nice. (Think of Gandhi—or Jesus.) Saints may not enjoy all the same things as other people, and perhaps a few of them have been melancholy; but an exceptional capacity for joy is more characteristic of them. (For all his asceticism, one thinks again of St. Francis.) There are joys (and not minor ones) that only saints can know. And as for attractiveness, the people we think of first as saints were plainly people who were intensely interesting to almost everyone who had anything to do with them, and immensely attractive to at least a large proportion of those people. They have sometimes been controversial, but rarely dull; and their charisma has inspired many to leave everything else in order to follow them.

Wolf may have set herself up, to some extent, for such contrasts, by conceiving of moral sainthood purely in terms of commitment or devotion to moral ends or principles. There are other, less voluntary virtues that are essential equipment for a saint: humility, for instance, and perceptiveness, courage, and a mind unswayed by the voices of the crowd. The last of these is part of what keeps saints from being bland or lacking in individuality.

In order to understand how Wolf arrives at her unflattering picture of the moral saint, however, we must examine her stated conception of moral sainthood.

II. Wolf's Argument

Wolf states three criteria for moral sainthood, and they are not equivalent. (1) In her third sentence she says, "By *moral saint* I mean a person whose every action is as morally good as possible." (2) Immediately she adds: "a person, that is, who is as morally worthy as can be" (p. 419). Her words imply that these two characterizations amount to the same thing, but it seems to me that the first expresses at most a very questionable test for the satisfaction of the second. The idea that only a morally imperfect person would spend half an hour doing something morally indifferent, like taking a nap, when she could have done something morally praiseworthy instead, like spending the time in moral self-examination, is at odds with our usual judgments and ought not to be assumed at the outset. The assumption that the perfection of a person, in at least the moral type of value, depends on the maximization of that type of value in every single action of the person lies behind much that is unattractive in Wolf's picture of moral sainthood; but I believe it is a fundamental error.

(3) On the next page we get a third criterion: "A necessary condition of moral sainthood would be that one's life be dominated by a commitment to improving the welfare of others or of society as a whole" (p. 420). Here again, while it might be claimed that this is a necessary condition of a person's, or her acts', being as morally worthy as possible, the claim is controversial. It has been held as a moral thesis that the pursuit of our own perfection ought sometimes to take precedence for us over the welfare of others. The utilitarian, likewise, will presumably think that many people ought to devote their greatest efforts to their own happiness and perfection, because that is what will maximize utility. Given a utilitarian conception of moral rightness as doing what will maximize utility, why shouldn't a utilitarian say that such people, and their acts, can be as morally worthy as possible (and thus can satisfy Wolf's first two criteria of moral sainthood) when they pursue their own happiness and perfection? Presumably, therefore, Wolf is relying heavily on her third criterion, as an independent test, when she says that such cases imply "that the utilitarian would not support moral sainthood as a universal ideal" (p. 427).

This third criterion is obviously related to Wolf's conception of morality. Later in her paper she contrasts the moral point of view with "the point of view of individual perfection," which is "the point of view from which we consider what kinds of lives are good lives, and what kinds of persons it would be good for ourselves and others to be" (p. 437). "The moral point of view . . . is the point of view one takes up insofar as one takes the recognition of the fact that one is just one person among others equally real and deserving of the good things in life as a fact with practical consequences, a fact the recognition of which demands expression in one's actions and in the form of one's practical deliberations" (p. 436f.). And moral theories are theories that offer "answers to the question of what the most correct or the best way to express this fact is" (p. 437).

This account of moral theory and the moral point of view is in clear agreement with Wolf's third criterion of moral sainthood on one central issue: Morality, for her, has exclusively to do with one's regard for the good (and perhaps she would add, the rights) of other persons. One's own dignity or courage or sexuality pose *moral* issues for Wolf only to the extent that they impinge on the interests of other people. Otherwise they can be evaluated from the point of view of individual perfection (and she obviously takes that evaluation very seriously), but not from the moral point of view. This limitation of the realm of the moral is controversial, but (without wishing to be committed to it in other contexts) I shall use 'moral' and 'morality' here in accordance with Wolf's conception.

It might still be doubted whether her third criterion of moral sainthood follows from her definition of the moral point of view. A utilitarian, for reasons indicated above, might argue that for many people a life not "dominated by a commitment to improving the welfare of others or of society as a whole" could perfectly express "recognition of the fact that one is just one person among others equally real and deserving of the good things of life." Dedication to the good of others is not the same as weighing their good equally with one's own. But if the former is not implied by the latter, it is the altruistic dedication that constitutes Wolf's operative criterion of moral excellence (though I suspect she looks to the equal weighing for a criterion of the morally obligatory). I do not wish to quibble about this. What interests me most in Wolf's paper is what she says about moral devotion, and weighing one's own good equally with the good of others (demanding as that may be) is something less than devotion.

Thus Wolf's three criteria of moral sainthood seem to me to be separable. The second (maximal moral worthiness of the person, rather than the act) probably comes the closest to expressing an intuitive idea of moral sainthood in its most general form. But the other two seem to be her working criteria. I take all three to be incorporated as necessary conditions in Wolf's conception of moral sainthood.

The center of Wolf's argument can now be stated quite simply. It is that in a life perfectly "dominated by a commitment to improving the welfare of others or of society as a whole" there will not be room for other interests. In particular there will not be time or energy or attention for other good interests, such as the pursuit of aesthetic or athletic excellence. The moral saint will not be able to pursue these interests, or encourage them in others, unless "by happy accident" they have an unusual humanitarian payoff (p. 425f.). But from the point of view of individual perfection we have to say that some of the qualities that the moral saint is thus prevented from fostering in herself or others are very desirable, and there are commendable ideals in which they have a central place. So "if we think that it is *as* good, or even better for a person to strive for one of these ideals than it is for him or her to strive for and realize the ideal of the moral saint, we express a conviction that it is good not to be a moral saint" (p. 426f.).

III. Sainthood and Religion

While those actual saints whom I have mentioned have indeed been ex-
ceptionally devoted to improving the lives and circumstances of other
people, it would be misleading to say that their lives have been "dominated by a commitment to improving the welfare of others or of society
as a whole." For sainthood is an essentially religious phenomenon, and
even so political a saint as Gandhi saw his powerful humanitarian concern
in the context of a more comprehensive devotion to God. This touches
the center of Wolf's argument, and helps to explain why actual saints are
so unlike her picture of the moral saint. Wolf's moral saint sees limited
resources for satisfying immense human needs and unlimited human desires, and devotes himself wholly to satisfying them as fully (and perhaps
as fairly) as possible. This leaves him no time or energy for anything that
does not *have* to be done. Not so the saints. The substance of sainthood
is not sheer willpower striving like Sisyphus (or like Wolf's Rational Saint)
to accomplish a boundless task, but goodness overflowing from a boundless source. Or so, at least, the saints perceive it.

They commonly have time for things that do not *have* to be done,
because their vision is not of needs that exceed any possible means of
satisfying them, but of a divine goodness that is more than adequate to
every need. They are not in general even trying to make their *every action*
as good as possible, and thus they diverge from Wolf's first criterion of
moral sainthood. The humility of the saint may even require that she
spend considerable stretches of time doing nothing of any great importance or excellence. Saintliness is not perfectionism, though some saints
have been perfectionistic in various ways. There is an unusual moral
goodness in the saints, but we shall not grasp it by asking whether any
of their actions could have been morally worthier. What makes us think
of a Gandhi, for example, as a saint is something more positive, which
I would express by saying that goodness was present in him in exceptional
power.

Many saints have felt the tensions on which Wolf's argument turns.
Albert Schweitzer, whom many have honored as a twentieth-century saint,
was one who felt keenly the tension between artistic and intellectual
achievement on the one hand and a higher claim of humanitarian commitment on the other. Yet in the midst of his humanitarian activities in
Africa, he kept a piano and spent some time playing it—even before he
realized that keeping up this skill would help him raise money for his
mission. Very likely that time could have been employed in actions that
would have been morally worthier, but that fact by itself surely has no

tendency to disqualify Schweitzer from sainthood, in the sense in which people are actually counted as saints. We do not demand as a necessary condition of sainthood that the saint's every act be the morally worthiest possible in the circumstances, nor that he try to make it so.

The religious character of sainthood also helps to explain how the saint can be so self-giving without lacking (as Wolf suggests the Loving Saint must) an interest in his own condition as a determinant of his own happiness. In fact saints have typically been intensely and frankly interested in their own condition, their own perfection and their own happiness. Without this interest they would hardly have been fitted to lead others for whom they desired perfection and happiness. What enables them to give of themselves unstintedly is not a lack of interest in their own persons, but a trust in God to provide for their growth and happiness.

IV. Should Everyone Be a Saint?

Even if it can be shown that the life of a Gandhi or a St. Francis is happier and more attractive than Wolf claims that the life of a moral saint would be, we still face questions analogous to some of those she presses. Would it be good if everyone were a saint? Should we all aspire to be saints?

Not everybody *could* be a Gandhi. He himself thought otherwise. "Whatever is possible for me is possible even for a child," he wrote.[2] This is a point on which we may venture to disagree with him. A life like his involves, in religious terms, a vocation that is not given to everyone. Or to put the matter in more secular terms, not all who set themselves to do it will accomplish as much good by humanitarian endeavor as Wolf seems to assume that any utilitarian can (p. 428). But perhaps some of us assume too easily that we could not be a Gandhi. In all probability there could be more Gandhis than there are, and it would be a very good thing if there were.

Wolf, however, will want to press the question whether there are not human excellences that could not be realized by a Gandhi, or even by someone who seriously aspired to be one, and whether it would not be good for some people to aspire to these excellences instead of aspiring to sainthood. My answer to these questions is affirmative, except for the 'instead of aspiring to sainthood'. Given the limits of human time and energy, it is hard to see how a Gandhi or a Martin Luther King, Jr., could at the same time have been a great painter or a world-class violinist. Such saints may indeed attain and employ great mastery in the arts of speaking and writing. But there are demanding forms of excellence, in

the arts and in science, for example, and also in philosophy, which probably are not compatible with their vocation (and even less compatible with
the vocation of a St. Francis, for reasons of life-style rather than time
and energy). And I agree that it is good that some people aspire to those
excellences and attain them.

But if it is right to conclude that not everyone should aspire to be a
Gandhi or a Martin Luther King or a St. Francis, it may still be too hasty
to infer that not everyone should aspire to sainthood. Perhaps there are
other ways of being a saint. That will depend, of course, on what is meant
by 'saint'; so it is time to offer a definition.

If sainthood is an essentially religious phenomenon, as I claim, it is
reasonable to seek its central feature (at least for theistic religions) in the
saint's relation to God. 'Saint' means 'holy'—indeed they are the same
word in most European languages. Saints are people in whom the holy
or divine can be seen. In a religious view they are people who submit
themselves, in faith, to God, not only loving him but also letting his love
possess them, so that it works through them and shines through them to
other people. What interests a saint may have will then depend on what
interests God has, for sainthood is a participation in God's interests. And
God need not be conceived as what Wolf would call a "moral fanatic"
(p. 425). He is not so limited that his moral concerns could leave him
without time or attention or energy for other interests. As the author of
all things and of all human capacities, he may be regarded as interested
in many forms of human excellence, for their own sake and not just for
the sake of their connection with what would be classified as *moral* concerns in any narrow sense. This confirms the suggestion that Gandhi and
Martin Luther King and St. Francis exemplify only certain types of sainthood, and that other types may be compatible with quite different human
excellences—and in particular, with a great variety of demanding artistic
and intellectual excellences. I do not see why a Fra Angelico or a Johann
Sebastian Bach or a Thomas Aquinas could not have been a saint in this
wider sense.

Now I suspect that Wolf will not be satisfied with the conclusion that
a saint could be an Angelico or a Bach or an Aquinas. And I do not think
that the sticking point here will be that the three figures mentioned all
dealt with religious subjects. After all, much of Bach's and Aquinas's
work is not explicitly religious, and it would be easy to make a case that
a saint could have done most of Cézanne's work. The trouble, I rather
expect Wolf to say, is that the forms of artistic and intellectual excellence
typified by these figures are too sweet or too nice or too wholesome to
be the only ones allowed us. There are darker triumphs of human creativi-

ty that we also admire; could a saint have produced them?

Not all of them. I admire the art of Edvard Munch, but I certainly grant that most of his work would not have been produced by a saint. I do not think that is a point against the aspiration to sainthood, however, nor even against a desire for universal sainthood. Who knows? Perhaps Munch would have painted even greater things of another sort if he had been a saint. But that is not the crucial point. Perhaps he would have given up painting and done something entirely different. The crucial point is that although I might aspire to Munch's artistic talent and skill, I certainly would not aspire to be a person who would use it to express what he did, nor would I wish that on anyone I cared about. In view not merely of the intensity of unhappiness, but also of the kind of unhappiness that comes to expression in Munch's art, it would be perverse to aspire to it, nobly as Munch expressed it. The lesson to be learned from such cases is that our ethical or religious view of life ought to allow for some ambivalence, and particularly for the appreciation of some things that we ought not to desire.

Van Gogh provides an interesting example of a different sort. There is much in his life to which one would not aspire, and his canvases sometimes express terror, even madness, rather than peace. Yet I would hesitate to say that a saint could not have painted them. The saints have not been strangers to terror, pain, and sadness. If in Van Gogh's pictures we often see the finite broken by too close an approach of the transcendent, that is one of the ways in which the holy can show itself in human life. Certainly Van Gogh wanted to be a saint; and perhaps, in an unorthodox and sometimes despairing way, he was one.

V. Is Morality a Suitable Object of Maximal Devotion?

Wolf's arguments lead her to reject an important received opinion about the nature of morality and about what it means to accept a moral theory: the opinion, namely, that it is "a test of an adequate moral theory that perfect obedience to its laws and maximal devotion to its interests be something we can whole-heartedly strive for in ourselves and wish for in those around us" (p. 435). There are two parts to the received opinion, as it has to do with perfect obedience and with maximal devotion. I cannot see that Wolf's arguments call in question the desirability of perfect obedience to the laws of morality, unless those laws make all good deeds obligatory (as in a rigorous act utilitarianism). Wolf seems on the whole to prefer the view that even nonmoral ideals to which it would be good to aspire ought not to involve the infringement of moral *requirements,* so she concludes that if (as she has argued) "we have reason to want people to live lives that are not morally perfect, then any plausible moral theory must make use of some conception of supererogation" (p. 438). What she clearly rejects in the received opinion, then, is the desirability of maximal devotion to the interests of morality.

In this I agree with her. We ought not to make a religion of morality. Without proposing, like Kierkegaard and Tillich, to define religion as maximal devotion, I would say that maximal devotion (like sainthood) is essentially religious, or at least that it has its proper place only in religion. Wolf is going too far when she says that "morality itself does not seem to be a suitable object of passion" (p. 424). But maximal devotion is much more than passion. And morality, as Wolf conceives of it, is too narrow to be a suitable object of maximal or religious devotion. Her reason (and one good reason) for thinking this is that a demand for universal maximal devotion to morality excludes too many human excellences.

Religion is richer than morality, because its divine object is so rich. He is not too narrow to be a suitable object of maximal devotion. Since he is lover of beauty, for instance, as well as commander of morals, maximal submission of one's life to him may in some cases (as I have argued) encompass an intense pursuit of artistic excellence in a way that maximal devotion to the interests of morality, narrowly understood, cannot. Many saints and other religious people, to be sure, have been quite hostile to some of the forms of human endeavor and achievement that I agree with Wolf in prizing. What I have argued is that the breadth of the Creator's interests makes possible a conception of sainthood that does not require this hostility.

There is for many (and not the least admirable) among us a strong temptation to make morality into a substitute for religion, and in so doing to make morality the object of a devotion that is maximal, at least in aspiration, and virtually religious in character. Such a devotion to morality, conceived as narrowly as Wolf conceives of it, would be, from a religious point of view, idolatry. The conclusion to which Wolf's arguments tend is that it would also be, from what she calls "the point of view of individual perfection," oppressive.

On the other hand, the loss of the possibility of sainthood, and of maximal devotion, would be a great loss. Wolf says, "A moral theory that does not contain the seeds of an all-consuming ideal of moral sainthood . . . seems to place false and unnatural limits on our opportunity to do moral good and our potential to deserve moral praise" (p. 433). This seems right, but I do not think it is just our indefinite (not infinite) opportunities and capacities that generate the all-consuming ideal. There are other departments of human life (such as memorization) in which our potential to deserve praise is indefinite but in which it would be bizarre to adopt an all-consuming ideal. The fact is that many of the concepts that we use in morality were developed in a religious tradition, and to tear them loose entirely from a context in which something (distinct perhaps from morality but including it) claims maximal devotion seems to threaten something that is important for the seriousness of morality.

It may not, in other words, be so easy to have a satisfactory conception of morality without religion—that is, without belief in an appropriate object of maximal devotion, an object that is larger than morality but embraces it.

Notes

1. *The Journal of Philosophy,* 8 (August 1982), pp. 419–39. Page numbers in parentheses in the text refer to Wolf's article.

2. M. K. Gandhi, *Gandhi's Autobiography: The Story of My Experiments with Truth,* trans. Mahadev Desai (Washington, D.C.: Public Affairs Press, 1948), p. 7.

12

Pure Love

In a standard handbook of teachings of the Roman Catholic Church we find the statement,

> There is a habitual state of love for God, which is pure charity without admixture of the motive of self-interest. Neither fear of punishments nor desire of rewards have any more part in it. God is no longer loved for the sake of the merit, nor for the sake of the perfection, nor for the sake of the happiness to be found in loving Him (Denzinger, 1911: par. 1327).

This is not a surprising proposition to find in a compendium of Christian beliefs. The surprising thing is that it is not there to be endorsed, but to be condemned as "rash, scandalous, bad sounding, offensive to pious ears, pernicious in practice," or "even . . . erroneous." It is a fairly accurate quotation from Fénelon's *Explanation of the Maxims of the Saints Concerning the Interior Life,*[1] and is the first of the propositions from that book that were condemned by Pope Innocent XII in 1699 in the denouement of the famous dispute between Fénelon and Bossuet.

It is not my purpose here to tell the story, or sift through all the rights and wrongs, of that aftershock of the quietist controversy. Fénelon attracts my attention because he articulated an extreme form of an ideal of disinterested love which has been attractive to Christians in many times and places. Ideals, like metals, reveal some of their properties most clearly

An earlier version of this paper was read at the annual meeting of the American Society of Christian Ethics in January 1979. The ideas in it have been discussed with a number of individuals and groups, and provided approximately half of the substance of the thirty-second annual Willson Lectures at Southwestern University in March 1979. I am particularly indebted to Rogers Albritton, David Blumenfeld, John Giuliano, and Warren Quinn for their comments. I also particularly prize Giles Milhaven's comments, but have not altered the paper in the light of them, since it appears (in its first publication) with his response.

when stretched or pressed, and I believe that reflection on Fénelon's views will shed light on the relations between love and various sorts of self-concern.

I. Holy Indifference

Fénelon distinguishes three basic types of love for God.

(1) Love "for the gifts of God distinguished from him, and not for himself, may be called, *merely servile love*." Fénelon has little to say about it because, as he remarks, it is not love of God at all, strictly speaking (Fénelon, 1697:13f., 1f., my italics).

(2) *Concupiscential love* is "that love wherewith God is loved only as the only means and instrument of happiness," as "the only object, the sight of which can render us happy" (Fénelon, 1697:14, 2f.). It is the lover himself, rather than God, who is the "ultimate end" of this sort of love. But in concupiscential love it is at least by the vision of God himself that one seeks to be happy, whereas in merely servile love one seeks satisfaction in gifts much more separate from God.

(3) *Charity* is love of God for himself. Its "formal object . . . is the goodness or beauty of God taken simply and absolutely in itself, without any idea that is relative to us" (Fénelon, 1697:42). Many passages in Fénelon's works suggest that charity consists in desiring that God's will be done, desiring it for its own sake, as an ultimate end.

Fénelon distinguished two intermediate states in which concupiscential love for God is mingled with charity. His conception of these states is complex and subtle, and changed significantly during the two-year period of intense controversy with Bossuet. We shall not be concerned with them, however, but only with the contrast between concupiscential love and the *pure* state of charity, unmingled with other motives, which Fénelon, following St. Francis de Sales, calls *holy indifference*.

In calling this state "indifference" he does not mean that it is "a stupid insensibility, an inward inactivity, a non-willing, . . . [or] a perpetual equilibrium of the soul." On the contrary, "as [that] indifference is love itself, it is a very real and very positive principle. It is a positive and formal will which makes us really will or desire every volition of God that is known to us" (Fénelon, 1697:51). Fénelon quotes with approval St. Francis de Sales as saying,

Indifference . . . loves nothing except for the sake of the will of God. . . . The indifferent heart is like a ball of wax between the hands of its God, to receive in like manner all the impressions of the eternal good pleasure. It is a heart without choice, equally disposed to everything, without any other object of its will but the will of its God. It does not set its love on the things that God wills, but on the will of God that wills them (Fénelon, 1697:55f.; quoted, pretty accurately, from Sales, 1969:770 [bk. IX, ch. 4]).

The state of pure love is one of indifference because in that state the soul is indifferent to all created things, and specifically to her own good, except insofar as she believes that God's will is concerned. "The indifferent soul no longer wills anything for herself by the motive of her own self-interest" (Fénelon, 1697:49).

The most dramatic feature that characterizes the state of holy indifference is the sacrifice of eternal happiness. For one's eternal happiness is not excluded from the thesis that in this highest state of Christian perfection one wills *nothing* as an end in itself except that God's will be done. The logical consequence of the thesis had already been rigorously drawn by St. Francis de Sales (1969:770; bk. IX, ch. 4; partly quoted by Fénelon, 1697:56):

> In sum, the good pleasure of God is the supreme object of the indifferent soul. Wherever she sees it she runs "to the fragrance of" its "perfumes," and always seeks the place where there is more of it, without consideration of any other thing. . . . [The indifferent person] would rather have hell with the will of God than Paradise without the will of God—yes indeed, he would prefer hell to Paradise if he knew that there were a little more of the divine good pleasure in the former than in the latter; so that if (to imagine something impossible) he knew that his damnation were a little more agreeable to God than his salvation, he would leave his salvation, and run to his damnation.

Fénelon (1697:87) emphasizes the conditional aspect of this sacrifice. "It is certain that all the sacrifices which the most disinterested souls make ordinarily concerning their eternal happiness are conditional. One says, my God, if by an impossibility you willed to condemn me to the eternal pains of Hell without losing your love, I would not love you less for it. But this sacrifice cannot be absolute in the ordinary state."

Fénelon (1697:90, 87) does speak of an "absolute [i.e., unconditional] sacrifice of her own self-interest for eternity," which a soul in the state of holy indifference can make if persuaded "that she is justly reprobated by God." This absolute sacrifice was much more controversial than the conditional sacrifice, and Fénelon's exposition of it is tangled and tormented, and changed (I suspect) during the period of the controversy. It involves a very questionable claim about contrary beliefs being held in different "parts" of the soul. Fortunately our arguments need not depend on the doctrine of the absolute sacrifice: The conditional sacrifice of eternal happiness will provide us with plenty of food for thought.

The reason why the sacrifice of salvation cannot normally be unconditional is that Christians should believe that God does will their salvation. They should therefore will it too, not out of self-interest, but because God wills it. Hence Fénelon (1697:73) can speak of "the disinterested love that we owe to ourselves as to our neighbor for the love of God." Precisely here another important consequence of Fénelon's conception of holy indifference comes into view. On his account the disinterested desire for one's own salvation clearly is just a special case of the desire one ought to have for the salvation of all human beings, as willed by God. More generally, indeed, if all one wills as an end in itself is that God's will be done, one will regard oneself, volitionally, as just another person. One will not be special in one's own volitional eyes, except as the only agent that one can directly control.

> Souls attracted to pure love may be as disinterested with respect to themselves as to their neighbor, because they do not see or desire in themselves, any more than in the most unknown neighbor, anything but the glory of God, his good pleasure, and the fulfillment of his promises. In this sense these souls are like strangers to themselves . . . (Fénelon, 1697:106).

This neutralizing of the specialness of one's own self may be attractive to many moralists. It is a characteristic that Fénelon's theory shares with more than one ethical secular theory, including the most stringent form of utilitarianism. But my principal aim in this paper is to show that it does not belong in a theory of Christian love.

II. Some Objections

One of the first objections to Fénelon's views that is likely to occur to us is that the state of holy indifference, as he describes it, is psychologically impossible. Could we really have no desire for anything, for its own sake, except that God's will be done? Perhaps not, but we should realize that Fénelon's exclusion of self-interested desires from the state of pure love was not as sweeping as might appear from the statements quoted thus far. For having said that "the indifferent soul . . . has no longer any interested desire," he adds, " 'Tis true, that there remain in her still some involuntary inclinations and aversions, which she submits [to the will of God]; but she has no longer any voluntary and deliberate desires for her own interest, except on those occasions wherein she does not cooperate faithfully with all her grace" (Fénelon, 1697:49f.). There is an emphasis here on the voluntary as the only morally significant functions of the soul, which is congenial to the tradition within which Fénelon is working. The "voluntary and deliberate" desires, I take it, are conditional and unconditional choices, intentions, and resolutions. These can be in the indifferent soul, according to Fénelon, only to the extent that they are derived from a decision that in every possible (or even impossible) situation, she would choose whatever would best fulfil the will of God. The "involuntary inclinations and aversions," on the other hand— the desires that we know we have, not because we decide on them but because we feel them—are seen as assailing the command post of the soul from outside, so to speak, and may be self-interested even in a perfectly indifferent soul, provided they are controlled and not allowed to influence choice. The indifferent soul will normally have, for example, both a natural, self-interested, involuntary aversion to physical illness, and a deliberate intention to do, ordinarly, what is necessary to avoid or cure physical illness. But the intention will be based on the belief that God commands us to care for our health, and will not be influenced in the least by the aversion. This extreme separation between impulse and will strikes me as both unrealistic and undesirable, but I will not bear down on that point here. When I ascribe to Fénelon views about desires, they should be understood to be about *voluntary* desires, unless otherwise indicated.

I shall be more concerned here with a series of objections in which Fénelon's opponents claimed that his views would exclude from the Christian ideal some of the most important Christian virtues—particularly hope, penitence, gratitude, and even the desire to love God. Some of the fiercest controversy raged about the theological virtue of *hope*. Because he held that even salvation, or eternal happiness, is not desired with a self-interested desire in the state of pure love, Fénelon was accused of leaving no room for this virtue in the highest state of the Christian life in this world; and he was at pains to defend himself against the charge. The indifferent or fully disinterested soul, he insists, will still hope for her own salvation. In hoping, she will will to be saved. But this is not "a falling away from the perfection of her disinterestment," nor "a return to the motive of self-interest." For "the purest love never prevents us from willing, and even causes us to will positively, everything that God wills that we should will" (Fénelon, 1697:44). "Whoever loves from pure love without any mixture of self-interest . . . wills happiness for himself only because he knows that God wills it, and that he wills that each of us should will it for his glory" (1697:26f.). "Then I will that which really is, and is known by me to be, the greatest of all my interests, without any interested motive determining me to it" (1697:46). As the controversy progressed, Fénelon (1698:12) added that in holy indifference we would desire our own salvation "precisely for the reason that it is our good, since it is for this reason that God wills it, and for which he commands us also to will it. Therefore . . . precisely the reason that it is our good, really moves and excites the will of man" in hoping for the intuitive vision of God. But if, on this account, the indifferent soul desires her salvation because it is her own good, she desires her own good only because God desires it—she desires it only in order that his desires may be satisfied.

The indifferent soul can will, conditionally, that she be saved *if* God wills it. And believing that God does will it, she can detach the consequent and will that she be saved, *since* God wills it. But it is hard to see how she can will that God will her salvation. For she could hardly want God to will her salvation solely in order that his will might be done. I have not found any place where Fénelon explicitly draws this conclusion. It would probably have seemed damaging, since the desire it would exclude seems to be central to much of Christian piety and prayer. But despite the strangeness of this consequence of Fénelon's position, I do not think this is the most promising point at which to try to show that he excludes something that is important for Christian ethics to maintain.

III. Self-concern, Self-interest, and the Desire to Love God

Fénelon's opponents charged that he would not have even charity itself to be sought for as a virtue (Noailles et al., 1698:224). They dwelt much less on this objection than on that about hope, but they struck here a much more sensitive spot in Fénelon's position—one at which I believe that he himself was driven into inconsistency. Fénelon inherited from St. Francis de Sales a strong suspicion against desires in which one aims ultimately at one's own virtue or perfection or even one's own love for God. St. Francis de Sales (1969:785 [bk. IX, ch. 9]; cf. p. 1549 [first draft]) had spoken of the danger of coming to love one's love for God instead of loving God. And Fénelon (1697:10f.) declared that in pure charity God is no longer loved "for the sake of the merit, nor for the sake of the perfection . . . to be found in loving him." Yet they certainly also thought that we ought to want to be virtuous, and that the chief point of virtue we ought to desire is to love God with charity.

The only way of reconciling these concerns that is consistent with the general thesis that the only thing is desired for its own sake in pure love is that God's will be done, is to say that in pure love the soul does indeed want to love God, but only because (as she believes) he wills that we love him. Yet Fénelon was not in fact prepared to accept every consequence of this view, as can be seen in his treatment of

(A) the desire that God's will be done,

and

(B) the desire that I love and obey God.

We might suppose that these desires could never be opposed to each other. But such a conflict seems at least thinkable. Fénelon accepts a distinction between God's *signified will*, revealed to us primarily in his commandments and counsels, which is often violated, and his *good pleasure*, contrary to which nothing happens. It is not just God's signified will, but his good pleasure, that the indifferent soul wants to be done. Suppose it were God's good pleasure that my heart be hardened so that I would hate him and disobey his signified will. In that case it would seem that my hatred and disobedience are what God would really want, rather than the love and obedience that he commands. So if my heart is in holy indifference, shouldn't I desire, conditionally, that I should hate and disobey God if it were his good pleasure?

Fénelon's first response will be that the supposition of God's actively willing my sin is impossible. Sins that happen, though not contrary to God's good pleasure, are not willed but only permitted by God, according to Fénelon's theology, and God's "permissive will" is not proposed as a rule for even the indifferent soul (Fénelon, 1697: article XVIII, True). Nonetheless, Fénelon does demand of the indifferent soul a conditional desire regarding another impossible supposition—that God would torment her forever in hell though she loved him purely. I cannot see any good (or indeed any morally tolerable) reason for thinking that that supposition is any less impossible than the supposition of God's wanting me to hate and disobey him. So if we are to have conditional preferences regarding impossible suppositions, it would seem that the indifferent soul ought to will that she should hate and disobey God if that were his good pleasure.

But Fénelon vehemently rejects any such desire. This is most explicit in his treatment of "the ultimate trials" in which an indifferent soul makes an absolute or unconditional sacrifice of her own self-interest for eternity. Even in that case, he says,

> She loves God more purely than ever. Far from consenting positively to hate him, she does not consent even indirectly to cease for a single instant

from loving him, nor to diminish in the least her love, nor to put ever to the increase of that love any voluntary bounds, nor to commit any fault, not even a venial fault (Fénelon, 1697:91).

It would be blasphemous to say that a soul in trials "may consent to hate God, because God will have her hate him; or that she may consent never more to love God, because he will no more be beloved by her; or that she may voluntarily confine her love, because God will have her to limit it; or that she may violate his law, because God will have her to transgress it" (Fénelon, 1697:93f.).

Even a conditional desire to hate God if he should will it seems to be ruled out by saying that the indifferent soul "does not consent even indirectly" to cease, diminish, or limit her love for God. And, in the course of his controversy with Bossuet, Fénelon stated explicitly that the conditional sacrifice envisaged by St. Francis de Sales is a sacrifice of one's supernatural happiness (which consists in the eternal rapture of an intuitive vision of God, accompanied by all the gifts of body and soul), but is not a sacrifice of "the love that we necessarily owe to God in every state" (Fénelon, 1838a:89 [letter V, sec. 3]; cf. 1838b:134 [letter III, sec. 5]).

There is thus an important difference between Fénelon's treatment of (B), the desire that I love and obey God, and his treatment of

(C) the desire that I be happy rather than miserable eternally, if I have charity.

It is impossible that God should will the opposite of either (B) or (C), according to Fénelon. Yet he holds that if my love were pure, I should desire conditionally to be miserable eternally, without ceasing to have charity, if God willed it. Even so, he denies that I should desire conditionally to hate or disobey God, or even to lessen my love for him, if God willed it. This difference in the conditional desires of the soul in pure love can be accounted for only on the supposition that the soul has desire (B) independently of (A), the desire that God's will be done. For if I desired to love and obey God only in order that his will might be done, it would seem that I should want to cease loving and obeying him if he willed it. If I ought not to have that conditional desire, then presumably my loving and obeying God is something that I would desire at least partly for its own sake if I were a perfect Christian.

One might try to avoid this conclusion by supposing that desire (B) ought to be derived from

(D) the desire that as many people as possible love and obey God.

On this account I ought not to desire my own loving God for its own sake, but only as a means to the satisfaction of (D). But this view is not suggested by Fénelon, and would require him to say that I ought to have a conditional desire to hate God if that would result in more other people coming to love and obey him. But he would surely refuse to say that, and so is still left with the conclusion that my loving and obeying God is something I ought to want at least partly for its own sake.

But if part of what I am to desire for its own sake is not only that God's will be done, but also that *I* love and obey God, then it seems that my love for him is not to be completely disinterested: There is to be an element of self-concern in it. Thus Fénelon seems forced to admit an element of self-concern even in perfect love for God.

Of course the fact that even Fénelon did not manage consistently to exclude all self-concerned attitudes from the state of holy indifference does not prove that there is a rightful place for self-concern in pure or perfect love; however, I think in fact there is. Not to care, literally not to care at all, whether I will be one who loves or hates God, so long as God's will will be done, would not be an attitude of love toward God on my part, but of something much more impersonal.[2]

Perhaps Fénelon would not have been too troubled by this. What he meant to insist on most of all was the ideal of a love for God completely free of *self-interest*. To desire, for its own sake, to be related in any way to another person is self-concerned, in the sense that it is aiming ultimately at a state of affairs that essentially involves oneself. I suspect Fénelon would say that while the desire to be one who loves and obeys God is self-concerned in this broad sense, it is not self-interested in the sense that concerns him.

This response has some plausibility. In wanting to love or serve God, or someone else, one is not necessarily aiming at one's own advantage. It may be part of one's desire that one wants to give up something, or make some sacrifice of one's own advantage, for the beloved. Fénelon is particularly interested in a desire to love and obey God even if one were eternally miserable. Such desires are concerned in part with the desirer, but it would seem strange, in many cases, to call them "self-interested." This suggests that not all self-concerned desires are self-interested; self-interest is a species of self-concern.

Which species is not easy to say, however. There is perhaps a broad sense in which it is self-interested to desire anything *for one's own sake*. But 'for one's own sake' is a very vague expression, and no account of it, or of a broad sense of 'self-interested', that has occurred to me seems really satisfactory. I prefer therefore to use 'self-interested' in a narrower sense. Historically, to speak of a person's "interest" is to speak of his good on the whole: A state of affairs is "in his interest" if and only if it is good for him, on the whole, that it should obtain. I think this agrees well enough with Fénelon's use of "interest" ('*intérêt*'). We may say, then, that a desire is *self-interested,* in the strict or narrower sense, if and only if it is a desire in which one aims ultimately at one's own good on the whole. Butler (1970:101, 104 [sermon XI]) adopts a sense very much like this for 'interested'. (When I speak of a desire in which one *aims ultimately* at an end or state of affairs X, I mean a desire for X for its own sake, or at least partly for its own sake; or a desire for something else for the sake of X, where one does desire X at least partly for its own sake.) Even this narrower conception of self-interestedness is not without its problems, for it is doubtful whether anyone has a satisfactory conception of a person's good. But let us ignore that problem for present purposes. We do speak with some confidence of states of affairs being good (or bad) for a person on the whole—whether we are entitled to that confidence or not.

Fénelon's position can be modified, in terms of this distinction between self-concern and self-interest, to make it consistent. He could say that Christian love ought to be completely free of self-interested desire, though not completely free of self-concern. This certainly would be a modification of his views, as it involves abandoning the thesis that one who has perfect charity wants nothing for its own sake except that God's will be done. But I think the weaker claim is much more plausible than the stronger, and is sufficient to account for much of what Fénelon wanted to say.

In particular, the Salesian and Fénelonian suspicion against love for one's own love of God can be interpreted as something less than a complete rejection of self-concerned desires to love God. This may be done in at least three ways.

(a) Most obviously, Fénelon may still consistently object to desires in which love for God is desired not for its own sake but as a means to one's own good. Similarly, St. Francis de Sales was particularly worried that one might begin to prize one's love for God for the sake of the pleasure that one found in it. Wanting pleasure for oneself is not necessarily a self-interested motive, in the narrower sense defined above; for one can pursue one's own pleasure without pursuing one's own good on the whole, as in smoking a cigarette, or eating a hot fudge sundae, that one thinks will be enjoyable but bad for one. But it seems to be consistent to maintain that in perfect charity one's love for God would be desired for its own sake, but one's own pleasure, as well as one's own good, would not.

I do not mean to suggest that St. Francis de Sales does maintain this explicitly. When he speaks of the danger of loving one's love of God, "not for the good pleasure and satisfaction of God, but for the pleasure and satisfaction that we ourselves derive from it" (Sales, 1969:785f. [bk. IX, ch. 9]), he considers only the possibilities that the love is desired for the lover's pleasure and that it is desired for God's pleasure. He is correct in pointing out that love for God could be desired primarily as a pleasant experience of one's own, and that that would be a perversion. I agree with him about this, though I do not think there is necessarily anything wrong with wanting, for its own sake, to *enjoy* loving God, so long as one's interest in the subjective pleasure is subsidiary to one's desire for the objective relationship. But it is just this desire for the objective relationship that St. Francis de Sales fails to mention. Desiring charity as pleasing to God is not the only alternative to desiring it for one's own pleasure. Love for God can also be desired for its own sake as a relation to God; and I think some aspects of the Salesian position imply that it ought to be desired in that way.

(b) Another characterization of the perversion that St. Francis de Sales fears is that "instead of loving this holy love because it tends toward God who is the beloved, we love it because it proceeds from us who are the lovers" (Sales, 1969:785 [bk. IX, ch. 9]). More vividly, as he wrote in an earlier draft of his *Treatise,*

> Who does not see that [in this perversion] it is no longer God that I regard, but from God I have returned to myself, and that I love this love because it is mine, not because it is for God (Sales, 1969:1550).

The point of these statements is not obvious, but we may conjecture that it has to do, not with what is *desired* in love, but with what is *admired*. Our interest in loving God is perverted when the focus of our admiration shifts from God's perfection, from his worthiness to be loved, to our own possible perfection. This seems to be correct, and is consistent with the view that our own righteousness and love for God are among the ends that we ought to desire at least partly for their own sake.

(c) A sense of proportion provides a final, and reasonable, ground of suspicion against one's interest in one's own love for God, and more broadly in one's own virtue. Even if self-concerned desires to love and obey God, and to be morally and religiously perfect, have a rightful or indeed a necessary place in the best Christian piety, it is clear that they all too easily assume too large a place. It is sinfully self-centered to care too much about one's own perfection in proportion to one's concern for the good of other people and the glorification of God in his whole creation. If one aims ultimately *only* at one's own perfection, one's attitude is not one of love for God. In this way it would indeed be possible to love one's (supposed) love for God instead of loving God.

IV. Penitence and Gratitude

The suggestion that Christian love ought to be completely free of self-interested desire, but not completely free of self-concern, can be tested against other Christian virtues, to see if it is consistent with a satisfactory account of them. It works out very well in the case of *penitence*. It was charged that Fénelon overthrew "the proper and intrinsical motive of repentance" by holding that redeemed souls ought to engage in penitential behavior, "not for their own purification and deliverance, but as a thing that God wills" (Noailles et al., 1698:226). Insofar as the accent falls here on 'deliverance', implying that in penitence one should have a self-interested motive, fearing some loss or diminution of one's own good, this criticism shows an ignoble misunderstanding of the nature of penitence. In this respect Fénelon's sharp retort seems fully justified: "You annihilate the acts of perfect contrition, where one makes oneself suffer for one's sin, not for the sake of the happiness that one desires, but for the sake of the righteousness that one loves in itself" (Fénelon, 1838a:87 [letter IV, sec. 20]; cf. 1838b:143 [letter III, sec. 12]). The value of penitence is not enhanced by self-interest.

But penitence is certainly self-concerned. For it involves remorse, and remorse is not just regret that something bad has happened; it is being particularly sorry that one has done something bad *oneself*. The best sort of penitence involves wanting, for its own sake, not to be a wrongdoer. In penitence one cannot regard oneself as "just another person." Insofar as the accent, in the charge against Fénelon, falls on 'purification', implying that in penitence one's own moral or religious improvement should be sought as an end in itself, the objectors seem to have a correct view of penitence. It is a view that Fénelon himself appears to share, in proposing "the righteousness that one loves in itself" as the right motive of penitence. And it requires the admission of self-concern, though not necessarily of self-interest, to the Christian ideal.

Thus far we have not found any Christian virtue that requires self-interest. But we have yet to consider *gratitude*. Fénelon's opponents charged that he omits mention of gratitude as a motive of love toward God (Noailles et al., 1698:252). He responded that gratitude is useful in the earlier stages of the spiritual life, by helping us to see and attend to the perfections of

God, and by diminishing concupiscence and increasing grace: "finally, in the most perfect state, the acts of . . . thankfulness become more and more frequent, but that is because they are commanded by charity" (Fénelon, 1838b:132 [letter III, sec. 2]). This answer fails to come to grips with the problem. Where acts of thankfulness have to be commanded by charity—a charity not motivated by benefits received (ibid.)—there cannot be much real gratitude.

The first question to ask here is whether the occasion of gratitude must be something that is good for the grateful person and that he desires *ultimately because* it is good for him. Certainly one cannot appropriately be said to be *grateful* to just anyone for just any good deed that he does. Suppose a stranger risks his life to save the life of a child who is equally a stranger to you. No matter how much you admire the hero, or how much you feel for the child, it would be odd to say that you are *grateful* to the hero. You are not sufficiently involved. But you need not be *benefited* by the act for which you are grateful. You may be grateful to a second person for doing something for a third person at your request, even though it is not you but the third person who is benefited. Your request involves you enough to render both the fact and the concept of gratitude appropriate in such a case.

But would God's answers to our prayers for others provide adequate occasion for Christian gratitude to God? I think not. The Christian is supposed to be conscious of God's goodness *to him,* and grateful for that. And this is not an arbitrary demand. It is rooted in the needs of love. You might be very grateful to me for my making a contribution in your name to your favorite charity. But such a gift does not fully take the place of giving you something for your own benefit or pleasure. The good and happiness of the beloved are central ends in themselves for love. The full expression of love requires some actions that aim ultimately at those ends; and one ought to respond to such acts with gratitude.

Christians are supposed to be grateful to God for acting to promote their good. In the best sort of gratitude one must like something about what the benefactor did or meant to accomplish. And in gratitude to God it won't do to like only "the thought behind" the deed, as if he were a cousin who had knitted you a sweater of the wrong size. God makes no such mistakes. So it seems in the best sort of gratitude to God one must like one's own good: one must prefer that it have been promoted rather than not. And I think one must prefer it for one's own sake; that is, the preference must be self-interested. Suppose one were glad to have had one's own good promoted, but only as a means, saying to oneself, "This will help me glorify God," or "This will enable me to do a lot of good for other people." Such an inability to accept a gift *for oneself,* when one's own good was the chief goal of the giver, is *ungrateful.*

This argument does not show that the grateful Christian ought pursue his own good as an end in itself, but only that he ought to like its having been promoted when it has been promoted by God. It is a self-interest already satisfied, rather than a striving self-interest that is required here. But it is a sort of self-interest, favoring one's own good for its (and one's) own sake.

Our review of the motivational requirements of several Christian virtues suggests that certain sorts of self-concern hold an important place in the Christian life; and that self-interest does indeed hold a place there, but a much less important place than some other sorts of self-concern. The right approach to Christian self-denial is not by an attempt at complete exclusion of self-interest or self-concern, but by a subtler study of their right and wrong relation to other motives.

V. Eros in Agape

Our discussion thus far has been about love for God, but it can also be applied to love for fellow human beings. The purest and ethically most interesting sort of love for another person is often identified with *benevolence*—that is, with desire for the other person's good. The natural extension of this view to the case of love for God is to identify perfect love for God with the desire that God's will be done.

Similarly, the contrast between Agape and Eros is popularly seen as a special case of the contrast between altruism and self-interest. Agape, Christian love, is identified with benevolence, and Eros is identified with self-interested desire for relationship with another person.[3] Benevolence is a motive that can hardly be praised too highly, and the contrast between altruistic and self-interested desires is legitimate and useful. But it has too often been treated as a dichotomy. That is, it is too often assumed, particularly where personal relations are in question, that what is desired is desired either for one's own good or for another person's good. The conception of love, and particularly of Eros, has suffered much from being forced into this dichotomy.

For Eros need not be either self-interested or altruistic. This is not a claim about what Plato (for example) meant, but about the character of the attitudes that we would normally recognize as concrete paradigms of Eros. The central case of Eros is passionate desire for a personal relationship. And such desire for a personal relationship need not be based on the belief that it would be good for anyone. This is most obvious in the case of a tragic or destructive Eros. There are doubtless instances in which a close personal relationship is strongly desired by both of the parties to it although neither of them believes it will be good for either of them. Perhaps if they truly love each other they will prefer on balance to break off the relationship; but that does not change the fact that they have a desire for the relationship—a desire which is neither self-interested nor altruistic in the present sense.

It is happily more usual in human relations that the lover believes that the relationship he desires would be good both for him and for the beloved. But it is *not* usual for the lover to desire the relationship only because he believes it would be good for one or both of them. Indeed if he desires the relationship in such a way that he would have no interest in it at all if he did not think it would be beneficial, we may doubt that he really loves. Eros is not based on calculations or judgments of utility or benefit, and must therefore at least partly escape classification as self-interested or altruistic. The mistake, in trying to force love into a dichotomy of self-interest and altruism, is a failure to recognize a desire for a relationship for its own sake as a third type of desire that is not just a combination or consequence of desire for one's own good and desire for another persons' good. It is indeed this third type of desire, which is self-concerned but not self-interested in the sense explained above, that is most characteristic of Eros.

Thus the identification of Eros with self-interested desire for personal relationships is in error; and so is the identification of Agape with benevolence. The ideal of Christian love includes not only benevolence but also desire for certain kinds of personal relationship, for their own sakes. Were that not so, it would be strange to call it "love." It is an abuse of the word 'love' to say that one *loves* a person, or any other object, if one does not care, except instrumentally, about one's relation to that object. Even St. Francis de Sales (1969:843 [bk. X, ch. 10]) said that "if . . . there were an infinite goodness . . . with which we could not have any union or communication, we would certainly esteem it more highly then ourselves, . . . and . . . we could have mere wishes to be able to love it; but strictly speaking we would not love it, because love has to do with union. . . ."

In saying that love involves caring about one's relationship with its object in a way that benevolence does not, I have in mind a wide variety of relationships, and not just those intimate social relationships that we think of first in connection with love. To take an example that is closely related to Fénelon's ideas: The lover commonly will want to *serve* the beloved: to satisfy his desires or promote his well-being. It may be thought that the benevolent person also wants to serve, by promoting the happiness of the object of his benevolence. But that is not quite right. The benevolent person need not care who promotes the well-being of the one whom he wishes well, so long as it is promoted. But to the lover it is not indifferent who promotes the good of his beloved. He wants to be the one who serves his beloved—or at least one of those who do.

Similarly the lover not only desires that misfortune and annoyances should not befall his beloved; he is particularly concerned that *he* not cause harm or displeasure to his beloved. And in general it is normally a part of love to want one's own actions and their consequences to express one's love. That this is true of love for God as well as love for fellow human beings seems to be one of the factors that led Fénelon into inconsistency.

The claim that Christian love—New Testament Agape—is not solely benevolence can be supported by at least two arguments from the Bible.

(1) Whatever else Agape may be in the New Testament, it is first of all God's love for us. And God's love for us is surely seen as involving a desire for certain relationships between God and us, for their own sakes and not merely as good for us. The jealous husband of Israel (Jeremiah 2:1–3:5; Hosea 2), he made the whole human race so that they might seek and find him (Acts 17:26–7). He desires our worship and devotion. Why did Christ give himself up for the Church? Because he loved her and wanted to present her to himself in splendor as a bride (Ephesians 5:25–7). No doubt it would be possible to interpret all of this on the hypothesis that God desires to be related to us only because it will be good for us. But I think that is implausible. The Bible depicts a God who seems at least as interested in divine-human relationships as in human happiness per se. Even Anders Nygren, who is most emphatic about the unselfishness of Agape, presents it as one of the distinctive characteristics of Agape that it creates *fellowship* between God and human beings. But if such fellowship is desired for its own sake by God, God's desire is self-concerned inasmuch as the object of the desire involves him as essentially as it involves us. And would we have it otherwise? Let him who would rather be the object of benevolence than of love cast the first stone.

(2) The New Testament sets a very high value on reconciliation and friendly relations between people. Loving enemies and strangers seems to be first of all a matter of desiring good for them, but also of greeting them (Matthew 5:43–7). Christians are to "greet one another with a kiss of love [Agape]" (I Peter 5:14). The incentive of love is to lead them to be in harmony with each other (Philippians 2:1–2). One might try to

explain this on the hypothesis that reconciliation, harmony, and friend-ship are to be pursued solely out of benevolence, as being good for the other persons involved. But that seems a strained interpretation. There is no reason to think that reconciliation and friendly relations are always a benefit to people, except insofar as they are worth pursuing for their own sake. Perhaps a good fight would sometimes be better for people. The Christian interest in harmonious relations, as a goal of love, seems to go beyond any merely instrumental value they may have. And I believe that moral intuition, as well as scriptural authority, favors regarding the desire for friendly relations, for their own sake, as a good motive.

Conceived as I have argued they ought to be, Eros and Agape are not opposites. Eros is generally present as a strand in love. It is the lover's desire for relationship with the beloved. It may be self-interested, but it need not be. It manifests itself most fully in a desire for the relationship for its own sake, and not just for the good of either party. Benevolence, the desire for the good of the beloved, is also present as a strand in love. I have argued that Agape is not to be identified with this strand. It in-cludes both strands. Specifically, Agape includes a sort of Eros—not every sort of Eros, for there are certainly selfish, sick, and destructive forms of Eros that have no place in the Christian ethical ideal. One of the dis-tinguishing characteristics of Agape is the kind of Eros that it includes: the kind of relationship that is desired in Agape.

It is a striking fact that while benevolence (the desire for another per-son's well-being) and Eros, as a desire for relationship with another per-son, seem to be quite distinct desires, we use a single name, 'love' or 'Agape', for an attitude that includes both of them, at least in typical cases. Why do we do this? I find it a tempting hypothesis that the central element in Agape, the element that holds the concept together, is the agapic type of Eros. In an exemplary case of Agape the lover wants a certain type of relationship with the beloved. That relationship includes mutual benevolence. Thus benevolence is desired in agapic Eros. Desir-ing benevolence is not the same as having it, but there is at any rate a natural affinity between benevolence and agapic Eros, which springs from the nature of agapic Eros.

To say that the agapic type of Eros is the *central* element in Agape, in this sense, is not to deny that benevolence is *ethically* the most *im-portant* element in Agape. Benevolence is not only the most important, but also the most *essential* element in Agape. There cannot be Agape at all without benevolence; but when it is demanded of me that I have Agape toward the starving millions of Bangladesh, or even toward a multitude of strangers in my own city, perhaps no more of Eros is demanded of me than that I should want *not* to have *un*friendly relations with them—which is hardly enough to count as Eros. Ethically important (indeed necessary) as it is, however, I think that Agape with so little Eros in it should be seen by Christians as only an incomplete and fragmentary participation in the fullness of God's Agape.

Notes

1. Fénelon, 1697. I quote always from this first edition. The critical edition (Fénelon, 1911) presents a revised text made but not published by Fénelon, though the first edition can be reconstructed from Cherel's apparatus. The first edition seems to me the more important document. I have allowed my translations to be influenced in a number of cases by the language of a rather good contemporary English translation, which exists in at least two significantly different (and differently paginated) editions (*The Maxims of the Saints Explained, concerning the Interior Life*. London: H. Rhodes, 1698, and London: G. Thompson, R. Dampier, W. Manson, and J. Bland, n.d.).

2. This argument is an objection to the ideal of holy indifference as caring about nothing for its own sake except that God's will be done. It is not so clearly an objection to what Fénelon called 'holy resignation', in which one prefers the accomplishment of God's will above all other ends although one does desire some other ends for their own sakes. The conditional sacrifices follow from holy resignation as well as from holy indifference, and I am not offering an opinion here as to what Fénelon ought to have said about the conditional sacrifices.

3. There is much in Nygren (1969) to encourage this interpretation of the distinction, though it is not fully explicit in Nygren and does not fit everything he says about Agape. It fits his conception of Eros better. Nygren's discussion, however, is less focused on the ends of diverse loves than on their causes and conditions.

References

Butler, Joseph. 1970. *Fifteen Sermons Preached at the Rolls Chapel*. Edited, with Butler's *Dissertation on the Nature of Virtue,* by T. A. Roberts. London: S.P.C.K.

Denzinger, Heinrich. 1911. *Enchiridion symbolorum, definitionum, et declarationum de rebus fidei et morum*. Editio undecima quam paravit Clemens Bannwart. Freiburg: Herder.

Fénelon, François de Salignac de la Mothe. 1697. *Explication des maximes des saints sur la vie intérieure*. Paris: Pierre Aubouin, Pierre Emery, and Charles Clousier.

———. 1698. *Instruction pastorale de Messire Franc. de Salignac de la Mothe*

Fénelon . . . touchant son livre des maximes des saints. Edition nouvelle, corrigée & augmentée. Amsterdam: Henri Wetstein.

————. 1838a. *Lettres à Mgr. l'évêque de Meaux, en réponse aux divers écrits ou mémoires sur le livre intitulé* Explication des maximes des saints. In 1838c.

————. 1838b. *Lettres en réponse à celle de Mgr. l'évêque de Meaux.* In 1838c.

————. 1838c. *Oeuvres de Fénelon, Archévêque de Cambrai,* précédées d'études sur sa vie, par M. Aimé-Martin. Tome II. Paris: Firmin Didot Frères.

————. 1911. *Explication des maximes des saints sur la vie intérieure.* Édition critique publiée d'après des documents inédits par Albert Cherel. Paris: Bloud.

Noailles, Louis Antoine de, Jacque-Bénigne Bossuet, and Paul Godet Desmarais. 1698. *Declaratio . . . circa librum cui titulus est:* Explication des maximes des saints sur la vie intérieure, etc. Text dated Paris, August 6, 1697. Republished, with facing French translation, among the "additions" to a "new edition" of Fénelon, 1697. Amsterdam: Henri Wetstein.

Nygren, Anders. 1969. *Agape and Eros.* Translated by Philip S. Watson. New York and Evanston, Ill.: Harper & Row.

Sales, St. François de. 1969. *Traité de l'amour de Dieu.* In *Oeuvres,* ed. André Ravier. Paris: Gallimard (Bibliothèque de la Pléiade).

PART FOUR

THE METAPHYSICS
OF THEISM

13

Has It Been Proved That All Real Existence Is Contingent?

I

It is believed by many philosophers (i) that no proposition asserting the existence of something—or at least no proposition asserting that something has the kind of real existence that God must be supposed to have, if he exists—can be logically necessary. And it is widely believed (ii) that belief (i) has been established so conclusively that arguments for the logically necessary existence of such a real thing can be rejected out of hand, without further examination, on the ground that such logically necessary existence is known to be impossible. The present essay is an attack on what I take to be the most important arguments for the second of these beliefs. Its aim is strictly limited, in at least two respects.

(A) I do not attempt to show here that any real thing does have logically necessary existence; I only argue that it has not been shown that none can have it. I am not even claiming that there are no good reasons for thinking that all real existence is indeed logically contingent. What I do maintain is that no such reasons are so conclusive as to constitute a refutation, in advance, of any argument purporting to show that the real existence of something is logically necessary.

(B) My own interest in the subject is rooted in an interest in the conception of God's existence as logically necessary. But this essay is not concerned with specifically theological problems about necessary existence, such as might arise from some of the attributes traditionally ascribed to God. Neither is it concerned with arguments against *God*'s necessary existence which might be based on such problems. It deals only

I am indebted to many (particularly including Marilyn McCord Adams, Nelson Pike, and a reader for the *American Philosophical Quarterly*) for helpful discussion and criticism of earlier versions of this essay.

with arguments for the general doctrine that all real existence must be logically contingent.

I would like to be able to prove conclusively that that doctrine cannot be proved true, that the most one can do to support the doctrine is to rebut arguments offered for necessary existence. It would follow that the doctrine cannot be used to refute arguments for logically necessary existence but requires for its own support the refutation of any such argument that may be offered. Unfortunately I seem to be in a position like that myself. For short of proving that the existence of some real thing is logically necessary (which I shall not attempt to do here), I see no way of demonstrating conclusively that my own thesis is correct. All I can do is to try to rebut the principal arguments offered in support of the claim that it has been proved that all real existence is logically contingent. It seems to me that there are three such principal arguments, or types of argument, which I shall discuss in sections II, III, and IV.

II

In part IX of Hume's *Dialogues Concerning Natural Religion,* we find the classic instance of a type of argument which we may call the 'But surely I can conceive' type of objection to logically necessary existence.

> Nothing, that is distinctly conceivable, implies a contradiction. Whatever we conceive as existent, we can also conceive as non-existent. There is no Being, therefore, whose non-existence implies a contradiction.[1]

The adverb 'distinctly' must do quite a lot of work if the first premise of this argument is to be plausible. It would normally be thought that one can have a fairly clear conception of something, and mistakenly believe it to be possible, even though it is in fact self-contradictory (for instance, the trisection of the angle by Euclidean methods, or a general decision procedure for the predicate calculus). It may be replied that such conceptions are not *distinct*. If we tried, for example, to conceive, step by step, a correct Euclidean construction for the trisection of the angle, we could not bring it off. A distinct conception, then, will be one which does not imply a contradiction and which is so full that anyone who has it has conclusive grounds for believing that it does not imply a contradiction. There are such conceptions, of course. There are, for example, Euclidean constructions whose possibility can be established by conceiving them step by step.

Distinct conceptions in this sense can also be found outside the realm of logical and mathematical proof. I think there is reason to suppose that *imagination* is the type of conception which Hume had principally in mind in the quoted passage. And in some cases imagination provides conclusive grounds for believing that what is imagined is logically possible, although in other cases it does not. The extent to which imaginability does or does not establish possibility is important to our argument—enough so that I think it will be worthwhile to consider a range of cases.

(1) I can imagine a triangular red patch beside a square blue patch. This provides me with conclusive grounds for believing it logically possible that a triangular red patch and a square blue patch should appear to me side by side. For in this case virtually nothing is asserted in the proposition to be proved possible except a bare description of the images occurring in the imagination experience. What we have here is essentially an inference from the actuality of a certain experience to its possibility.

(2) I can imagine that there is a unicorn in my garden right now, and I think I can imagine it in such a way as to have very good reason to believe it logically possible for there to have been a unicorn there now. For I can live through, in my imagination, experiences which would surely have left no reasonable doubt that there was a unicorn in my garden right now. And these imagined experiences form, so to speak, a coherent story. Yet this case is different from that of the color patches, in that I am imagining something that is definitely not the case. There is therefore no straightforward argument from actuality to possibility here.

(3) I can imagine the nonexistence or extinction of lions, by imagining a safari to Africa during which we see no lions, and imagining that our guide explains that lions have become extinct. I don't doubt that it is logically possible for lions to become extinct, but imagining it in this way does not provide very good grounds for believing it possible. For I have not imagined any experience which would positively exclude the continued existence of lions. There could be stealthy lions lurking in some bushes that we did not explore carefully enough; and what a guide says (even an honest and generally knowledgeable guide) may be false.

(4) I can imagine myself discovering an effective general decision procedure for the predicate calculus. I can imagine this with a wealth of anecdotal detail, though I cannot imagine, step by step, a sound proof of such results. In this case what I imagine myself doing is logically impossible. Perhaps it will be objected that really I have only imagined myself *believing* I had discovered an effective general decision procedure. But I think it is quite in keeping with the meaning of the word 'imagine' to say that I imagined myself really discovering it.

It is clear, then, that we can sometimes conceive of something in such a way as to leave no reasonable doubt of its possibility. This may be done in some cases by imagination; and in the case of logical and mathematical proofs and constructions, it may be done by conceiving them step by step in detail. These are important methods for establishing possibility. But just as clearly, not every conception establishes the possibility of that which is conceived in it.

We want to know whether it can be established, by what we may call "the method of distinct conception," that *everything* which can be conceived to exist can also (without logical impropriety) be conceived not to exist. This could not be established by distinctly conceiving the nonexistence of one thing after another. For there would always remain things whose nonexistence we had not yet conceived; and we would not have proved that their nonexistence is also logically possible.

I think probably the only way in which the method of distinct conception could yield a general proof that nonexistence is logically possible in *every* case would be by providing a proof that a state of affairs is logically possible in which nothing would exist at all. And it does not seem to me likely that such a state of affairs can be conceived in such a way as to exclude all rational doubt of its logical possibility. How could anything we might imagine prove anything about the possibility of a state of affairs in which nothing would exist either to be a subject of experience or to have imaginable properties? It would be absurd to suppose that we could live through, in imagination, experiences which would establish with certainty that nothing at all existed, since at least the experiences themselves, and/or an experiencer, would have to exist. Perhaps it will be suggested that we can imagine experiences which would leave no reasonable doubt that at some time prior to the experiences nothing at all had existed. This at least is not patently absurd, but I think it is very doubtful. I suppose we might be able to imagine experiences which would justify us in being quite sure that before a certain time there had not existed any physical objects of any type with which we were familiar. But I do not see how such experiences could establish, beyond a shadow of a doubt, that previously there had not existed anything at all—not even God, angels, devils, Platonic Forms, numbers (if they are properly said to exist), time itself (if it is properly said to exist), or tiny physical particles of a type which we had not yet discovered.

So I think it unlikely that one could prove, by the method of distinct conception, that nonexistence is logically possible in *every* case. I also think it unlikely that the method will provide a proof in some of the particular cases which have most interested philosophers. For instance, how would one distinctly conceive the nonexistence of an omniscient being (or the existence of one, for that matter)? What imaginable experience would exclude all rational doubt that there is, or that there is not, a being that knows absolutely everything? That would probably have to be the experience of proving either that the existence of such a being is logically necessary or that its existence is logically impossible. But neither of those experiences can be *distinctly conceived* in the requisite sense unless there is a sound proof to be found for one of those conclusions.

It may be suggested that the existence of any conscious being can be more directly imagined by imagining thoughts and perceptions that it might have. Its nonexistence could hardly be conceived by imagining a total absence of thoughts and perceptions. What would it be to imagine that? But perhaps its ceasing to exist could be imagined by imagining the "fading out" of the thoughts and perceptions which one imagines as constituting its consciousness, and by not imagining after them any other thoughts and perceptions which one would ascribe to the same conscious being.

No doubt such an exercise in imagination is possible. But exactly what could one prove by it about the possible existence or nonexistence of an omniscient being? (a) One could prove to oneself that such thoughts as one has imagined (or at least very similar ones) are possible. For one has actually had very similar ones in imagining them, and what is actual is possible. (b) On the same grounds, one could prove to oneself that it is possible for such thoughts to "fade out." (c) That one can *regard* a set of such thoughts as constituting part of the consciousness of an omniscient being is also something that can be established on the ground that what is actual is possible. (d) Similarly, it can be established that one can *regard* the fading out of such thoughts as representing the ceasing to exist of an omniscient being. (e) And one can prove to oneself that a state of one's mind is possible which one *regards* as representing the nonexistence of an omniscient being because one is not imagining any thoughts which one ascribes to an omniscient being.

But such an exercise in imagination would not prove (c') that it is logically possible for an omniscient being to exist or to have such thoughts as were imagined for it. Nor would it prove (d') that it is logically possible for an omniscient being to cease to exist, or (e') that the nonexistence of an omniscient being, or of any other conscious being, is logically possible. For from the fact that one can *regard* one's thoughts as representing such and such a state of affairs, it does not follow that that state of affairs is logically possible. The possibility claims (c'), (d'), and (e') may indeed have considerable initial plausibility, but they have not been proved true by the method of distinct conception.

I conclude that the method of distinct conception will probably fail the opponent of logically necessary existence, in two ways. (1) It will not yield a general proof that real existence is never logically necessary. (2) Neither will it provide particular proofs of the logical possibility of non-existence in all those cases in which some philosophers have asserted logical necessity of existence. For instance, it does not yield a proof that it is logically possible that there exists no omniscient being.

This does not show that belief in the contingency of all real existence cannot in any way be supported by conceptions of the nonexistence of things. To many philosophers, for instance, it has seemed intuitively plausible that there is no logical impropriety in the conception of a state of affairs in which nothing would exist at all. I do not deny that any such plausibility counts in favor of the claim that no real existence is logically necessary—so long as no conclusive proof of the logically necessary existence of some real thing has been discovered. Even if an argument for the logically necessary existence of some real being is brought forward which is not conclusive but which has some force, that force must naturally be weighed against any considerations, including intuitive plausibilities, which there may be on the other side. What I do deny is that such intuitive plausibility can rightly serve as a refutation, in advance, of any argument for logically necessary existence.

III

Another influential type of argument against the possibility of logically necessary existence can be introduced by the following simile. Imagine oneself a quality control officer in a shoe factory, inspecting the finished shoes as they come off the assembly line. If one has at least a rudimentary knowledge of what feet are like and how shoes are meant to fit them, one can tell some things, but not everything, about any foot that a given shoe will fit, just by examining the shoe. For instance, one can tell whether it is a left or right foot, but not whether or not the person it belongs to is married. If the shoe is very badly made, one may be able to tell, just by looking at it, that there is no foot that it will fit. But no matter how well made a shoe is, one cannot tell just by looking at the shoe that there *is* a foot that it fits. In order to know that, one must also examine feet, until one finds a foot that the shoe fits.

This is just a simile, of course, and will not bear pressing hard at all points. But I think we may say that it is very common for philosophers to think of concepts as related to things in much the same way that shoes are related to feet. Specifications, so to speak, are built into the concepts as well as into shoes. In order to "satisfy" the concept, a thing must have certain properties which are the "defining properties" of the concept. Knowing what the defining properties are is the largest part of understanding the concept. Simply by understanding and considering the concept, therefore, it is possible to know some things, though not everything, about anything that will satisfy the concept. Those things which consideration of concepts alone can tell us about whatever things may satisfy them are logically necessary truths. Those things which we cannot learn from concepts alone are held not to be logically necessary.

This picture of the matter suggests that existence cannot be logically necessary, although nonexistence can be. It is normally supposed that 'There exists an F' is true if and only if the concept of F is satisfied. And a concept, like a shoe, can be "so badly made" that we can see, just by examining it, that nothing could possibly satisfy it. This is the case when a concept is self-contradictory, when it specifies incompatible defining properties for its instances. But there is no such thing as a concept being "so well made" that we can see, just by considering it, that it must be satisfied. For to say that a concept is satisfied is to say that a certain agreement obtains between it and something else. And in order to know that such an agreement obtains, we must examine not only the concept but also the something else. Therefore, it is claimed that it cannot be logically necessary that a certain concept is satisfied, or that there exists something of a certain sort, since logically necessary truths are truths which can be known by consideration of concepts alone.

I believe that this line of thinking underlies a very large proportion of the arguments commonly given for the contingency of all assertions of existence. Many of these arguments turn on the claim that existence is not a predicate, or not a property. If existence is not a property at all, it cannot be a defining property. It is concluded that since existence cannot be built into a concept as a defining property, assertions of existence cannot be logically necessary or analytic. Such an argument could hardly be expressed more clearly than it is by Paul Edwards, when he writes,

> To say that there is a necessary being is to say that it would be a self-contradiction to deny its existence. This would mean that at least one existential statement is a necessary truth; and this in turn presupposes that in at least one case existence is contained in a concept. But only a characteristic can be contained in a concept and it has seemed plain to most philosophers since Kant that existence is not a characteristic, that it can hence never be contained in a concept, and that hence no existential statement can ever be a necessary truth.[2]

The same sort of argument can be stated, however, without reliance on the doctrine that existence is not a predicate or property. Jerome Shaffer has argued that 'exists' functions in some contexts as a predicate, and even as a defining predicate. For instance, 'Historical persons have at some time existed' (as opposed, say, to fictitious characters, who have never existed) is tautological.[3] But being tautological, Shaffer argues, it cannot tell us whether there have actually been any historical persons or not. An assertion that there is, or has been, something of a certain sort, Shaffer calls an *extensional assertion*.

> Why is it that extensional assertions cannot be tautological? Because they do not merely tell us what the requirements are for being an *A* but, starting with these requirements, tell us whether anything meets these requirements.[4]

The crucial assumption in Shaffer's argument, as in Edwards', is that a tautological or logically necessary truth can tell us only what the requirements are for a thing to satisfy a certain concept.

This is a mistaken assumption. 'If it is raining, it is raining' is a tautology, but does not tell us what the requirements are for anything to satisfy a certain concept. There are a number of ways in which a proposition may be logically necessary. Some universal affirmative propositions are logically necessary because the predicate term is a defining property of the subject term (e.g., 'All husbands are married'). Some negative existential propositions are logically necessary because of the self-contradictoriness of the predicate which they say is unsatisfied (e.g., 'There are no unmarried husbands'). All that Edwards' and Shaffer's arguments, and others like them, succeed in showing is that a proposition that there is something of a certain sort cannot be logically necessary in either of *these* ways. But it does not follow that there is *no* way in which the existence of a thing can be logically necessary, for we do not know that these are the only ways in which a proposition can be logically necessary. Indeed, as I have just pointed out, we know that they are not the only ways.

My objection to arguments like those of Edwards and Shaffer can perhaps be made clearer with the aid of a somewhat different application of the simile of shoe-fitting, an application suggested by the idea that a logically necessary truth is a proposition which is true about all logically possible worlds. It may be said that concepts (or predicate-concepts, at any rate) are made to fit things or objects. But we may equally well say that propositions are made to fit states of affairs, or possible worlds. If a proposition of the form 'There is no *F*' is logically necessary, we may say it is necessary because the concept of *F* is "so badly made" that it could not fit, or correctly describe, any possible individual. Alternatively, we could say that the *proposition* 'There is an *F*' is "so badly made" that it could not fit, or correctly describe, any possible state of affairs. Now suppose it is claimed that a proposition of the form 'There is a *G*' is logically necessary. Obviously this claim could not be explained by saying that the concept of *G* is so badly made that it could not fit anything; for what is claimed is that there must be something that it fits. But why couldn't it be that 'There is a *G*' is logically necessary because its contradictory, the *proposition* 'There is no *G*', is so badly made that it could not fit any possible world?

As long as we think only in terms of the relation between things and concepts of things, it may seem as if there is no way of expressing what a logically necessary affirmative existential proposition would be. But in terms of the relation between possible worlds and propositions we can say that a logically necessary affirmative existential proposition (like any other logically necessary proposition) would be a proposition which is true about all possible worlds and whose contradictory fails to describe any possible kind of world. Thus we can say that 'If it is raining, it is raining' is logically necessary because its contradictory, 'It is not the case that if it is raining, it is raining', is logically defective and could not describe any possible world.

In fairness I must point out, of course, that a negative existential proposition could not be logically defective in the same way as 'It is not the case that if it is raining, it is raining'. For the latter proposition is truth-functionally self-contradictory. But negative existential propositions are not truth-functional tautologies. Neither can affirmative existential propositions be theorems of quantification logic—at least not in a system of quantification logic valid in empty domains, in which '$(\exists x)(Fx)$' ['There exists an *x* such that *Fx*'] does not follow from '$(\forall x)(Fx)$' ['For every *x*, *Fx*'].

I anticipate that someone will object that the ways in which I have already admitted that an affirmative existential proposition could not be logically necessary are the only ways in which they can see that any proposition could be logically necessary. They can see how a proposition can be logically necessary by virtue of truth-functional propositional logic, by virtue of a quantificational logic valid in empty domains, by virtue of the defining properties of a predicate-concept, or by virtue of self-contradictoriness of a predicate-concept; but they cannot see any other way. And therefore they do not see how the existence of anything could be logically necessary. Perhaps it would be fairest to interpret arguments such as those of Edwards and Shaffer as intended to form part of a larger argument of this sort.

Certainly, if one does not see *how* any proposition of a certain form or type could be logically necessary, that may be a good reason for believing that no such proposition is logically necessary. But it hardly constitutes a conclusive proof. For how are we to know that there is not some other, as yet unconsidered, way in which a proposition of that form or type can be logically necessary? Surely it has not been proved that logical analysis must consist only in truth-functional and quantificational logic and the analysis of predicates.

Many arguments have been advanced by philosophers for the logically necessary existence of God, or of Platonic Forms, or of numbers, or other entities. Such an argument, if successful, might be expected to show us a way in which it can be logically necessary that there exists something of a certain sort. Perhaps it would establish, for instance, that such a conclusion followed from a theory of general scope in philosophy of mathematics, philosophy of logic, or metaphysics, and that the theory could be shown by some sort of logical analysis to be necessarily true. The claim that there is no way in which an affirmative existential proposition could be logically necessary might be to some extent confirmed by the refutation of arguments for the logically necessary existence of one entity or another. But it is by its nature a claim which is always liable to refutation by a new argument for logically necessary existence. It would therefore be question-begging to treat that claim as providing a refutation of any argument for logically necessary existence.

IV

It is often said that what is wrong with *a priori* arguments for the existence of God is that you can't legitimately get from mere concepts to reality in that way. As J. N. Findlay has said, "It is not thought possible to build bridges between mere abstractions and concrete existence."[5] I suspect that behind most such objections lies a fear that acceptance of the existence of any real thing as logically necessary would compromise the conviction that what reality is, is independent of human thought, choice, and activity. This fear makes sense if, like many modern philosophers, one holds that "necessity in propositions merely reflects our use of words, the arbitrary conventions of our language" (as Findlay again has put it).[6]

At first sight it might seem that a conventionalist view of logical necessity gives grounds to fear that the independence of reality from human linguistic activity will be compromised by the admission of any logically necessary truths at all. For it seems plausible to suppose that every truth is a partial determination of what reality is. What reality is, is determined by some negative existential truths as well as by affirmative existential truths: for instance, by the fact that there are no unicorns as well as by the the fact that there are horses. Why, then, isn't the independence of reality from language compromised by the logical necessity of negative as well as affirmative existential truths?

It may be plausible, however, to assume a certain asymmetry between existence and nonexistence at this point, and to say that whereas reality is determined in part by the existence of *any* real thing, it is determined by negative existential truths only if they are contingent. That there are no unicorns is a determination of reality, because there might possibly have been unicorns; it depends on extralinguistic factors whether there are any or not. That there are no unmarried husbands is not a determination of reality, because "unmarried husband" is just a linguistic monstrosity which has not been given any descriptive function. But the existence of a real being, such as God, must in any case be a partial determination of what reality is. For even if we suppose that his existence is logically necessary, and that 'There is no God' is a linguistic monstrosity which has not been given any descriptive function, God himself, as a real being, must be supposed to be a part of reality, and his existence would therefore have to be a constituent of what reality is. Perhaps we should say that 'what reality is' means 'which of all logically possible real things (or kinds of real thing) exist'. This formulation seems to have the result we were looking for: What reality is would be determined, in part, by the existence of a logically necessary real being, but not by the nonexistence of a logically impossible thing.

By speaking of "real things" here we leave open the possibility that some things, such as numbers, might be thought to have logically necessary existence without reality being determined thereby. For it might be held that such things are not real things, and that they exist, not in reality, but in some "purely conceptual realm." But something which (like God) is conceived of as acting causally on real human beings and physical objects must presumably exist as a real thing if it exists at all. What reality is would be determined, in part, by the necessary or contingent existence of any such thing.

I do not mean to endorse the position that I have just been sketching. I have simply been trying to develop, as plausibly as possible, what I take to be the thinking behind certain common objections to logically necessary existence. The argument suggested by this thinking can be formulated as follows.

> (A) What reality is, is not (even in part) something that merely reflects our use of words.

(B) If it is a truth that there exists (or that there does not exist) a real thing of a certain logically possible kind, that is part of what reality is.

(C) Logically necessary truths merely reflect our use of words.

(D) Therefore, it is in no case a logically necessary truth that there exists a real thing of a certain kind.

This is the kind of argument on which one would have to rely to substantiate the claim (made by Findlay in the article quoted above) that if logically necessary truth "merely reflects our use of words," then the existence of a real being cannot be logically necessary.

"The correct reply" to this line of argument, as Norman Malcolm has written, "is that the view that logical necessity merely reflects the use of words cannot possibly have the implication that every existential proposition must be contingent. That view requires us to *look at* the use of words and not manufacture *a priori* theses about it."[7] What does seem to follow from the doctrine that logical necessity merely reflects our use of words is that the existence of God, or of some other real thing, could be logically necessary if such words as 'God', 'real', and 'exists' were used in certain ways, and would not be logically necessary if the relevant words were used in other ways. Whether the relevant words are in fact used in such a way that the existence of a certain real thing is logically necessary is something that can be discovered only by investigating how the words are used. Arguments for the logically necessary existence of God, or of any other real thing, could presumably be construed as playing a part in that investigation, as attempts to show us that in fact words are used in such a way that it is logically necessary that a certain real thing exists. To insist that what reality is is not (even in part) something which merely reflects our use of words, and that therefore every argument for the logically necessary existence of a real thing must be counted as refuted in advance, would be to prejudge the results of the investigation, illegitimately. No doubt the thesis that reality is independent of our language, as stated in proposition (A), is intuitively very plausible. But such intuitive plausibility cannot justify a claim to have refuted in advance every argument which purports to show that words are used in such a way that some real existence is logically necessary.

If we assume that proposition (B) is correct, we can draw certain conclusions about the relations between propositions (A) and (C). (C) does not imply that (A) is false. For (C) leaves open the possibility that words may not in fact be used in such a way as to make any real existence logically necessary. But given (B), (C) does imply that whether (A) is true or false depends on how we use words. For the truth or falsity of (A) will depend on whether we do or do not use words in such a way that some real existence is logically necessary. This means that the type of conventionalism expressed in (C) implies, in conjunction with (B), that if what reality is is not (even in part) something that merely reflects our use of words, that fact is itself something that depends on our use of words.

This conclusion, that whether (A) is true or not depends on our use of words, will probably seem objectionable to any philosopher who is determined to adhere to (A) because of its intuitive plausibility. It seems to me that the conviction that reality is not dependent on our language gives to those who hold it less reason for rejecting the possibility of logically necessary real existence than it gives for rejecting the doctrine that logically necessary truths merely reflect our use of words. Findlay has given the argument a somewhat different turn, in a work more recent than the article quoted above. He is now inclined to accept, and no longer to reject, arguments for the logically necessary existence of a real perfect being. But because he still holds strongly to some such principle as (A), he thinks that the acceptance of logically necessary real existence requires the rejection of the doctrine that logical necessity merely reflects our use of words.[8]

There is more than one way, then, in which the truth of the conjunction of (A), (B), and (C) may be called into question. The point that I would emphasize, however, is that as we have seen, the view of necessary truth expressed in (C) does not allow (A) to be so certain as to provide a conclusive refutation, in advance, of any argument for logically necessary real existence.

V

In this essay I have discussed three types of argument against the possibility of logically necessary existence. In each case my criticism followed the same pattern. I allowed that the objection to logically necessary existence rests on premises which may have considerable plausibility so long as no cogent argument for the logically necessary existence of any real thing has been found. But I argued that the premises of the objection are such that it would be question-begging to regard them as conclusively established in advance of detailed consideration of any argument that might be offered for the logically necessary existence of any real thing. In section II, I argued that this is true of objections based on a claim to be able to conceive distinctly the nonexistence of anything at all. In section III, I argued that it is true of objections based on the claim that there is *no way* in which an affirmative existential proposition could be logically necessary. And in section IV, I argued that it is true of objections based on the fear that the independence of reality from human language will be compromised if logically necessary real existence is admitted.

I do not claim that these are the only possible types of objection to logically necessary real existence. But I think they are the most interesting and influential types of objection that I have encountered. And none of them establishes conclusively that all real existence is logically contingent.

Notes

1. P. 189 in the Library of Liberal Arts reprint of Norman Kemp Smith's edition of the *Dialogues*.

2. Paul Edwards, "The Cosmological Argument," reprinted (from *The Rationalist Annual for the Year 1959*) in Donald R. Burrill, ed., *The Cosmological Arguments: A Spectrum of Opinion* (New York, 1967), p. 116. Similar arguments can be found in John Hick, "A Critique of the 'Second Argument'," in John Hick and Arthur McGill, eds., *The Many Faced Argument* (New York, 1967), p. 342; and in Terence Penelhum, "Divine Necessity," *Mind*, 69 (1960), p. 180.

3. Jerome Shaffer, "Existence, Predication, and the Ontological Argument," *Mind*, 71 (1962), p. 318.

4. Ibid., p. 323.

5. J. N. Findlay, "Can God's Existence Be Disproved?" *Mind*, 57 (1948), p. 176.

6. Ibid., p. 182.

7. Norman Malcolm, "Anselm's Ontological Arguments," *Philosophical Review*, 69 (1960), p. 55.

8. J. N. Findlay, *The Trancendence of the Cave* (London and New York, 1967), p. 88: "These ideas will, of course, forbid us to hold any merely empty, verbal doctrine of necessity, nor is there any reason, other than sheer epistemological dogma, why we should accept such a doctrine."

14

Divine Necessity

The subject of this paper is the doctrine of divine necessity: the belief that God's existence is necessary in the strongest possible sense—that it is not merely causally or physically or hypothetically, but logically or metaphysically or absolutely necessary. When I use 'necessary' (and its modal relatives) below, I shall normally be using it in this strong sense (and them in corresponding senses). I will not attempt to prove here that God's existence is necessary, nor even that God exists, though some theoretical advantages of theistic belief will be noted in the course of discussion. Nor will I try to explain exactly *how* God's existence can be necessary. I believe the most plausible form of the doctrine of divine necessity is the Thomistic view that God's existence follows necessarily from his essence but that we do not understand God's essence well enough to see how his existence follows from it. What I will attempt is to refute two principal objections to the doctrine of divine necessity: two influential reasons for thinking that the existence of God, or indeed of any concrete being, could not be necessary.[1]

I

Many philosophers have believed that the proposition that a certain thing or kind of thing exists is simply not of the right *form* to be a necessary truth. They think that necessity cannot be understood except as consisting in *analyticity* and that existential propositions cannot be analytic. It has

I am indebted to a number of colleagues and students, and especially to Marilyn McCord Adams, for helpful discussion of these topics. This paper was prepared for an American Philosophical Association symposium, December 29, 1983. Thomas P. Flint was the respondent; his comments have been helpful in revising the notes for the present edition.

become notorious that the notion of analyticity itself is difficult to analyze; but for present purposes it seems fair to say that an analytic truth
must be of one of the following three sorts. (1) It may be a (broadly
speaking) conditional proposition of the form $\ulcorner p \supset q \urcorner$ [$\ulcorner$If p then $q\urcorner$] or
$\ulcorner (x)(Fx \supset \phi x)\urcorner$ [$\ulcorner$For every x, if Fx then $\phi x\urcorner$], where q is a correct
analysis or partial analysis of p, or ϕ of F. As has often been noted, such
conditional propositions do not say that anything exists. (2) A proposition
that follows formally from such conditional analyses will also be analytic,
but will still not say that any particular thing or kind of thing exists. (3)
Theorems of formal logic are usually counted as analytic, but they too
will not say that any particular thing or kind of thing exists. It would be
very questionable to use in this context a system of logic that would not
be valid in an empty domain and in which '$(\exists x)(Fx \vee \sim Fx)$' ['There
exists an x such that Fx or not Fx'], for example, is a theorem; but even
in such a system it will not be a theorem that there exists a thing of any
particular sort (that is, of any sort to which a thing could fail to belong).
So in none of these three ways could it be analytic that a certain particular
thing or kind of thing exists.

I am prepared to grant that existential propositions cannot be analytic
in any of these ways, but I do not see any good reason to believe that
all necessary truths must be analytic. Philosophical work in the past generation has given us cause to doubt the identification of necessity with
analyticity. There are in the first place the well-known difficulties in understanding the notion of analyticity itself, and in the second place it has
come to seem clear to many of us that there are necessary truths *de re*
that are not exactly analytic. What I wish to emphasize here, however,
is an even more fundamental point. The identification of necessity with
analyticity has retained its grip on so many philosophers because it has
seemed to them to provide the only possible explanation of the meaning
of 'necessary'. But in fact it provides no explanation at all of the meaning
of 'necessary', and should never have been thought to provide one.

To see this it will be helpful to begin with an account of necessity that
is even older than the one in terms of analyticity. A necessary truth, it
has been said, is one whose negation implies a contradiction. Let us think
about this, beginning with the limiting case of a proposition p whose
negation *is* a formal contradiction. Such a proposition is, no doubt, necessary; and the fact that its negation is a contradiction gives us reason
to believe that p is necessary. For a contradiction can't be true, and hence
a proposition whose negation is a contradiction can't be false. But this
does not explain what 'necessary' means here. A contradiction *can't* be
true; that is, it is necessarily false. And when we say that a contradiction

is *necessarily* false, surely we are saying more than just that it is a contradiction. This "more" is precisely what we want explained, but it is not explained by saying that a necessary truth is one whose negation implies a contradiction.

The plot thickens when we think about a necessary truth q whose negation is not a contradiction but *implies* a contradiction. Semantically understood, 'implies a contradiction' presumably means "*can't* be true unless a contradiction is." But 'can't' here involves the very notion of necessity that we are trying to analyze: 'can't be' means "necessarily is not." Thus the use of 'implies a contradiction', semantically understood, in the analysis of necessity renders the analysis viciously circular. Suppose, then, that we give a syntactical or purely formalistic account of implication, so that what we mean when we say that not-q (the negation of q) implies a contradiction is that it stands in a certain formal relation to a contradiction. This relation, I grant, gives us reason to believe that not-q can't be true and, hence, that q is necessarily true. But this again cannot explain what 'necessary' means here. We say that not-q can't be true; that is, it is necessarily false. And when we say this, we surely mean more than just that not-q stands in this formal relation to a contradiction. We mean that something else is true about not-q because it stands in this relation to a contradiction. Indeed our belief that this "something else" is true of propositions that stand in this formal relation to a contradiction, but is not true of all propositions that stand in certain other formal relations to a contradiction, is presumably what would guide us, in our syntactical analysis, to interpret implication in terms of certain formal relations and not others. Involved in this something else is precisely the notion of necessity that we want explained. It is not explained by saying that a necessary truth is one whose negation implies a contradiction.

Consideration of the identification of necessity with analyticity will lead to a similar conclusion. Of the three sorts of analytic truths mentioned above, let us begin with theorems of formal logic. No doubt all the theorems of a good or valid or semantically satisfactory system of formal logic are indeed necessary truths. But it would be circular to appeal to this fact to explain what we mean by 'necessary' here; for what makes a system of formal logic good or valid or semantically satisfactory is at least in part the necessary truth of all its theorems (or of all substitution instances of its theorems).

Perhaps it will be objected to me here that the notion of a valid or semantically satisfactory logical system need not presuppose the notion of *necessary* truth—that it is enough for the validity of a logical system if all its theorems and all their substitution instances are in fact true, provided that the theorems contain no nonlogical constants. On this view the analyticity (and hence necessity) of truths of logic is to be understood in terms of their being true solely by virtue of their logical form, and being true solely by virtue of their logical form is to be understood in terms of the actual (not necessary) truth of all propositions that have that logical form. We might find it difficult to understand the notion of logical form without presupposing the notion of logical necessity, but quite apart from that, this view will not be plausible if there are any logical forms all of whose substitution instances are true, but not in every case necessarily true. And it is not obvious that there are no such "contingently valid" logical forms, as we might call them. Consider, for example, the proposition that something exists. If we may express it as '$(\exists x)(x = x)$' ['There exists an x such that x is identical with x'], it is the only proposition of its logical form; and it is certainly true. Yet a number of philosophers have been convinced that it is a contingent truth. I am not convinced of that, but I think it would be ridiculous to argue that it must be a necessary truth *because* it is both actually true and the only proposition of its logical form (and hence is of a logical form all of whose substitution instances are true). So it seems to me implausible to suppose that the meaning of 'necessary truth' is to be understood in terms of the actual truth of all instances of a logical form.

Indeed it should not require elaborate argument to show that no such analysis is plausible. For when we say that all the instances of a certain logical form are *necessarily* true, we surely mean more than that they *all are* true. We mean that they can't be false.

Turning from theorems of formal logic, let us consider another sort of analytic truth. 'All husbands are married' is an analytic truth if anything is. It is analytic because 'married' is a correct partial analysis of 'husband' ('married man' being a correct complete analysis of 'husband'). But this does not explain what we mean by 'necessary' when we say it is a necessary truth that all husbands are married. For in the first place it is not clear that we can understand the notion of a *correct analysis* without presupposing the notion of necessity. When asked what we mean by saying that 'married man' is a correct analysis of 'husband', our first response is likely to be that we mean that by 'husband' we *mean* "married man." But this is not an adequate explanation. For there is surely a sense in which by 'God' we *mean* "the Creator of the universe"; yet 'God (if he exists) is the Creator of the universe' is not an analytic truth—or at any rate not a necessary truth—since God could have chosen not to create any universe. In order to maintain that 'All husbands are married' is analytic (and necessary) because by 'husband' we mean "married man," we will therefore have to distinguish the sense in which by 'husband' we *mean* "married man" from the sense in which by 'God' we *mean* "the Creator of the universe." The former sense will imply a *necessary* equivalence, and the latter won't; but I don't see how to distinguish the two senses without presupposing the notion of necessity that concerns us (or the corresponding notion of possibility). This argument (which is a variation on W. V. Quine's argument about analyticity[2]) would need more discussion if I were going to rely heavily on it; but that is not my intention.

My main argument is of a kind that should be familiar by now. Suppose we could understand the notion of a correct analysis without presupposing the notion of necessity (or any of that family of modal notions). In that case, it seems to me, when we say that 'All husbands are married men' is a necessary truth, we are saying more than just that it expresses a correct analysis. We are saying that it *can't* be false, in the same sense in which we say that theorems of a valid formal logic can't be false. This is a property that correct analyses have in common with theorems of a valid formal logic. As a common property, it must be distinct both from the property of expressing a correct analysis and from the property of being a theorem of a valid formal logic. And we could not plausibly claim to have explained what necessity is by saying it is the disjunctive property of expressing a correct analysis *or* being a theorem of a valid formal logic. For why should that disjunctive property possess an importance not possessed by, say, the disjunctive property of being a theorem of formal logic *or* asserted by Woody Allen? Presumably because correct analyses and theorems of valid formal logics have something in common *besides* the disjunctive property—namely their necessity, the fact that they can't be false.

If the foregoing arguments are correct, the meaning of 'necessary' cannot be explained in terms of analyticity. Of course it does not follow that there are any necessary truths that are not analytic. But the principal ground for believing that all necessary truths must be analytic is exploded. And I think it is plausible to suppose that there are necessary truths that do not belong to any of the three types of analytic truth identified above. Not to mention necessities *de re*, let us consider

(T) Everything green has some spatial property.

This seems to be a necessary truth, and is not a theorem of anything we would ordinarily recognize as formal logic. It is more controversial whether 'has some spatial property' is a correct partial analysis of 'green'; but I think it is not. For I do not think there is a satisfactory complete analysis of 'green' of which 'has some spatial property' is a part. This point can be backed up by the following observation. In the case of 'husband', which has 'married man' as a satisfactory complete analysis and 'married' as a correct partial analysis, we can easily say what would be otherwise like a husband but not married: an unmarried man. But if we ask what would be otherwise like a green thing but with no spatial property, there is nothing to say, except that it is obvious that there cannot be any such thing. This suggests that the impossibility of separating greenness from spatiality is not rooted in any composition of the concept of green out of spatiality plus something else—and hence that the necessary truth of (T) cannot be explained as based on correct *analysis*. Perhaps some will complain that I am insisting here on an unreasonably strict interpretation of 'analysis' and 'analytic'. It is enough for the analyticity of (T), they may say, if (T) is true "solely by virtue of the meanings of its terms." But this criterion, cut loose from any precise conception of analysis, is so vague as to be useless for any serious argument (not to mention that it may presuppose the notion of necessity). In particular, I defy anyone to show that existential propositions cannot be true solely by virtue of the meanings of their terms.

Now of course I have not proved that the existence of God, or of any other particular being or kind of being, is necessary. What I think can be shown by such arguments as I have been presenting is that we are not likely to get a satisfying analysis of necessity from which it will follow that such existence cannot be necessary. That is because we are not likely to get a satisfying analysis of necessity at all. I think we have a good enough grasp on the notion to go on using it, unanalyzed; but we do not understand the nature of necessity as well as we would like to. Such understanding as we have does not rule out necessity for existential propositions. Aquinas's supposition that God's existence follows necessarily from his essence although we do not see how it does is quite compatible with the state of our knowledge of the nature of necessity.

II

Another objection to the doctrine of divine necessity is that if God exists his existence is too real to be necessary. Many philosophers believe that absolute necessity is "logical" or "conceptual" in such a way as to be confined to a mental or abstract realm and that it cannot escape from this playground of the logicians to determine the real world in any way. On this view necessary truths cannot be "about the world," and cannot explain any real existence or real event, but can only reveal features of, or relations among, abstract or mental objects such as concepts or meanings. They cannot govern reality, but can only determine how we ought to think or speak about reality.

If, on the other hand, it is a necessary truth that God exists, this must be a necessary truth that explains a real existence (God's); indeed it provides the ultimate explanation of all real existence, since God is the creator of everything else that really exists. Thus if God's existence follows from his essence in such a way as to be necessary, his essence is no mere logicians' plaything but a supremely powerful cause. This is a scandal for the view that necessary truths cannot determine or explain reality.

This view is extremely questionable, however. It is not, I think, the first view that would suggest itself to common sense. If we think about the role that elaborate mathematical calculations play in scientists' predictions and explanations of, say, the movements of the planets or the behavior of a rocket, it seems commonsensical to say that the necessary truths of mathematics that enter into those calculations also contribute something to the determination of the real events and form part of the explanation of them. The doctrine that necessary truths cannot determine or explain reality is also not the only view that has commended itself to philosophers. The extremely influential Aristotelian conception of a "formal cause," for example, can be understood as the conception of a cause that governs the action of a real thing by a logical or quasi-logical necessity. It is far from obvious that necessary truths cannot cause or explain any real existence or real event; why should we believe that they can't?

I suspect that the most influential ground for the belief that necessary truths are not "about the world" is epistemological. This motive is clearly articulated by A. J. Ayer, when he writes that if we admit that some necessary truths are about the world,

> we shall be obliged to admit that there are some truths about the world which we can know independently of experience; that there are some properties which we can ascribe to all objects, even though we cannot conceivably observe that all objects have them. And we shall have to accept it as a mysterious inexplicable fact that our thought has this power to reveal to us authoritatively the nature of objects which we have never observed.[3]

The main assumptions of this argument seem to be, first, that if necessary truths are about the world, we can sometimes know that they apply to objects that we have not experienced; and second, that if we know something about an object, there must be some explanation of how it comes to pass that our beliefs agree with the object. Both of these assumptions are plausible. Ayer seems to make a third assumption, with which I will disagree, that the only way in which agreement of our beliefs with a real object can be explained is through experience of that object. (Ayer mentions as an alternative, but only to dismiss it, "the Kantian explanation"—presumably that our mind imposes necessary truths on the world.[4]) From these three assumptions it follows that necessary truths are not about the world.

Before we draw this conclusion, however, we should ask whether our knowledge of necessary truths is any more explicable on the view that they reveal only features or relations of abstract or mental objects such as concepts or meanings. I think it is not. For if necessary truths reveal features or relations of thoughts, they reveal features or relations of thoughts that we have not yet thought, as well as of those that we have thought. If I know that modus ponens is a valid argument form, I know that it will be valid for thoughts that I think tomorrow as well as for those I have thought today. If this is a knowledge of properties and relations of the thoughts involved, the question how I can know properties and relations of thoughts I have not yet experienced seems as pressing as the question how I could know properties and relations of objects outside my mind that I had not yet experienced. The retreat to abstract or mental objects does not help to explain what we want explained.

The prospects for explanation are not any better if we accept an idea that Ayer espouses in *Language, Truth and Logic*. He says that necessary truths (which he regards as all analytic) "simply record our determination to use words in a certain fashion," so that "we cannot deny them without infringing the conventions which are presupposed by our very denial, and so falling into self-contradiction" (84). I grant that there is no special problem about how we can know the determinations, intentions, or conventions that we have adopted for the use of words. But that is not all that we know in knowing necessary truths that will govern our thoughts tomorrow. We also know what follows (necessarily) from our determinations and which intentions would (necessarily) be inconsistent with other intentions, tomorrow as well as today. We know, in Ayer's words, what "we *cannot* deny . . . without infringing" our conventions or determinations. And we are still without an explanation of how we can know these properties of thoughts we have not yet experienced.

Given that we know things about our future thoughts which we have not learned from experience of them, it is reasonable to suppose that we have a faculty for recognizing such truths nonempirically. We would expect a theory of natural selection to provide the most promising naturalistic explanation of our possessing such a faculty. True belief is in general conducive to survival; hence individuals with a hereditary ability to recognize truths will have survived and passed on their hereditary ability to their descendants. This does indeed provide a possible explanation of our having the perceptual ability to recognize truths about our physical environment. Perhaps it also gives an acceptable explanation of our possessing the power to recognize simple truths of arithmetic. The ability to count, add, subtract, and multiply small numbers correctly has survival value. We may well suppose that under the conditions prevailing during the formative periods of human evolution, humanoids that usually or systematically made gross errors about such things would have been less likely to survive and reproduce themselves. (Be it noted, however, that this argument seems to assume that the *truth* of arithmetical propositions makes a difference to what happens in the world. This assumption seems to fit better with the view that necessary truths can determine reality than with the contrary opinion.) But there are aspects of our knowledge of necessary truths for which this evolutionary explanation is less satisfying. That is particularly true of the knowledge of modality which most concerns us in this discussion. During the formative periods of human evolution, what survival value was there in recognizing necessary truths as necessary, rather than merely as true? Very little, I should think. Logical or absolute necessity as such is a philosophoumenon which would hardly have helped the primitive hunter or gatherer in finding food or shelter; nor does it seem in any way important to the building of a viable primitive society. Those of us who think we have some faculty for recognizing truth on many of the issues discussed in this paper can hardly believe that such a faculty was of much use to our evolving ancestors; nor is there any obvious way in which such a faculty, and its reliability, are inevitable by-products of faculties that did have survival value.[5]

The prospects for explanation of our knowledge of necessary truth may actually be brighter on the view that necessary truths can determine and explain reality. For then we may be able to appeal to an explanation in terms of formal cause. For example, we might suppose that it is simply the nature of the human mind, or perhaps of mind as such, to be able to recognize necessary truths. Then the explanation (and indeed the cause) of our recognizing necessary truths as such would be that this recognition follows necessarily from the nature of our minds together with the fact that the truths in question are necessary.

I do not believe the explanation I have just sketched. We are too easily mistaken about necessary truths and too often unable to recognize them. And there is too much reason to believe that other mechanisms or causal processes are involved in our knowing them. But I do seriously entertain the hypothesis that there is a mind to whose nature it simply pertains to be able to recognize necessary truths. Indeed I am inclined to believe that such a mind belongs to God.

And that opens the way for another explanation of our knowledge of necessary truths: an explanation in terms of divine illumination. Suppose that necessary truths do determine and explain facts about the real world. If God of his very nature knows the necessary truths, and if he has created us, he could have constructed us in such a way that we would at least commonly recognize necessary truths as necessary. In this way there would be a causal connection between what is necessarily true about real objects and our believing it to be necessarily true about them. It would not be an incredible accident or an inexplicable mystery that our beliefs agreed with the objects in this.

This theory is not new. It is Augustinian,[6] and something like it was widely accepted in the medieval and early modern periods. I think it provides the best explanation available to us for our knowledge of necessary truths. I also think that that fact constitutes an argument for the existence of God. Not a demonstration; it is a mistake to expect conclusive demonstrations in such matters. But it is a theoretical advantage of theistic belief that it provides attractive explanations of things otherwise hard to explain.[7]

It is worth noting that this is not the only point in the philosophy of logic at which Augustinian theism provides an attractive explanation. Another is the ontological status of the objects of logic and mathematics. To many of us both of the following views seem extremely plausible. (1) Possibilities and necessary truths are discovered, not made, by our thought. They would still be there if none of us humans ever thought of them. (2) Possibilities and necessary truths cannot be there except insofar as they, or the ideas involved in them, are thought by some mind. The first of these views seems to require Platonism; the second is a repudiation of it. Yet they can both be held together if we suppose that there is a nonhuman mind that eternally and necessarily exists and thinks all the possibilities and necessary truths. Such is the mind of God, according to Augustinian theism. I would not claim that such theism provides the only conceivable way of combining these two theses; but it does provide one way, and I think the most attractive.[8]

There are many things that I have not explained, and indeed do not know how to explain, about the necessity of God's existence and the necessity of his knowledge of necessary truths. But I hope I have given some reason to believe that the doctrine of divine necessity does not saddle us with problems about either the nature or the knowledge of necessity which could be avoided, or solved more advantageously, on views incompatible with divine necessity.

Notes

1. I have treated this subject before. The two objections roughly correspond to the second and third discussed in "Has It Been Proved That All Real Existence Is Contingent?" (chapter 13 in this collection). I do not substantially disagree with what I said there, but what is said here is different and, I hope, goes deeper.

2. *From a Logical Point of View*, 2d ed. (New York: Harper Torchbooks, 1963), pp. 20–46.

3. *Language, Truth and Logic*, 2d ed. (New York: Dover, n.d.), p. 73.

4. Ibid., p. 73. Induction is another way in which beliefs are extended beyond experience. It would not be plausible, however, to say that the beliefs that concern us here are based on induction from experience—and there may also be comparable problems in explaining why our inductive processes are reliable with regard to future events (which have not influenced them).

*5. It might be objected that the concept of logical or metaphysical necessity is so fundamental that the ability to apply it correctly would have had survival value even during the relevant period of evolutionary history. Some philosophers would analyze other types of necessity in terms of logical or metaphysical necessity. For instance, the physically necessary might be analyzed as what is logically necessary given the physical laws of the actual world and its present state. Even if that is the best analysis of physical necessity, however, it does not follow that our primitive progenitors must have been able to recognize logically necessary truths as such in order to recognize physical possibility and impossibility. For the way in which we recognize a fact does not necessarily express its correct analysis. Our remote ancestors on whom natural selection is supposed to have operated with such dramatic effects are unlikely to have had *any* analysis of what they meant when they said, for example, 'The deer cannot see us from here'. Teachers of philosophy have much experience of the fact that it is quite possible to have a functioning concept of the practically possible without having a developed capacity to discriminate logical modalities from other modalities. I still find it hard, therefore, to see how the *accuracy* of any tendencies they may have had toward distinguishing logical from other modalities would have made any difference to the survival of our hunting-and-gathering ancestors.

*6. Edward Mahoney has pointed out to me that the theory I have sketched here is Augustinian only in a rather broad sense. It agrees with Augustine in explaining our knowledge of necessary truths in terms of God's action on us. Augustine's theory of divine illumination has God intervening, so to speak, in each event of logical or mathematical knowledge; whereas what I have presented is an account of God giving us an innate capacity to judge rightly about such matters. Such innatism is perhaps more Cartesian than Augustinian. I do not mean to express a decided preference for one of these theories over the other.

And how far they are incompatible depends on issues, not discussed here, about the divine activity in creating and conserving the world.

*7. The ability to discriminate logically necessary truths from other sorts of truths is only one of several abilities on which essentially similar epistemological arguments for theism can be based. There are quite a variety of not obviously empirical cognitive capacities that we take ourselves to have but that are not easily explained by natural selection because they are quite different from any that are likely to have functioned during the relevant evolutionary period. I suspect that what we call "philosophy" and theoretical physics both consist largely of the exercise of such capacities.

If our possession of them is to be explained by natural selection, presumably it must be as a more or less mechanical consequence of capacities that helped our remote ancestors to survive. Perhaps there is reason to suppose that the thinking of theoretical physicists is based on some of the same brain structures that the first humans used in thinking about their very different problems of hunting, toolmaking, and social organization. But the fact that a piece of cerebral equipment produced good results in those primitive tasks does not explain why it produces good results in theoretical physics, or in philosophy (which is what we want explained). The tasks that a computer performs are so interrelated that a machine that performs simple ones accurately in a certain way can be expected to perform much more complex ones accurately, because the complex ones are performed by iteration of the simple ones. But it doesn't seem likely that there is such a relationship among all the tasks that a human mind performs, at least among those that concern us here.

8. One readily available classic text in which this point is exploited as the basis for an argument for the existence of God is Leibniz's *Monadology*, sections 43 and 44. Alvin Plantinga makes similar use of it at the conclusion of his presidential address, "How to Be an Anti-Realist," *Proceedings of the American Philosophical Association*, 56 (1982), pp. 47–70. My general indebtedness to the philosophy of Leibniz in the second part of this paper is great.

15

The Logical Structure
of Anselm's Arguments

In this essay I offer a formal analysis of Anselm's arguments for the existence of God in the *Proslogion* and in his reply to Gaunilo. I do not attempt to show here that the arguments are compelling, or that they are not. What I try to do is discover in each argument, so far as possible, a valid logical form, to exhibit the relations of the arguments to each other, and to show how they depend on certain doctrines in logic or the philosophy of logic. Anselm's arguments are far from dead, and in this paper I hope to provide a logical map, so to speak, of some ground that is still very much fought over.

The first two sections of the paper are concerned with the most famous of Anselm's arguments, the argument of chapter 2 of the *Proslogion*. In section I, I formulate a version of the argument in modern logical symbolism, and state the assumptions about existence and predication on which the argument seems to me to depend. Gaunilo's criticism of Anselm was directed very largely against the ontological presuppositions of the *Proslogion* 2 argument; and in section II, I try to show how Gaunilo's famous "lost island" counterexample proves that the assumptions stated in section I must be modified, if not rejected. In his reply to Gaunilo, Anselm introduced two new arguments for the existence of God that do not depend on assumptions about predication. I discuss one of these arguments in section III; it seems to me to be at least a better argument than the argument of *Proslogion* 2. Analysis of this argument from the reply to Gaunilo leads to the conclusion that the crucial question about logically necessary divine existence is whether it is possible. Section IV is devoted to an analysis of Anselm's argument in the third chapter of the *Proslogion* and its relation to the other arguments.

I am indebted to my wife, Marilyn McCord Adams, for helpful criticism and discussion of drafts of this paper.

I

I wish to show, first of all, that the following four propositions from chapter 2 of Anselm's *Proslogion* can be understood as the premises and conclusion of a formally valid argument.

(1) There is, in the understanding at least, something than which nothing greater can be thought.

(2) If it is even in the understanding alone, it can be thought to be in reality also,

(3) which is greater.

(4) There exists, therefore, . . . both in the understanding and in reality, something than which a greater cannot be thought.[1]

The structure of the argument is complicated, and I think the apparatus of modern quantification logic may help us to state it precisely. In my formalization of the argument, the notions of existence in the understanding, existence in reality, and comparative greatness will be expressed by predicate constants as follows.

'Ux' for 'x exists in the understanding'
'Rx' for 'x exists in reality'
'Gxy' for 'x is greater than y'

I have found it necessary also to introduce the notion of a *magnitude,* as follows.

'Qxy' for 'x is the magnitude of y'

I interpret 'can be thought' as meaning 'is logically possible', which I think is accurate enough for the purposes of the argument, and I express this notion by means of the possibility operator,

'M', for 'it can be thought that' or 'it is logically possible that'.

The property of being something than which nothing greater can be thought will be expressed as the property of having a magnitude such that it is not possible for anything to have a greater magnitude. This property is so complex that the argument will be easier to follow if we define a function '$\phi(x,m)$' as follows.

'$\phi(x, m)$' = df. 'Qmx & $\sim$ M$(\exists y)(\exists n)(Gnm$ & $Qny)$'

Now we can write '$(\exists m)(\phi (x, m))$' for 'x is something than which nothing greater can be thought'.

The four propositions which I have quoted from Anselm will be symbolized as follows.

(1) $(\exists x)(\exists m)(Ux$ & $\phi(x, m))$

(2) $(x)(m)([Ux$ & $\phi(x, m)] \supset$ M $Rx)$

(3) $(x)(m)([\phi(x, m)$ & $\sim Rx] \supset \sim$ M $\sim [Rx \supset (\exists n)(Gnm$ & $Qnx)])$

(4) $\therefore$ $(\exists x)(\exists m)(Ux$ & Rx & $\phi(x, m))$

The symbolization of the third proposition calls for some explanation. All Anselm said was 'which is greater'. This could be taken to mean that anything which exists in reality is greater than anything which does not; this is a claim to which Anselm would probably have assented. But it could also mean just that the being under discussion (that than which nothing greater can be thought) would be greater if it existed than if not; this is all the argument requires, and I am assuming this minimal interpretation in symbolizing the argument. On this interpretation Anselm is claiming that if such a being does not exist in reality, it *would* be greater if it did exist in reality. The counterfactual conditionality of this claim poses another problem for us in symbolizing the argument. I have taken Anselm to be committed to the view that the reality of an unsurpassably great being *logically implies* its having a magnitude greater than it has if it does not exist in reality.

Anselm's argument is a *reductio ad absurdum*. "If, therefore, that than which a greater cannot be thought is in the understanding alone, that very thing than which a greater cannot be thought is something than which a greater can be thought. But certainly this cannot be."[2] In my formalization I follow the same *reductio* strategy. The denial of what is to be proved is introduced as a premise, which is later removed by conditionalization with a self-contradictory consequent. The rules and conventions of quantification logic followed in the formalization are mainly those of Quine's *Methods of Logic,* though a modal operator is used in ways of which Quine would not approve.[3]

$\left\{\begin{array}{l}\end{array}\right.$ (1) $(\exists x)(\exists m)(Ux$ & $\phi(x, m))$	Premise
* (2) $(x)(m)([Ux$ & $\phi(x, m)] \supset$ M $Rx)$	Premise
(3) $(x)(m)([\phi(x, m)$ & $\sim Rx] \supset \sim$ M $\sim [Rx \supset$ $(\exists n)(Gnm$ & $Qnx)])$	Premise
* (4) Ua & $\phi(a, b)$	(1), EI (a, b)
* (5) $[Ua$ & $\phi(a, b)] \supset$ M Ra	(2), UI
* (6) M Ra	(4), (5), TF
* (7) $[\phi(a, b)$ & $\sim Ra] \supset \sim$ M $\sim [Ra \supset (\exists n)$ $(Gnb$ & $Qna)]$	(3), UI
* (8) $\sim Ra \supset \sim$ M $\sim [Ra \supset (\exists n)(Gnb$ & $Qna)]$	(4), (7), TF
** (9) $\sim Ra$	Premise
**(10) $\sim$ M $\sim [Ra \supset (\exists n)(Gnb$ & $Qna)]$	(8), (9), TF
**(11) M $(\exists n)(Gnb$ & $Qna)$	(6), (10), modal inference

**(12)	$(\exists\ y)$ M $(\exists\ n)(Gnb\ \&\ Qny)$	(11), EG
**(13)	M $(\exists\ y)(\exists\ n)(Gnb\ \&\ Qny)$	(12), see below
**(14)	$Ua\ \&\ Qba\ \&\ \sim$ M $(\exists\ y)(\exists\ n)(Gnb\ \&\ Qny)$	(4), definition of 'ϕ (,)'
**(15)	M $(\exists\ y)(\exists\ n)(Gnb\ \&\ Qny)\ \&\ \sim$ M $(\exists\ y)(\exists\ n)$ $(Gnb\ \&\ Qny)$	(13), (14), TF
* (16)	$\sim Ra \supset$ [M $(\exists\ y)(\exists\ n)(Gnb\ \&\ Qny)\ \&\ \sim$ M $(\exists\ y)(\exists\ n)(Gnb\ \&\ Qny)$]	(9), (15), Conditionalization
* (17)	Ra	(16), TF
* (18)	$Ua\ \&\ Ra\ \&\ \phi\ (a,\ b)$	(4), (17), TF
* (19)	$(\exists\ x)(\exists\ m)(Ux\ \&\ Rx\ \&\ \phi\ (x,\ m))$	(18), EG

I think the inferences in this argument are clearly correct. With two exceptions they are justified by generally accepted rules of propositional and predicate logic. The inference of step (11) from steps (6) and (10) has the form '$\sim$ M $\sim (p \supset q)$ and M p; therefore M q'; this seems to me intuitively to be a valid form, and I believe it could be justified in any system of modal logic that would be likely to be used in this context. The inference of (13) from (12) is an instance of the principle that 'M $(\exists\ x)\psi(x)$' follows from '$(\exists\ x)$ M$\psi(x)$'. This principle is commonly accepted in systems of modal logic with quantifiers, and rightly so. For surely if something is such that it is possible that *it* should satisfy a certain function, then it is possible that *something* should satisfy that function. If there is a good reason for rejecting the *Proslogion* 2 argument, it must be based on some objection to one or more of the premises.

I will not attempt to discuss here all of the objections which have been or could be raised against the premises. For instance, I will not consider all the possible reasons for denying that a thing could be any better or **greater** if it existed than if it did not. What I do want to discuss are certain **general** principles about existence and predication which are presupposed in the formulation and assertion of the premises of the *Proslogion* 2 argument. It is because of its dependence on these presuppositions, which may plausibly be said to belong to the field of ontology, that I think this argument deserves its traditional designation as "ontological." The following assumptions about existence and predication seem to be involved in the argument.

(i) Predication does not presuppose real existence. That is, a thing can have properties, and can be the subject of true predications, without existing in reality. (Anthony Kenny has shown, in recent publications,[4] that this is also presupposed in Descartes's ontological argument, and that Descartes was aware of the presupposition—more clearly aware of it, I think, than Anselm was.) In terms of the predicate calculus used in my formalization of the argument, this means that the universe of discourse over which the variables range is not restricted to things that exist in reality. Obviously, if the universe of discourse were assumed to include only real things, the first step of the argument could not without circularity be asserted as a premise. The philosopher who is most often mentioned as having held the position that predication does not presuppose real existence is Alexius Meinong. According to him, when I think about something which does not really exist, what I am thinking about is something which not only has properties even though it does not really exist, but also would have properties even if no one ever thought about it. A thing need not exist either in the understanding or in reality to be included in Meinong's universe of discourse. Anselm's formulation of his argument, however, is consistent with the supposition that his universe of discourse is restricted to things which either exist in reality or are actually thought about.

(ii) There is another respect in which Anselm is less liberal than Meinong. He clearly assumes that the universe of discourse includes no object with contradictory predicates, whereas Meinong admits such objects (for example, the round square). If it were not assumed that self-contradictory objects are excluded from the universe of discourse, Anselm's *reductio ad absurdum* argument would collapse. For even if unreality and being a being than which a greater cannot be thought are inconsistent properties, it would not follow that the same object could not possess both.

(iii) A thing which exists in the understanding truly possesses all the properties which are contained or implied in its concept or definition. If we form a consistent description or conception of something, then whether or not it exists in reality, there is something (which at least exists in the understanding) which truly has all the properties which are included or implied in the description or conception. This appears to be presupposed for the justification of premise (1). From the fact that we understand the conception of a being than which nothing greater can be thought, Anselm infers that there is, in the understanding at least, something which has the property of being something than which nothing greater can be thought.

(iv) One and the same thing can exist both in the understanding and in reality. Or perhaps it would be better to say that its properties are not qualified as had in the understanding or had in reality; they are simply had. At any rate, the argument, as stated so far, does not use any apparatus for qualifying properties as had in the understanding or had in reality. And it is essential to the argument to assume both that the same thing can exist in the understanding and in reality, and that it must have at least the same *defining* properties in reality as in the understanding.

(v) Existence and nonexistence in reality and existence in the understanding are predicates or properties, and it is legitimate to treat them formally in the same way as other predicates. This is obviously assumed in the argument; and at least it cannot fairly be objected that existence in reality is already expressed by the particular or "existential" quantifier, and therefore ought not to be treated as a predicate. For existence in reality is not expressed by the "existential" quantifier, if it is assumed that the universe of discourse is not restricted to things that exist in reality.

It will be convenient, though perhaps inelegant, to refer to this set of assumptions about existence and predication as "assumptions (i–v)."

II

The importance of Anselm's ontological assumptions was not overlooked by his first critic, Gaunilo. Indeed, almost the whole of Gaunilo's little essay can be read as a discussion of the *Proslogion* 2 argument in terms of its ontological presuppositions. He seems to hold that one is not obliged to admit that any subject of predication truly has a given property unless one is first persuaded that such a being exists in reality.[5]

Gaunilo's most famous argument is also, in my judgment, his best. The counterexample of the lost island shows quite clearly that assumptions (i–v) must be rejected or at least modified. We can form a consistent description of an island, including in the description profitable and delightful features which are not in fact possessed by any island or country known to man. We can also include in the description the property of being the most excellent of all lands or countries. When I hear and understand this description, there must, according to assumptions (i–v), exist in my understanding an island which truly has all the properties contained or implied in the description. But then, Gaunilo claims, this island must, on Anselm's principles, exist in reality too. For suppose it does not; then "whatever other land exists in reality, will be more excellent than it."[6] Thus the island which exists in my understanding will be both the most excellent (because that is contained in its description) and not the most excellent, which is impossible. In this way, Gaunilo suggests, something which surely does not in fact exist could be proved to exist if Anselm's assumptions about existence and predication were accepted.

I shall attempt a symbolization of this argument, so that the extent of the similarity between it and the *Proslogion* 2 argument may appear more clearly. Three new predicate symbols are required.

'Ix' for 'x is an island'
'Lx' for 'x is a land or country'
'Px' ascribes to x the profitable and delightful features attributed by legend to the lost island.

The proof follows the *reductio ad absurdum* pattern of *Proslogion* 2, but is shorter.

$$
\begin{cases}
\text{(1)} & (\exists x)(Ux \;\&\; Ix \;\&\; Px \;\&\; \sim(\exists y)(Ly \;\&\; Gyx)) \\
* \{ \text{(2)} & (\exists x)(Lx \;\&\; Rx) \\
\text{(3)} & (x)(y)([Lx \;\&\; Rx \;\&\; Iy \;\&\; \sim Ry] \supset Gxy)
\end{cases}
$$

	(1) $(\exists x)(Ux \;\&\; Ix \;\&\; Px \;\&\; \sim(\exists y)(Ly \;\&\; Gyx))$	Premise
	(2) $(\exists x)(Lx \;\&\; Rx)$	Premise
	(3) $(x)(y)([Lx \;\&\; Rx \;\&\; Iy \;\&\; \sim Ry] \supset Gxy)$	Premise
*	(4) $Ub \;\&\; Ib \;\&\; Pb \;\&\; \sim(\exists y)(Ly \;\&\; Gyb)$	(1), EI (b)
*	(5) $La \;\&\; Ra$	(2), EI (a)
*	(6) $(La \;\&\; Ra \;\&\; Ib \;\&\; \sim Rb) \supset Gab$	(3), UI
*	(7) $\sim Rb \supset Gab$	(4), (5), (6), TF
**	(8) $\sim Rb$	Premise
**	(9) Gab	(7), (8), TF
**	(10) $La \;\&\; Gab$	(5), (9), TF
**	(11) $(\exists y)(Ly \;\&\; Gyb)$	(10), EG
**	(12) $(\exists y)(Ly \;\&\; Gyb) \;\&\; \sim(\exists y)(Ly \;\&\; Gyb)$	(4), (11), TF
*	(13) $\sim Rb \supset [(\exists y)(Ly \;\&\; Gyb) \;\&\; \sim(\exists y)(Ly \;\&\; Gyb)]$	(8), (12), Conditionalization
*	(14) Rb	(13), TF
*	(15) $Ub \;\&\; Rb \;\&\; Ib \;\&\; Pb \;\&\; \sim(\exists y)(Ly \;\&\; Gyb)$	(4), (14), TF
*	(16) $(\exists x)(Ux \;\&\; Rx \;\&\; Ix \;\&\; Px \;\&\; \sim(\exists y)(Ly \;\&\; Gyx))$	(15), EG

The principal departure here from the pattern of the *Proslogion* 2 argument is that whereas Anselm spoke of a being whose greatness could not *possibly* be surpassed, Gaunilo speaks only of an island to which no country is *in fact* superior. Because of this difference, it is not necessary to use the concept of a magnitude in formulating the lost-island argument, and no possibility or necessity operator enters into the symbolization. Anselm criticized Gaunilo severely for having written as if God were characterized in the *Proslogion* as the greatest of all beings rather than as a being than which a greater cannot be thought. So far as I can see, this criticism is the only reason that Anselm gives for rejecting the lost-island counterexample.[7] Anselm's complaint is in large measure justified. The difference between the two concepts is important in some connections, and Gaunilo does not make it clear that he grasps the distinction.

But it is not at all obvious that this failure on Gaunilo's part vitiates the lost-island counterexample. Although it does not have exactly the same form as Anselm's argument, the lost-island argument seems to be well constructed for the purpose of deriving an absurd conclusion from assumptions (i–v). In particular, the first premise of the lost-island argument does seem to be justifiable, if it is true that whenever we understand a consistent description, there exists in the understanding something which has all the properties contained in the description. The second premise, that some land or country exists in reality, is obviously true. The third premise of the lost-island argument appears to have been accepted by Anselm. It expresses a more sweeping claim about the superiority of the real to the unreal than is found in the third premise of my formulation of the *Proslogion* 2 argument. But Anselm raised not a murmur of protest when Gaunilo in effect attributed to him the still more sweeping assumption that *whatever* exists in reality is greater than *anything* that does not.[8] And the conclusion, that the lost island exists in reality, is validly implied by the three premises. Thus it was far from unreasonable for Gaunilo to suggest that the reality of the lost island could be proved on the basis of Anselmian assumptions.

But Gaunilo's counterexample is much more complicated than it needs to be, if its purpose is to discredit assumptions (i–v). A simpler form of counterexample was suggested by Caterus when he argued that the (real) existence of a lion could be proved from the concept (really) *existent lion* in the same way as Descartes had proved the existence of God from the concept of God.[9] According to assumption (v), real existence is a property or predicate and can legitimately be treated as such in descriptions. And according to assumptions (i–iii), for every consistent description that is understood, there is some subject of which all the properties contained or implied in that description can be truly predicated. Scandalous conclusions can easily be drawn from these assumptions, along the lines suggested by Caterus. 'Really existent lion', 'really existent unicorn', and 'really existent golden mountain' are consistent descriptions, which are understood. Therefore there exist, in the understanding at least, subjects which have all the properties contained or implied in these descriptions. These subjects must be, of course, a lion, a unicorn, and a golden mountain; and they must all really exist.

$(\exists x)(Ux \ \& \ x \text{ is a lion } \& \ Rx)$

$(\exists x)(Ux \ \& \ x \text{ is a unicorn } \& \ Rx)$

$(\exists x)(Ux \ \& \ x \text{ is a mountain } \& \ x \text{ is golden } \& \ Rx)$

These propositions seem to be reached by substantially the same reasoning as the first premise of the *Proslogion* 2 argument, but real existence is already asserted in them; no further premises are needed. Assumptions (i–v) thus provide us with a short way to prove the real existence of anything we can think of whose description is consistent. Clearly that set of assumptions must be rejected or significantly altered.

There is more than one alteration which might be proposed to meet the objection. Descartes held, in effect, that it is only of *simple* concepts that we are entitled to assume that they are satisfied by some subject of predication.[10] This strikes me as a somewhat ad hoc modification of assumptions (i–v). It also seems to me doubtful whether Descartes's concept of God really is simple in a way in which the concept *existent lion* is not. Perhaps the following approach would be more promising for Anselm.

The problem which Gaunilo and Caterus have spotted in assumptions (i–v), we may say, is that this set of assumptions permits us to prove, from concepts alone, things which obviously are not conceptual truths. This fault might be at least partially remedied by a modification of the assumption that if a description which is understood is consistent, there must be something (real or unreal) which truly has all the properties contained or implied in the description. The application of this assumption is to be restricted to descriptions which are meant to be understood as containing only properties which belong *necessarily* to their common subject. A description which is understood to contain properties which belong contingently to their subject need not be assumed to be satisfied by anything, real or unreal.

Anselm's argument in *Proslogion* 2 seems to survive this restriction. For though Anselm does not explicitly say there that the property of unsurpassable greatness belongs to its subject necessarily, surely he assumes that it does, and would not object to being understood in that sense. But the restriction seems to dispose of the existent lion, the existent unicorn, and the existent golden mountain. In order to satisfy our new requirement, they would have to be conceived of as the *necessarily existent* lion, the *necessarily existent* unicorn, and the *necessarily existent* golden mountain. But whereas it seems clear that the descriptions 'existent lion', 'existent unicorn', and 'existent golden mountain' are consistent, it is by no means clear, and perhaps not even plausible, that the descriptions 'necessarily existent lion', 'necessarily existent unicorn', and 'necessarily existent golden mountain' are consistent and describe things that are logically possible. And Anselm has made no commitment to admit the inconsistent or logically impossible into his universe of discourse.

Similarly, a description of the form 'island which is *P* and the best of all lands or countries' may plausibly be taken to describe something logically possible, but the same cannot be said for a description of the form 'island which is *necessarily P* and *necessarily* the best of all lands or countries'. Thus our restriction seems likely to rid Anselm of Gaunilo's lost island.

It is not clear that this modification of assumptions (i–v) eliminates all the existence proofs that one might want to eliminate. In particular, the existence of an *F* can still be proved, for any value of *F*, if 'necessarily existing *F*' is a consistent description. But that is probably as it ought to be. For quite independently of any doctrines about predication, there is reason to suppose that if it is logically possible that the existence of a certain thing is logically necessary, then that thing does exist; this will be shown in the next section of this paper, with particular reference to the necessary existence of God.

I cannot conclude the present section with any triumphant vindication of Anselm. I certainly have not proved, nor have I attempted to prove, that the ontological assumptions needed for the *Proslogion* 2 argument can be justified. I have discussed only one of several objections that are often raised against the doctrine that things which do not really exist can be subjects of true predication.[11] Even the reply which I have suggested to the lost-island objection may give rise to further problems which have not been explored here. And if all apparent difficulties internal to the doctrine can be resolved, we might still wonder whether there are compelling reasons to accept it rather than some alternative way of thinking about predication. At least in the present state of philosophical research, it seems to me that one would find it advantageous to free one's arguments from dependence on such controversial ontological assumptions.

III

Apparently it seemed so to Anselm, too; for in the first chapter of his reply to Gaunilo, having noted that Gaunilo refuses to accept the principle that what is understood exists in the understanding, Anselm advances two arguments which, so far as I can see, depend neither on that principle nor on the assumption that predication does not presuppose real existence. Both of them are stated as arguments for the proposition that if something than which a greater cannot be thought can even be thought to exist, it must exist.[12] If we add to this conclusion the premise that such a being can at least be thought to exist, we can draw the further conclusion that it does exist. Anselm obviously expects his readers to supply this additional premise and draw the further conclusion.

I shall not discuss the first of the two arguments. It turns on issues in the philosophy of time, rather than the philosophy of logic.[13] That fact sets it apart from the arguments with which this essay is principally concerned.

The second argument is stated in the following words, and may be divided in three steps.

(1) For no one who denies or doubts that there exists something than which a greater cannot be thought denies or doubts that if it did exist, its nonexistence, either in actuality or in the understanding, would be impossible. For otherwise it would not be that than which a greater cannot be thought.

(2) But as to whatever can be thought and does not exist—if it did exist, its nonexistence, either in actuality or in the understanding, would be possible.

(3) Therefore if that than which a greater cannot be thought can even be thought, it cannot be nonexistent.[14]

This is one of the most ingenious and fascinating of Anselm's arguments. In its Anselmian form it turns on complex and partly counterfactual conditionals. And it is very difficult to tell whether the argument is sound, or even whether it is formally valid, because the logic of counterfactual conditionals is so obscure. It is possible, however, to get an argument with a clearer logical structure if we look behind the counterfactual conditionals for more basic assumptions on which steps (1) and (2) may plausibly be supposed to rest.

In the first step Anselm makes a claim which has the following conditional structure. (I use 'g' as a propositional *constant* to represent 'God exists' or 'There exists a being than which nothing greater can be thought'.)

(Even) if it is false that g, (still) if it were true that g, it would not be possible that not-g.

Anselm justifies this claim by observing that anything which did exist but whose nonexistence was possible "would not be that than which a greater cannot be thought." Evidently this first step is based on an assumption about the concept of a being than which nothing greater can be thought. Anselm believes it follows from that concept, and is therefore a necessary truth, that if such a being exists at all its existence is logically necessary. This belief can be symbolized as follows, if we use 'N' as a necessity operator with the meaning 'it is logically necessary that' or 'it cannot be thought that not'.

$$N(g \supset Ng)$$

From this proposition it certainly does follow that even if it is false that g, still it would be impossible that not-g (that is, necessary that g) if it were true that g.

In the second step Anselm claims, in effect, that the following is true about every affirmative existential proposition 'p' (and therefore, by implication, about 'g').

If it is possible but false that p, then if it were true that p it would still be possible that not-p.

Anselm offers no justification for this claim. But we may observe that some systems of modal logic contain a principle from which it follows that what Anselm asserts here about affirmative existential propositions is true about all propositions. The principle to which I refer is sometimes called Brouwer's Axiom, and can be expressed in the form

$\sim p \supset NM \sim p.$

By substituting '$\sim p$' for 'p' in this formula, and applying the rule of double negation, we could get '$p \supset NM\ p$', which is an alternative form of Brouwer's Axiom. But it will be more convenient for us to use the 'If it is false that p' form. In either of these equivalent forms Brouwer's Axiom expresses the view that the actual state of affairs, whether positively or negatively described, would have been at least a possible state of affairs, even if any other possible state of affairs had been actual instead. From this view it obviously follows that if it is false (though possible) that p, then even if it were true that p it would still be possible that not-p—which is what Anselm asserts in step (2) about affirmative existential propositions.

I do not mean to suggest here that Brouwer's Axiom is a logical principle of undoubted validity; it is in fact a somewhat controversial principle. We shall return to that point. But first I want to offer a formal proof that Anselm's conclusion, '$M\ g \supset g$', does follow from '$N(g \supset N g)$' in a system of modal logic which contains Brouwer's Axiom. There are at least two known systems of modal propositional calculus in which the proof that I shall give would be formally correct. One of these is the very widely used system S5, in which Brouwer's Axiom is not normally used as an axiom but is provable as a theorem. The other is a somewhat weaker system, called "the Brouwersche System" by Saul Kripke, of which Brouwer's Axiom is a characteristic axiom.[15]

It will simplify the proof if possibility operators are eliminated in favor of necessity operators. ('N' is equivalent to '$\sim M \sim$', and 'M' to '$\sim N \sim$'.) Thus Brouwer's Axiom will be stated as '$\sim p \supset N \sim N p$' instead of '$\sim p \supset NM \sim p$', and the conclusion as '$\sim N \sim g \supset g$' instead of '$M\ g \supset g$'. In addition to Brouwer's Axiom, the argument will appeal to several rules of inference which are part of the classical nonmodal propositional calculus as well as of the relevant modal systems, and to the following two modal principles.

(T1) $N (p \supset q) \supset N(\sim q \supset \sim p)$
(T2) $N (p \supset q) \supset (N p \supset N q)$

(T1) is provable as a theorem in the two modal systems mentioned above; and (T2), which is also contained in them, is commonly treated as one of their axioms. Here is the proof:

(1) $N (g \supset N g)$ Premise
(2) $N (g \supset N g) \supset N (\sim Ng \supset \sim g)$ Substitution in (T1)

(3) $N (\sim N g \supset \sim g)$	(1), (2), *modus ponens*
(4) $N (\sim N g \supset \sim g) \supset (N \sim N g \supset N \sim g)$	Substitution in (T2)
(5) $N \sim N g \supset N \sim g$	(3), (4), *modus ponens*
(6) $\sim g \supset N \sim N g$	Substitution in Brouwer's Axiom
(7) $\sim g \supset N \sim g$	(5), (6), hypothetical syllogism
(8) $\sim N \sim g \supset g$	(7), transportation, double negation

This argument can easily be extended to form a proof of the existence of God, by the addition of the premise (which Anselm obviously meant his readers to supply) that the existence of a being than which nothing greater can be thought is at least possible. The argument continues as follows.

(9) $\sim N \sim g$	Premise
(10) $\therefore g$	(8), (9), *modus ponens*

This proof is similar to an argument presented in modern modal logical notation by Charles Hartshorne.[16] The chief difference is that Hartshorne's argument uses, instead of Brouwer's Axiom, the principle ' $\sim N p \supset N \sim N p$ ', which is a characteristic axiom of S5 but is not contained in the Brouwersche System at all.[17] This difference is formally interesting, but practically of little or no importance; for there is not likely to be any good reason for accepting one of the two principles in the present context which would not also be a good reason for accepting the other.

Hartshorne calls his argument a "modal argument" for the existence of God; and that also seems a good name for the similar argument introduced by Anselm in chapter 1 of his reply to Gaunilo, because it is an argument that lends itself to formal paraphrase as primarily an argument in modal propositional logic. I think it is better not to call these arguments "ontological" because, unlike the argument of *Proslogion* 2, they need not depend on any assumptions at all about the relation of existence to predication. They do not presuppose that things which do not really exist can have predicates. They do not presuppose that existence, or existence in reality, is a predicate, nor even that necessary existence is a predicate. For their structure does not depend on predicate logic at all, but only on modal and nonmodal propositional logic. Obviously it is a great advantage to Anselm to be able to dispense with those controversial assumptions about predication.

Perhaps it will be objected, however, that Anselm's modal argument has compensating disadvantages of its own in the doctrines of modal logic which it assumes. I have already noted that there has been controversy over the question whether it is legitimate to use systems of modal logic containing Brouwer's Axiom. Doubtless some of this controversy is due to a failure of philosophers at first to appreciate that the question 'What is the correct system of modal logic?' is misconceived. The modal terms 'necessary' and 'possible' have more than one sense, and are sometimes used rather vaguely. Whether a given system of modal logic is valid or not depends on the interpretation that is assigned to its modal operators.

For instance, the interpretation of the necessity operator 'N' might be determined, or partially determined, by any one of the following semantical rules.

(R1) 'N p' is true if and only if 'p' is true about all possible worlds.
(R2) 'N p' is true if and only if 'p' is true solely by virtue of the meaning rules of our language being what they are.
(R3) 'N p' is true if and only if 'p' is logically provable.

Saul Kripke has shown that if (R1) is assumed, and if it is further assumed that just the same worlds would be possible no matter what world were actual, S5 (and therefore also the Brouwersche System) must be accepted as valid. I think there is also good reason to believe that if the interpretation of 'N' is determined by (R2), S5 and the Brouwersche System are valid. In particular, it seems that if it is not the case that a certain proposition is true solely by virtue of the meaning rules of our language being what they are, that itself is something that could not be otherwise, the meaning rules of our language being what they are. Therefore, according to (R2), '$\sim$ N $p \supset$ N $\sim$ N p', the controversial axiom of S5, is valid; and if it is, so is Brouwer's Axiom, '$\sim p \supset$ N $\sim$ N p'. On the other hand, if the interpretation of 'N' is determined by (R3), it is plausible to suppose that '$\sim$ N $p \supset$ N $\sim$ N p' is not valid; for what is not logically provable may not be provably unprovable. But 'N $p \supset$ N N p', a characteristic axiom of the modal system S4, presumably would be valid, since what can be proved can thereby be proved provable. And it is known that if 'N $p \supset$ N N p' is valid and '$\sim$ N $p \supset$ N $\sim$ N p' is not valid, Brouwer's Axiom is not valid either.[18]

All of this bears on the modal arguments for the existence of God, as follows. We are talking about arguments which derive the conclusion 'g' from the premises 'N ($g \supset$ N g)' and '$\sim$ N $\sim g$' in some system of modal propositional calculus. I have stated such an argument, which is formally correct in S5 and the Brouwersche System. Because the argument uses the Brouwersche Axiom, however, it is not formally correct in S4. Indeed, it can be proved that '[N ($p \supset$ N p) & ~ N ~ p] $\supset p$' is not a valid formula in S4,[19] so that S4 cannot be used to derive 'g' from 'N ($g \supset$ Ng)' and '~ N ~ g'. But it seems to me extremely plausible to suppose that the interpretation of the necessity operator in the modal arguments for the existence of God can rightly be regarded as determined by (R1) or (R2), and that S5 or the Brouwersche System is therefore valid in the context with which we are concerned. I do not claim that this conclusion is absolutely certain, but I think it is so plausible that the disadvantages of assuming Brouwer's Axiom in this context are rather small. They are quite inconsiderable in comparison with the disadvantages of the assumptions about existence and predication which are involved in the ontological argument of *Proslogion* 2.

This gives us some reason to suppose that Anselm's modal argument for the existence of God is a better argument than the *Proslogion* 2 argument. The logical doctrines assumed in the modal argument are less questionable than those assumed in the ontological argument. Therefore the modal argument is at least the better argument of the two unless its premises are decidedly less plausible than those of the *Proslogion* 2 argument. And I believe the premises of the modal argument are not less plausible than the premises of *Proslogion* 2. I will not attempt to prove that this belief of mine is right, but I will develop one line of thought which may tell in its favor.

The modal argument for the existence of God, in the last form in which I stated it, has two premises.

N ($g \supset$ N g)
~ N ~ g

(Modal axioms are not properly premises, but part of the logical apparatus.) The second premise says that it is possible that God exists. But what sort of God? If the rest of the argument is sound, it is a logically necessary God whose existence is here assumed possible. If God cannot exist at all unless it is necessary that God exist, then the claim that God's existence is possible implies that it is possible that it is necessary that God exists. This proposition, that it is possible that it is necessary that God exist (~ N ~ N g) is what any supporter of the modal argument must defend in trying to justify the premise that God's existence is possible. An alert critic of the argument will not let him get away with less. But if the proposition '~ N ~ N g' is granted, no other premise is needed in order to prove the existence of God by a modal argument. All that is needed is Brouwer's Axiom and two truth-functional rules of inference (*modus tollens* and double negation). The proof is extremely simple.

(1) $\sim N \sim N\, g$ Premise

(2) $\sim g \supset N \sim N\, g$ Substitution in Brouwer's Axiom

(3) $\therefore \sim \sim g$ (1), (2), *modus tollens*

(4) $\therefore g$ (3), double negation

This reasoning shows two things about the proposition '$\sim N \sim N\, g$'. First, '$\sim N \sim N\, g$' is already, in effect, a premise in Anselm's modal argument for the existence of God. Second, '$\sim N \sim N\, g$', all by itself, as sole premise, is sufficient for a proof of the existence of God, if the use of Brouwer's Axiom in these arguments is justified. If we are given this one premise of the modal argument, we do not need any other premise to prove the existence of God.

I will add a third point. '$\sim N \sim N\, g$' is a proposition which must be maintained by anyone who holds that the existence of God is logically necessary. For if it is necessary that God exist, it is possible that it is necessary that God exist; whatever is the case is also possible. Very commonly one assumes without question that what one is trying to prove is at least logically possible. But in the present case, what is to be proved follows by a very short argument from the proposition that it is possible. The crucial question, therefore, about logically necessary divine existence is the question of possibility: the question whether it is logically possible that it is logically necessary that God exist. Other premises can properly support belief in logically necessary divine existence only insofar as they support belief in its possibility.

Let us return to the comparison of the merits of the modal and ontological arguments. This at least can be said. The *Proslogion* 2 argument has probably never been defended except as part of a program for proving the logically necessary existence of God. It could be of value for a proof of that conclusion only if it helped to make more plausible the claim that it is logically possible that God's existence is logically necessary. It seems to me very unlikely that it would help in that way. Indeed, I think it is correct to say that although the modal argument for the existence of God helps us to see that the question of possibility is the crucial question about logically necessary divine existence, neither the modal nor the ontological argument provides us with grounds for answering it.

IV

When commentators have looked in Anselm for a "second ontological argument," possibly better than the argument of *Proslogion* 2, they have commonly looked for it in a passage which I have not yet discussed, in the third chapter of the *Proslogion*. It is generally acknowledged that Anselm did not intend to present there a second, independent argument for the existence of God, but to prove an additional proposition about the being which was already proved to exist in chapter 2. It is suggested, however, that the argument which Anselm uses for this purpose can be adapted to form an independent proof of God's existence.

In fact, there is an argument in the third chapter of the *Proslogion* which is capable of more than one interpretation and could be used to prove more than one conclusion. I will begin my discussion of it by stating a formal pattern of reasoning which is pretty much the same for all the interpretations and uses of the argument. Then I will discuss briefly three different uses to which this pattern of reasoning has been put by Anselm and his admirers.

Two premises are stated in *Proslogion* 3, in the following terms.

(1) For it can be thought that there exists something which cannot be thought not to exist,

$M (\exists x)(\sim M \sim Rx)$

(2) which is greater than what can be thought not to exist.

$(x)(m)([Q \; mx \; \& \; M \sim Rx] \supset \sim M \sim (y)[\sim M \sim Ry \supset (\exists n)(Gnm \; \& \; Qny)])$

Under any interpretation of the argument a third premise is required, which is not stated in *Proslogion* 3 but must be carried over from chapter 2. This premise says that some subject of predication has the property of being something than which nothing greater can be thought.

(3) $(\exists x)(\exists m)(Qmx \; \& \sim M (\exists y)(\exists n)(Gnm \; \& \; Qny))$

This formula might be interpreted as saying that some *really existing* subject of predication has the property of unsurpassable greatness. Or it might be understood, like the first premise of the *Proslogion* 2 argument, as asserting only that some subject of predication, which may or may not exist in reality, has the property of unsurpassable greatness. The choice between these two interpretations determines the ontological presuppositions of the argument and is important in relation to some of its uses, but it makes no difference to the formal structure of the argument.

The argument, like that of *Proslogion* 2, is presented by Anselm in *reductio ad absurdum* form. This will be carried over into the formalization of the argument. A thesis to be refuted will be introduced as a premise which will subsequently be removed by conditionalization with a self-contradictory consequent.

$\left\{\begin{array}{l}\end{array}\right.$

* (1) M ($\exists$ x)($\sim$ M $\sim$ Rx)   Premise

(2) (x)(m)([Qmx & M $\sim$ Rx] $\supset$ $\sim$ M $\sim$ (y)   Premise
[$\sim$ M $\sim$ Ry $\supset$ ($\exists$ n)(Gnm & Qny)])

** (3) ($\exists$ x)($\exists$ m)(Qmx & $\sim$ M ($\exists$ y)($\exists$ n)(Gnm &   Premise
Qny))

** (4) Qba & $\sim$ M ($\exists$ y)($\exists$ n)(Gnb & Qny)   (3), EI (a, b)

** (5) [Qba & M $\sim$ Ra] $\supset$ $\sim$ M $\sim$ (y)[$\sim$ M $\sim$ Ry   (2), UI
$\supset$ ($\exists$ n)(Gnb & Qny)]

** (6) M $\sim$ Ra $\supset$ $\sim$ M $\sim$ (y)[$\sim$ M $\sim$ Ry $\supset$ ($\exists$ n)   (4), (5), TF
(Gnb & Qny)]

*** (7) M $\sim$ Ra   Premise

*** (8) $\sim$ M $\sim$ (y)[$\sim$ M $\sim$ Ry $\supset$ ($\exists$ n)(Gnb &   (6), (7), TF
Qny)]

*** (9) $\sim$ M $\sim$ [($\exists$ x)($\sim$ M $\sim$ Rx) $\supset$ ($\exists$ y)($\exists$ n)   (8), see below
(Gnb & Qny)]

***(10) M ($\exists$ y)($\exists$ n)(Gnb & Qny)   (1), (9), modal infer-
ence

***(11) M ($\exists$ y)($\exists$ n)(Gnb & Qny) & $\sim$ M ($\exists$ y)   (4), (10), TF
($\exists$ n)(Gnb & Qny)

** (12) M $\sim$ Ra $\supset$ [M ($\exists$ y)($\exists$ n)(Gnb & Qny) &   (7), (11), condition-
$\sim$ M ($\exists$ y)($\exists$ n)(Gnb & Qny)]   alization

** (13) $\sim$ M $\sim$ Ra   (12), TF

** (14) Qba & $\sim$ M ($\exists$ y)($\exists$ n)(Gnb & Qny) &   (4), (13), TF
$\sim$ M $\sim$ Ra

** (15) ($\exists$ x)($\exists$ m)(Qmx & $\sim$ M ($\exists$ y)($\exists$ n)(Gnm &   (14), EG
Qny) & $\sim$ M $\sim$ Rx)

The inference of step (10) from steps (1) and (9) has the form '$\sim$ M $\sim$ (p $\supset$ q) and M p; therefore M q', which, as I said in section I, seems to me intuitively to be valid under any interpretation of the possibility operator which would fit the present context. It is obvious that (9) follows validly from (8) when we realize that (8) means 'It is necessary that if anything exists necessarily, then *it* has a magnitude greater than b', and (9) means 'It is necessary that if anything exists necessarily then *something* has a magnitude greater than b'.

We turn now to the three uses of this pattern of reasoning.

(A) In *Proslogion* 3 Anselm seems to intend to prove an additional proposition about a being who has already, in the second chapter, been proved to exist in reality. It is not said in chapter 2 that the being of unsurpassable greatness exists necessarily. Neither is it clear that the *Proslogion* 2 argument, if successful, must establish its conclusion with logical necessity. For it depends on the claim that someone has a concept of an unsurpassably great being. And for all that is said in chapter 2, that claim may well be only contingently true. So Anselm is trying to prove something new about the unsurpassably great being when he argues in chapter 3 that such a being "exists so truly that it cannot even be thought not to exist." He may be seen as building on the foundation laid in the second chapter. And in that case premise (3) of the *Proslogion* 3 argument may be interpreted as asserting the real existence that is supposed to have been proved in *Proslogion* 2. Under this interpretation, of course, the chapter 3 argument inherits all the weaknesses of whatever argument it depends on for the justification of its existential premise.

(B) It is easy to see how the *Proslogion* 3 argument may be regarded as being, in its own right, a distinct argument for the existence of God. Its conclusion states that something has the property of unsurpassable greatness and necessarily has real existence. This conclusion clearly implies that such a being really exists; for what necessarily has real existence does have real existence.

But if the argument of *Proslogion* 3 is to be an additional proof of the real existence of God, it cannot without circularity have a premise which presupposes or explicitly asserts the real existence of God. Hence, the universe of discourse for the formalization of the argument must not be understood as restricted to things that really exist. For if the universe of discourse were restricted to real existents, premise (3) would already assert the real existence of a being than which a greater cannot be thought. This means that if the *Proslogion* 3 argument is to be interpreted as an independent and noncircular argument for the reality of God, it must be understood as resting on the assumption that predication does not presuppose real existence. Considered as a "second" proof of the real existence of God, the argument of *Proslogion* 3 is indeed an "ontological" argument, involving substantially the same assumptions about the relation of existence to predication as are involved in *Proslogion* 2.

(C) As I have already tried to show, Anselm assumes, in the first chapter of his reply to Gaunilo, that it is a necessary truth that if God exists at all, his existence is necessary: $N (g \supset N g)$. The argument of *Proslogion* 3 can be seen as providing reasons for this assumption. If the argument is used for this purpose, it is most convenient to regard the universe of discourse as restricted to real existents, so that the existential or particular quantifier '$(\exists x)$' can be read as 'There exists (in reality) an x such that'. A sixteenth step is added to the argument in which premise (3) is removed by conditionalization.

* (16) $(\exists x)(\exists m)(Qmx \,\& \sim M (\exists y)(\exists n)(Gnm \,\& \, Qny)) \supset (\exists x)(\exists m)(Qmx \,\& \sim M (\exists y) (\exists n)(Gnm \,\& \, Qny) \,\& \sim M \sim Rx)$ (3), (15), conditionalization

Now we have a formally valid argument from premises (1) and (2) for the conclusion that *if* there exists (in reality) something than which nothing greater can be thought, *then* there exists (in reality) something than which nothing greater can be thought, and which cannot be thought not to exist. This argument does not depend on the denial of the doctrine that predication presupposes real existence; for its variables range over real existents only. Neither do its premises assert or imply the real existence of an unsurpassably great being, since it no longer has an existential premise.[20] If (1) and (2) are necessary truths, as Anselm presumably believed them to be, the argument shows that (16), which follows from them, is also a necessary truth.

Even when we prefix a necessity operator to (16), however, we do not yet have 'N $(g \supset N g)$' but something of a quite different form. The antecedent of (16) says that a certain description is satisfied. But the consequent does not say it is necessary that that description is satisfied. It says that the description is in fact satisfied, and by an individual whose real existence is conceptually necessary. This might still leave open the possibility that in some possible world the description would not be satisfied, though the individual in question would of course exist, but without satisfying it. In order to rule out this possibility, Anselm would have to assume that any individual which is unsurpassably great must possess that property by conceptual necessity. That is, unsurpassable greatness must be an essential property of the individual in question, a property without which he could not be the individual he is. I am sure that Anselm does hold this (see *Monologion,* chapters 16–17). With this additional assumption, the argument of *Proslogion* 3 can be regarded as giving reasons, which may have been Anselm's original reasons, for accepting the proposition 'N $(g \supset N g)$'.

I shall not attempt here to evaluate in detail this argument for 'N $(g \supset N g)$'; but there is one more point that I do want to make about it. 'N $(g \supset N g)$' might be an important premise for someone who was trying to prove the *non*existence of God by a modal argument. J. N. Findlay once offered a modal *dis*proof of the existence of God,[21] which seems to have the following general form.

   (i) God cannot exist (in reality) at all unless he exists (in reality) by conceptual necessity.
   (ii) It is not possible for anything to exist (in reality) by conceptual necessity.
   (iii) Therefore it is not possible for God to exist (in reality) at all.

The point that I want to make is that anyone who used this atheistic argument could not consistently support its first premise by the argument of *Proslogion* 3. For premise (1) of the *Proslogion* 3 argument says that it is possible for something to exist in reality by conceptual necessity. And intuitively it seems highly plausible that that should be a premise in an argument for the proposition that an unsurpassably great being cannot exist (in reality) except by conceptual necessity. It would hardly be reasonable to regard a being's greatness as surpassable simply because it lacked a property which could not possibly be possessed by anything at all. But premise (ii) of the atheistic argument flatly denies that it is possible for anything to exist in reality by conceptual necessity; it is therefore inconsistent with one of the premises of the *Proslogion* 3 argument. Of course I have not proved here that the proponent of the atheistic argument cannot support its first premise at all. But at least he cannot consistently establish it by the use of the argument in *Proslogion* 3.

Notes

1. I am responsible for the translation of quotations from Anselm and Gaunilo in this essay. Latin text established by F. S. Schmitt and reprinted in M. J. Charlesworth's edition, translation, and commentary, *St. Anselm's Proslogion* (Oxford, 1965).

2. *Proslogion,* chapter 2.

3. Quine objects to the occurrence of modal operators within the scope of a quantifier. See his "Reference and Modality" (Essay VIII in his *From a Logical Point of View* [Cambridge, Mass., 1953]) and "Three Grades of Modal Involvement" (Essay XIII in his *The Ways of Paradox and Other Essays* [New York, 1966]). I am not persuaded that Quine's objection is correct, but I do not intend to discuss the issue here.

4. Anthony Kenny, *Descartes* (New York, 1968), chapter 7; a slightly longer version, with discussion by others, and Kenny's replies, in *Fact and Existence,* ed. Joseph Margolis (Oxford, 1969), pp. 18–62.

5. "On Behalf of the Fool," chapters 5–6.

6. Ibid., chapter 6.

7. For Anselm's rejection of the lost-island counterexample, see the beginning of chapter 3 and the end of chapter 5 of his reply to Gaunilo; in relation to the latter, see the rest of chapter 5.

8. In chapter 1 of "On Behalf of the Fool."

9. In the First Objections to Descartes's *Meditations* (pp. 7–8 in vol. II of the Haldane and Ross translation of *The Philosophical Works of Descartes* [New York, 1955]).

10. See the discussion of this point by Kenny, Malcolm, and Sosa in *Fact and Existence,* ed. Margolis, pp. 18–62.

11. See ibid., the contributions by Kenny and Bernard Williams, for additional objections.

12. 'Exist', in most contexts in these arguments from the reply to Gaunilo, obviously means 'exist in reality'.

13. The argument to which I am referring is the one which is expressed in the following passage, which I divide in four steps. "[1] For that than which a greater cannot be thought cannot be thought to exist except without a beginning. [2] But whatever can be thought to exist and does not exist can be thought to exist with a beginning. [3] Therefore it is not the case that that than which a greater cannot be thought can be thought to exist and does not exist. [4] Therefore if it can be thought to exist, of necessity it does exist" (pp. 168–70 in Charlesworth's text).

14. Page 170 in Charlesworth's text.

15. Kripke, "Semantical Analysis of Modal Logic I: Normal Propositional Calculi," *Zeitschrift für mathematische Logik und Grundlagen der Mathematik,* 9 (1963), pp. 67–96. See also C. I. Lewis and C. H. Langford, *Symbolic Logic,* 2d ed. (New York, 1959), p. 498, on the relation of Brouwer's Axiom to S5.

16. *The Logic of Perfection* (La Salle, Ill., 1962), pp. 50–1.

17. Actually Hartshorne uses an axiom equivalent to '$N (\sim N p \supset N \sim N p)$'; the initial necessity operator is not needed here. But that is a minor point.

18. This claim presupposes some other principles of modal logic which would not be controversial in this context. On the issues discussed in this paragraph, see the works cited in n. 16; also Saul Kripke, "A Completeness Theorem in Modal Logic," *Journal of Symbolic Logic,* 24 (1959), pp. 1–14; and E. J. Lemmon, "Is There Only One Correct System of Modal Logic?" *Proceedings of the Aristotelian Society,* supp. vol. 33 (1959), pp. 23–40.

19. This can most readily be shown by the method of semantic tableaux which is explained by Kripke in the two works cited above.

20. As the argument now stands, real existence is expressed in it by two different notations. It might be desirable when interpreting the argument in this way to replace 'Rx' consistently by '$(\exists z)(z = x)$'. This could be done without damage to the structure of the argument.

21. J. N. Findlay, "Can God's Existence Be Disproved?" *Mind,* 57 (1948), pp. 176–83. The article has been reprinted several times.

16

Flavors, Colors, and God

In this essay I will be presenting, and defending, an argument for the existence of God. It will not be a knockdown proof that would suffice by itself to settle the issue in favor of theism; at best it will contribute to a cumulative case. Knockdown proofs are rare in metaphysics; and while the existence of God is much more than a metaphysical issue, it is that also, and is like other metaphysical questions in this respect. But even where there are no absolutely conclusive demonstrations, considerations for and against can still be found. We can look for theoretical advantages and disadvantages, as we may call them, of a metaphysical position. The-oretical advantages of theism can be found in the possibility of theological explanations of facts otherwise hard to explain.

The argument I will present is quite simple in a way, and not partic-ularly original. It is a version of the argument from consciousness which was Locke's principal argument for theism,[1] and which has recently been so ably revived by Richard Swinburne as to claim a whole chapter of response in J. L. Mackie's apology for atheism.[2] Nonetheless, I think that it is still a neglected argument, and that some of its strengths can be brought out in new ways, first by placing it in a historical context, and second by concentrating on one particular aspect of consciousness.

1. The Question

Why do red things look the way they do (and not the way yellow things do)? And not less important, why do red things look today the way they

Discussions with Richard Healey and Terence Horgan, as well as written comments from George Pappas and Peter van Inwagen, have given rise to improvements in this paper. I am glad to express my gratitude, without burdening them with responsibility for anything I have said.

looked yesterday? Why does sugar taste the way it does (and not the way salt does)? And not less important, why does sugar taste today the way it did yesterday? These are instances of a more general question, but to discuss it we will need a general term for such things as the look of red and the taste of sugar. The usual term is 'phenomenal qualia', or 'qualia' for short.

Philosophers have debated much about the nature of phenomenal qualia. Are they properties of the mind, or of states of mind, or of something else that might be called a "sense datum" or "idea"? I don't think we have to know, for present purposes. It is enough that we know that experiencing the appearance of something red, the appearance of something yellow, the taste of sugar, the taste of salt, the smell of a rose, the smell of hydrogen sulfide, are kinds of experience that differ from each other in ways that cannot be analyzed in a definition, but with which most of us are vividly familiar. Kinds of experience that differ in those ways are, or are associated with, phenomenal qualia. (Some philosophers deny that there are any such things. I'm sure they are wrong. I will come to them in section VI, but will ignore them for the time being, in the confidence that everyone will recognize what I am talking about.)

Now I can state my general question: Why are phenomenal qualia correlated as they are with physical qualities?

II. The Obvious Attempt at a Scientific Explanation

One's first reaction to this question may be to think that the answer to it is well known and does not involve God. Red things look the way they do because they reflect red light (or more accurately, certain wavelengths of light) to our retinas, and that sort of light affects part of the retina, causing it to transmit certain electrical signals to the brain, setting up a certain pattern of electrical activity in the brain, which causes us to see red. Similarly sugar tastes the way it does because its chemical composition affects certain taste receptors in the tongue in such a way that they send electrical impulses to the brain that result in a certain pattern of electrical activity in the brain, which gives us the sensation of a sweet taste.

I assume that these scientific accounts are at least approximately true. The trouble with them is that they do not answer the question that I am asking. For suppose that the experience of seeing red is caused by brain state R, and the experience of seeing yellow by brain state Y (both R and Y being patterns of electrical activity). This correlation of the appearance of red with R, and of the appearance of yellow with Y, is an example of precisely the sort of thing I am trying to explain. That is, it is an example of the correlation of phenomenal qualia with physical qualities or states. We have merely explained one mental/physical correlation in terms of another.

Why does R cause me to see red? Why doesn't it cause me to see yellow—or to smell a foul odor? We do not imagine that R is itself red, or Y yellow. It is hard to conceive of any reason why a particular pattern of electrical activity would be naturally connected with the peculiar kind of experience that I call the appearance of red, rather than with that which I call the appearance of yellow. Indeed, it is hard to conceive of any reason why a pattern of electrical activity would be naturally connected with either of these appearances, rather than with no phenomenal qualia at all. Let us be clear that I am not denying that R and Y are in fact constantly *correlated* with the experience of red and yellow respectively. I am also not denying that R and Y *cause* me to experience red and yellow, respectively. What I want to know is why these relationships between brain states and phenomenal qualia obtain rather than others—and indeed why any such regular and constant relationships between things of these two types obtain at all.

The search for explanation does not normally stop with the discovery of a correlation. On the contrary, science mainly seeks to explain not particular events, but correlations and other general facts. If I want to find out why my car won't start this morning, I go to a mechanic, not a scientist. But I might go to a scientist to find out why water regularly boils at a lower temperature in Denver than in Los Angeles.

It is difficult, however, to see how science would even try to explain the correlation between phenomenal qualia and brain states (or whatever other physical states the qualia are most directly correlated with). For what science is geared up to do is to find laws governing physical states, described in terms of properties that are geometrical or electrical or at any rate quite different from phenomenal qualia. Whatever mechanisms of that sort we discover, the problem of why precisely these flavor experiences or color experiences should be associated with just those physical states will remain essentially the same.

III. The Aristotelian Explanation

At this point we might be tempted to say that we cannot imagine what *any* explanation of the correlation of phenomenal qualia with physical states would look like; and that might lead us to suspect that the request for an explanation of it is misconceived. The history of Western thought comes to the aid of our imagination at this point, however, enabling us to see what a solution to our problem might look like. The first solution we will examine is surely false, but it does at least make sense enough to show that there is something here that in principle invites explanation.

It is part of the Aristotelianism that dominated Western thought in the later Middle Ages.[3] One difference between Aristotelianism and modern thought is this. We do not think there is any quality in physical objects that resembles the peculiar qualities or qualia that make the difference between experiencing red and yellow, or between the taste of sugar and salt. We believe that those experiences are caused by physical properties of bodies that are not at all like our phenomenal qualia. But the typical opinion of Aristotelian Scholastics was that phenomenal qualia are similar to, and produced by, physical qualities that we perceive in bodies by means of the qualia. There is a qualitative "form" in the sugar that is like the quality of the taste of sugar that makes it different from the taste of salt. The quality of the appearance of red that makes it different from the appearance of yellow resembles a form or quality that is present on the surface of a typical ripe apple.

On this Aristotelian view, the answer to the question, why phenomenal qualia are correlated with just those physical qualities with which they are in fact correlated, is straightforward. They are the same (or, at any rate, similar) qualities, present materially in the bodies that are perceived, and immaterially to the mind that perceives. This correlation is not arbitrary but natural, perhaps almost self-explanatory.

Of course it's not quite as simple as that. We want to know how the redness gets from the apple to the mind. Redness, Scholastics thought, exists on the surface of the apple as a qualitative "Form." Forms function as properties of things, but that is not their only role in Aristotelian theory; they are also causal agents. They operate by something like infection. Forms or qualities spread from things that have them to things that previously did not. Heat transfer provides a good case for this conception of causal interaction. If a heated rock is placed in cool water, the form of heat is imparted to the water from the rock; or, more precisely, the form of heat in the rock causes a new, similar form in the water.

Something like this happens in sensation, which is, after all, a causal process. If I place my hand in hot water, a sensible form of heat is transmitted from the water to my hand. From there it is transmitted through my body to the place at which it is made present to my mind as a feeling of warmth. In seeing red there is an additional complication, for the red surface of the apple is not in immediate contact with my body. For this reason vision requires a "medium," something transparent, like air, to which a form, typically called a "sensible species," of red is initially imparted and through which it is transmitted to my eye. From the medium the form of red enters the liquid in my eyeball; thence it is transmitted through my body to the appropriate place to become present to my mind. Thus I see red. The feature of this causal history that explains the connection between physical states and phenomenal qualia is that similar forms of red are present at every stage of the process: on the surface of the apple, in the medium, in the eyeball, and in or to the mind.

This theory is fantastic, you will object. Aren't these sensible species and media too bizarre to be taken seriously? That is my initial reaction too. But if we think about them carefully, trying to set aside the prejudices engendered by our own education, I believe we can see that in their own context these Aristotelian ideas are no more bizarre or incoherent or absurd than the quanta and quarks of modern physical theory. In fact there is something very commonsensical and directly experiential about the Aristotelian theory. Can't you *see* the "form" of whiteness on the surface of this piece of paper? Of course you are not accustomed to call it that, but doesn't the peculiar quality of whiteness known only by sight appear to you to lie on the surface of the page?

Nonetheless we have good reason to reject the Aristotelian account of these matters. Its rejection, in the early seventeenth century, was an important part of the beginning of modern science. Galileo wanted to develop a *mathematical* science of nature. "Philosophy," he wrote, meaning what we mean by 'science',

> is written in this grand book, the universe, which stands continually open to our gaze. . . . It is written in the language of mathematics, and its characters are triangles, circles, and other geometric figures without which it is humanly impossible to understand a single word of it.[4]

But the Aristotelian physics of qualities was relatively unamenable to mathematization. If we consider them purely in themselves, and as phenomenal qualia (or qualitatively identical with phenomenal qualia), leaving out of account everything we now know or believe about physical qualities that are correlated with them (such as wavelengths of light), the qualities of red and yellow, or (worse yet) the qualities of sweet and green, stand in no obvious or easily measured geometrical or arithmetical relationship to each other. This point will become important later in our argument. It was also a motive for rejecting the infection conception of causation and the idea that the whole diverse array of sensible qualities are causal agents in nature.

One well-known type of causation lent itself magnificently to mathematical treatment. *Mechanical* interactions, in which bodies affect each other by impact, by virtue of their motions and their mutual contact, can be described and explained in terms of sizes, shapes, and motions which can be treated geometrically and arithmetically. Galileo, Descartes, and other seventeenth-century natural philosophers proposed to reduce all causation in nature to purely mechanical interactions. That would make geometrical properties, plus motion and rest, the sole causally relevant properties of physical objects.

The mechanistic theory was applied to the action of physical objects on our sense organs, and of the sense organs on the central nervous system, as well as to other causal interactions in nature. Sight, for example, was explained in terms of mechanical action on the retina by light, conceived as either a stream of minute particles or pressure in a subtle circumambient fluid. From the retina, visual data were transmitted by mechanical operation of the nerves to the brain. There, notoriously, things got more complicated—but more of that later.

It follows from this theory that even if resemblances of our phenomenal qualia are in physical objects, they do not *cause* our sensations. But in fact the whole idea of such physical resemblances of the qualia was given up as explanatorily superfluous—and worse, as something for which no mechanical explanation could be given (and for other reasons that were found). Thus the Aristotelian explanation of the correlation between the qualia and physical states was relinquished.

The progress of modern science has vindicated the rejection of Aristotelianism. Our science is no longer mechanistic in the seventeenth-century sense. It admits electrical charge, for instance, alongside size and shape, as a causally relevant physical property. But it has no use for Aristotelian "forms," nor for any sort of physical resemblance of phenomenal qualia. The Aristotelian solution of our problem is no longer a live option. Even if we adopted a "common-sense realism" about flavors, colors, and other "secondary qualities," as some contemporary philosophers have proposed, we would not thereby revive the Aristotelian scheme of causal explanation; and we would still face the question of how to explain the correlation of flavors, colors, etc. (in the objects as well as in the mind) with the electromagnetic states that modern science seems to have discovered.

IV. The Theological Alternative

In this rejection of Aristotelianism something interesting happened to those peculiar qualities we experience in seeing red and yellow and tasting sugar and salt. They were "kicked upstairs," as M. R. Ayers has put it, into the mind.[5] Galileo concluded that "tastes, odors, colors, and so on, are no more than mere names so far as the object in which we place them is concerned, and that they reside only in the consciousness."[6] Since the existence of the phenomenal qualia is so evident in sensation that it can hardly be denied, they are seen as features belonging exclusively to the mental realm, and absent from the physical. One of the ways in which the mind/body problem is more difficult for modern thought than for Aristotelianism is that there is for us no affinity between the mental and the physical with respect to these qualities and it becomes an unsolved problem again *why* phenomenal qualia are correlated as they seem to be with physical qualities.

How did early modern thinkers propose to explain this correlation? Theologically, for the most part. Descartes ascribed it to the arbitrary action of God, though he thought the mind/body relations that actually obtain had been designed by God with certain ends in view.

> The nature of man could indeed have been constituted by God in such a way that that same motion in the brain [which in fact causes me to feel a pain in my foot] would have presented whatever else you please to the mind. In particular, it could have displayed itself, insofar as it is in the brain, or insofar as it is in the foot, or in some place in between, or finally anything else whatever. But nothing else would have been as conducive to the preservation of the body.[7]

Locke dwells extensively on the need for theological explanation at this point:

> . . . the production of Sensation in us of Colours and Sounds, *etc.* by impulse and motion . . . being such, wherein we can discover no natural connexion with any *Ideas* we have, we cannot but ascribe them to the arbitrary Will and good Pleasure of the Wise Architect.[8]

> 'Tis evident that the bulk, figure, and motion of several Bodies about us, produce in us several Sensations, as of Colours, Sounds, Tastes, Smells, Pleasure and Pain, *etc.* These mechanical Affections of Bodies, having no affinity at all with those *Ideas,* they produce in us, (there being no conceivable connexion between any impulse of any sort of Body, and any perception of a Colour, or Smell, which we find in our Minds) we can have no distinct knowledge of such Operations beyond our Experience; and can reason no otherwise about them, than as effects produced by the ap-

pointment of an infinitely Wise Agent, which perfectly surpass our Comprehensions.[9]

The cautious Locke does not flatly assert that there cannot be a nontheological explanation; but he thinks a theological explanation is the only one that is accessible to us, and he seems quite prepared to embrace it.

This is in agreement with Locke's views about the relation of physical qualities to consciousness in general. He states, "Matter, *incogitative Matter* and Motion, whatever changes it might produce of Figure and Bulk, *could never product Thought.*"[10] Motion, shape, and size cannot explain the existence of thought. Neither can the geometrical structure of a system of bits of matter, "For unthinking Particles of Matter, however put together can have nothing thereby added to them, but a new relation of Position, which 'tis impossible should give thought and knowledge to them."[11]

The rejection of Aristotelianism thus left the most typical of early modern thinkers with a system of physical states of affairs and a system of mental states of affairs, utterly diverse from each other and correlated only by the will and power of God. The supernaturalism of this view of the world was not unnoticed in the seventeenth century, and was not unwelcome to most of the founders of modern thought. Aristotelianism in its less theological forms, on the other hand, offered the possibility of a more integrated naturalistic world view that would not need to appeal to voluntary acts of God to explain the interaction of corporeal and mental nature.

It was an audacious move to give up that possibility of integration by rejecting Aristotelianism and splitting the world into physical and mental states of affairs between which no natural connection could be seen. This has clearly been such a good move for the progress of science that we can hardly doubt that it has brought us closer to the truth. But we may wonder whether this step would have been taken in a culture in which theism was not taken more or less for granted, as it was in seventeenth-century Europe. Without a theological explanation of the correlation between phenomenal qualia and physical states, would it have seemed plausible to reject the Aristotelian doctrine of their affinity? At any rate, a theological explanation of the correlation was the main one that was offered; and I think it is the only promising one that has been proposed. It is a theoretical advantage of theism that it makes possible such an explanation.

A brief digression is in order before we conclude our historical survey. In this discussion of seventeenth-century thought I have focused on thinkers who were dualistic in their view of the relation between physical and mental states of affairs. There was of course also an important idealistic movement in early modern philosophy, represented by Leibniz and Berkeley—a movement to which I personally am very sympathetic. Idealism seems to solve our problem. Physical and mental states are correlated as they are because the physical states are constructed out of the mental ones. But this only accentuates another problem. Why do our perceptual states occur in the order in which they do? This cannot be explained in terms of the action of bodies, for bodies are constructed out of the very perceptual facts to be explained, according to the idealist. And it certainly is not plausible to regard it as sheer happenstance that our perceptions are such that we can regard them as representing an orderly world. Early modern idealists had recourse to a theological explanation at this point, and I do not think any other plausible explanation is available.[12] Idealism has at least as much need of God as dualism, and cannot offer an atheistic escape from the problem of phenomenal qualia.

V. The Impossibility of Any Scientific Explanation

The hardest philosophical work in this paper has been reserved for the final two sections, in which I must deal with the two main objections to my argument. The first is an objection to my claim that there is no prospect of a plausible alternative to a theological explanation of the correlation between phenomenal qualia and physical states, and in particular to my claim that natural science cannot provide such an explanation.

Many people, including many theologians, are deeply prejudiced against any theistic argument based on a claim that science cannot explain something. Immensely (and rightly) impressed by the success of modern science in explaining the phenomena of nature, they judge it reasonable to assume that any remaining "gaps" in the scientific explanation of the world can in principle, and very likely will in fact, be filled by the continuing advance of science. A "god of the gaps," postulated to account for things that science cannot yet explain, seems to them a monarch of an inexorably dwindling realm, and doomed to be dethroned. Shouldn't the track record of science lead us to assume that there is a purely natural, nontheological explanation of the correlation of phenomenal qualia with physical states—an explanation that scientists can, and probably eventually will, discover?

What I have to make clear in opposition to this objection is that it is not just that science has not *yet* found an explanation for the correlation between qualia and physical states. Science is headed in the wrong direction for finding such an explanation, and it would be silly to expect science to turn in another direction.

Here it will be convenient to follow Richard Swinburne in distinguishing between two types of explanation. "Scientific explanation" is explanation in terms of laws of nature. "Personal explanation" is explanation in terms of the powers and intentional actions of voluntary agents.[13] If such a deep structural feature of at least the conscious part of nature as the correlation of phenomenal qualia with physical states is to be explained by the action of a voluntary agent, the agent will pretty well have to have such knowledge and power, and such a creative role, as to count as a deity. So, assuming that the only available types of explanation are the scientific and the personal, the alternatives to a theological explanation of this correlation will be to leave it a brute, unexplained fact (which seems pretty implausible), or else to explain it by a law of nature.

What would a law of nature have to look like in order to explain this correlation? Many seventeenth-century thinkers would have said the law would have to indicate a "perspicuous," intuitively intelligible connection between the phenomenal and physical states. It also seemed to them unlikely that there could be such a connection. That is part of what Locke was saying in the passages I quoted in section IV. These views still seem rather plausible to me, and perhaps there is an echo of them in Swinburne's statement that "brain-states are such different things qualitatively from experiences, intentions, beliefs, etc. that a *natural* connection between them seems almost impossible."[14] But I will not insist on this line of argument, for perspicuity and intuitive satisfaction are widely distrusted as criteria of success in scientific explanation.

A more universally accepted requirement for adequacy of a scientific explanation of a correlation is that the law in terms of which it is explained must be more *general* than the correlation. The explanation will thus embed the correlation in a more comprehensive and powerful theory. In order to be general enough to explain the correlation, the law must correlate things that do or could occur more widely than the terms of the correlation to be explained. In this and other ways it must present a *simpler* view of the universe than we have with the correlation unexplained. And of course the explanation must not be circular: It must not presuppose any of the facts to be explained. These requirements will be enough for my argument.

For it seems impossible to obtain the requisite generality. Suppose again that R and Y are patterns of electrical activity in the brain that cause the phenomenal qualia of red and yellow, respectively. A more *general* law that explained these correlations would not mention R or Y or the specific qualia of red and yellow. It would be stated in terms of other, more general characteristics of physical and conscious states. But it would imply that a physical state whose description (in the more general terms) R uniquely satisfies is correlated with a conscious state whose description (in the more general terms) is uniquely satisfied by the phenomenal quale of red. Here we stumble on the first difficulty in the way of obtaining the desired generality: Are there such general descriptions that are uniquely satisfied by the various phenomenal qualia?

I can think of two ways of trying to obtain descriptions of particular phenomenal qualia in more general terms, on which a sufficiently general scientific law could operate. Neither will do the job. The first would be to try to analyze the qualia as structured complexes of a small number of simpler elements common to all or many of them. For example, it has been claimed that the phenomenal quale of orange is composed of qualia of red and yellow. Experimental evidence can be cited in support of this claim.[15] Perhaps the evidence could sustain an alternative interpretation; but the main point to be made here is that even if the phenomenal quale of orange can be constructed out of qualia of red and yellow, that will not go very far toward a solution of the problem. For the qualia, or phenomenal hues, of red and yellow are generally acknowledged to be simple rather than complex, and we still want an explanation of their correlation with physical states.

This objection might be avoided by a much more ambitious analysis of phenomenal qualia. Leibniz held that though we are unable to explain what red is, or what any other phenomenal quale is, except by exhibiting it, "yet it is certain that the concepts of these qualities are composite and can be analyzed, as is obvious since they have their causes."[16] His opinion seems to be that our perceptions of the so-called secondary qualities, such as colors, smells, and tastes, are confused perceptions of their physical causes, which on his mechanistic view are to be understood in terms of primary qualities, such as size, shape, position, and motion, of minute particles of matter. He argues for the analyzability of phenomenal qualia explicitly on the ground that it provides a solution to our problem.

> It is also the insensible parts of our sensible perceptions that make there to be a relationship between these perceptions of colors, warmths, and other sensible qualities and the movements in bodies that correspond to them; whereas the Cartesians, with our Author [Locke], penetrating as he is, conceive the perceptions that we have of these qualities as arbitrary—that is to say, as if God had given them to the soul according to his good pleasure without having regard to any essential relationship between these perceptions and their objects: an opinion that surprises me and seems rather un-

worthy of the wisdom of the author of things, who does nothing without harmony and without reason.[17]

On Leibniz's view there is a natural affinity between the phenomenal qualia and their physical causes, in that the former are representations (albeit confused) of the latter. There is an obvious similarity between Leibniz and Aristotelianism on this point. The natural affinity makes it easy to state a general law governing the correlation between the qualia and physical states (although Leibniz thinks it is indeed God who gives the law effect). The general law is that each perceiving substance has perceptions representing the state of its organic body (and indirectly representing other things insofar as its body, as affected by them, represents them too).

But Leibniz's theory still is liable to the objection that many (at least) of the phenomenal qualia seem quite simple. Indeed, I think this objection is fatal to the theory. We can simply see and taste that the phenomenal qualia of red and sweet are quite different from any perception of sizes, shapes, and motions as such, and do not have the structure of such a perception. Perhaps if our sensory powers were more acute, we would perceive the shapes of sugar molecules instead of tasting their sweetness as we now do; and that might be in some sense a less "confused" perception than we actually have. But it would be qualitatively different from our present sensation of sweetness. It would not be the phenomenal quale whose actual correlation with sugar stimulation of the tongue we are trying to explain.

If the analysis of phenomenal qualia as complexes of simpler qualities cannot plausibly be carried far enough to solve our problem, there may be another way of trying to obtain identifying descriptions of the qualia in sufficiently general terms. If they cannot be broken up into more fundamental elements, it might still be possible to find patterns of resemblance among them that would enable us to arrange them on a scale and assign a unique numerical value to each phenomenal quale. Phenomenal pitches of sound, even if simple, can be ordered on a scale; and practised persons with "perfect pitch" can assign quite definite proportionate values to the "distances" between pitches on the scale. Phenomenal hues of color, likewise, might be assigned real numbers according to their position in the spectrum. This suggests that our general, explanatory law could take the form of an algorithm for finding the numerical value of the corresponding phenomenal quale, given a numerical value determined by certain quantities in a physical state.

A law of this sort could presumably be put in the form,

L: If $F(p) = S(q)$, then p causes q,

where p ranges over suitable physical states of affairs, and q over phenomenal qualia and perhaps over conscious states in general.[18] $F(p)$ will be a non–ad-hoc function from physical properties of p to mathematical values, and $S(q)$ an independent, non–ad-hoc function from q to mathematical values from the same range. It is convenient to think of these values as real numbers, but in principle they could be ordered n-tuples of real numbers; ordered triples might be required as values of $S(q)$, for example, in order to represent the relations of color qualia in hue, brightness, and saturation. The functions must be non–ad-hoc, or the law will not explain the phenomena, but merely restate them. And $F(p)$ and $S(q)$ must be mutually independent, in the sense that for a given p and q, the values of F and S can in principle be determined without knowing whether p and q are correlated; otherwise the explanation would be circular.

Two difficulties confront this approach, one associated with $F(p)$ and the other with $S(q)$. We will begin with the former. In order for the law to have the requisite generality, p must range over a sufficiently broad class of physical states of affairs. It will be easier to understand this in an example. Suppose we are trying to explain the correlation of phenomenal qualia with patterns of electrical discharge in the brain. In this case perhaps p would range over all electrical discharges in the universe. If p ranged only over those electrical discharges that occur in the brain, then a law in terms of p would merely restate, and not explain, an important part of what is to be explained here. For we would still want to know why phenomenal qualia are correlated with electrical discharges in the brain, and not with others.

Let's assume that $F(p)$ is the voltage of p. That is not plausible, but it will provide a clear and simple initial illustration. Then the general law says that each mathematical value of $F(p)$—that is, each voltage—is equal to the mathematical value assigned by S to a phenomenal quale, or perhaps some other conscious or mental state, that is caused by, and found in association with, electrical discharges of the corresponding voltage.

The objection that will occur immediately to most of us is that this implies that all the electrical discharges in the universe are associated with phenomenal qualia, or with other mental states, as our brain states are associated with them. What, we may ask, do the spark plugs in the engine feel, as we start a car? Could we make them see yellow by supplying them with the appropriate voltage? This is a sort of panpsychism. It could conceivably be true. But it surely has *no more* intrinsic plausibility than theism, and a lot less explanatory power.

Perhaps, however, this panpsychist result is due to the crudity of identifying $F(p)$ with voltage. Any plausible account of $F(p)$ will be much more complicated. Might we not be able to find an acceptable account on which the value of $F(p)$ would turn out to be zero for all values of p that occur outside of central nervous systems? We could then interpret **L** as implying that if $F(p) = 0$, p has no associated mental state. To assume that this could be done in a plausible, non–ad-hoc way would be issuing a very large promissory note; but let us grant it for the sake of argument, and pass on to the difficulty associated with $S(q)$, which seems to me decisive.

There is no plausible, non–ad-hoc way of associating phenomenal qualia in general (let alone conscious or mental states in general) with a range of mathematical values, independently of their empirically discovered correlations with physical states. The independence requirement is crucial here. Assuming that there is indeed a correlation between phenomenal qualia and physical states, and a mathematical function $F(p)$ that expresses the variation in physical states with which variation in qualia is found to be correlated, we could of course just assign to each phenomenal quale q_i the value $F(p_i)$, where p_i is the physical state with which q_i is correlated. That would guarantee mathematical values to the qualia. But it would only *restate* the correlation of phenomenal and physical states; it would not *explain* it. For there would be a vicious circle in saying that q_i is causally correlated with p_i *because* $S(q_i) = F(p_i)$, when the only thing that attaches the value of $F(p_i)$ to $S(q_i)$ is the fact that q_i is causally correlated with p_i. In order for $F(p) = S(q)$ to *explain* the correlation of physical states with phenomenal qualia, $S(q)$ must be a mathematical expression of a dimension (or structured system of dimensions) that can be discerned in the qualia independently of the physical states, just as voltage (for example) is a dimension of electrical discharges that can be discerned independently of associated qualia.

How would we find such an independent dimension or way of associating phenomenal qualia in general with a range of mathematical values? We began with the suggestion that phenomenal pitches and hues could be assigned real numbers on the basis of their position on the scale and the spectrum. But what is thus begun cannot be carried to completion. For the sake of argument, let us set aside any doubts about whether there are colors (some browns, perhaps) that have no phenomenally natural position in a "color space" mathematically ordered on the dimensions of hue, brightness and saturation. Let us assume also that all the phenomenal qualia of sound can be assigned a phenomenally natural position in a "sound space" ordered on pitch, loudness, and perhaps one or more other dimensions. The chief difficulty with this strategy is that these orderings cannot be extended to the other sensory modalities, and are not naturally integrated with each other.

It is much harder, in the first place, to find such an ordering among the qualia of any of the other senses. Is there a spectrum of odors? Is there an objectively valid, phenomenally natural order in which the flavors of chocolate, anise, and hazelnut—or sweet, sour, bitter, and salty—should be placed? As for the sense of touch, the degrees of phenomenal warmth and cold can be arranged in scales; but is there any natural continuum on which we would arrange the feelings of a moderate warmth, a moderate coolness, and a gentle stroking of the skin—all of approximately equal strength and agreeableness—in such a way as to represent the qualitative differences among them?

The problem, moreover, does not end there. For even if we had, from a purely phenomenal point of view, a single uniquely valid spectrum for each sensory modality, we would still face the mind-boggling problem of finding a mathematical relationship between the qualia of the different modalities. And without such a relationship, our law of nature will not explain why certain brain states produce phenomenal qualia such as red, yellow, and blue, and others produce qualia such as sweet, sour, and salty.

This is a crucial point. There are certain structural analogies between the current "opponent process theory" of the physiology of color vision and the spectral ordering of hues.[19] This may provide some explanation of why the pattern of neuron firings in the central nervous system that is actually correlated with the perception of orange is naturally more suited to that correlation than to a correlation with the perception of red. But that does not contribute to an explanation of why the actual correlation obtains, unless we take it as given that this electrical process in the central nervous system is part of a process of vision of colors. But what explains that given? My desire for an explanation on this point, obviously, will not be satisfied by any account that deals only with the physical side of the correlation, telling us why these electrical events in the nervous system are responsive to differences in reflected light. What I want to know is why this or any other pattern of electrical discharges should be correlated with color qualia rather than with odor qualia, or with no qualia at all.

If a law of the form **L** is to explain this, it is required, at a minimum, that the function $S(q)$ should represent a phenomenally natural ordering of *all* phenomenal qualia. But is there a unique objectively valid spectrum in which all phenomenal qualia are ordered? Or at any rate a unique phenomenally natural order in which the taste of anise, perhaps, comes between blue and the smell of hydrogen sulfide? Surely not. There is no such comprehensive ordering that will generate a function $S(q)$ sufficiently nonarbitrary to serve as a suitable term in a plausible law of nature. The different sorts of phenomenal qualia are too diverse from each other for that.

Here we may recall that one important motive for kicking the phenomenal qualia out of the physical world and upstairs into the mind, in the seventeenth century, was that the qualia do not have the mathematical structures and relationships in terms of which the modern approach to science was setting out to interpret the physical world. Given the mathematical character of our science, the physical side of any general law correlating physical with phenomenal states must be expected to have a mathematical structure. But given that the system of phenomenal qualia does not have a similar mathematical structure, I do not see where we would find the common denominator between the phenomenal and the physical that such a law would require. This is what I had in mind in saying that science (for its own good and sufficient reasons) is headed in the wrong direction for finding an explanation of the correlation between phenomenal qualia and physical states.

VI. Materialism

Some may think that the real objection to everything that I have been saying is that I have been ignoring materialism. Aristotelianism explained the correlation between phenomenal qualia and physical states by identifying them. Materialism, it might be suggested, can do the same, but in a different way. Whereas the Aristotelian postulated a (causally efficacious) qualitative identity of phenomenal and physical qualities, the materialist can solve the problem by identifying the phenomenal qualia with their correlated brain states. Surely no problem remains of explaining the "correlation," if the correlated states are identical![20]

It is important, however, to be clear about what is being identified with what. The mind with the brain? I don't believe in that identification, but I can accept it here for the sake of argument. It is enough (indeed, more than enough) for my argument to say that there are phenomenal qualia, and that even if they are properties of brains, they are distinct from the physical properties of brains (or of anything else). That is, they are distinct from the properties studied by physics, such as geometrical and electrical properties.

For as long as that distinction of properties remains, we can still ask why brains that have those physical qualities also have these phenomenal qualia. Why don't they have other phenomenal qualia instead, or none at all? This is essentially the same explanatory problem that we started with, and the materialist claim that it is brains that are the subject of the phenomenal qualia does nothing to solve it.

This is not a novel insight. Locke is careful to state his theistic argument from consciousness in terms of a demand for the explanation of mental *properties,* rather than substances (being notoriously cagy about committing himself as to the identity or duality of mental and material substances). And Swinburne is quite explicit that his version of the argument depends only on a dualism of properties—though he is personally willing to accept a dualism of substances.[21]

Although these classic formulations of the argument from consciousness are stated in terms of a dualism of properties, I think that even that is more than the argument requires. For suppose a materialist claims that R and the phenomenal appearance of red are one and the same property of brains, identified as R on the basis of its place in the physical system, and as the appearance of red on the basis of the way it seems to us when our brains have it. We can still ask why R seems to us the way it does, rather than the way Y (the physical brain state which "is" the appearance of yellow) does. This is quite recognizably our original question, and it remains unanswered. And if the materialist replies (implausibly, to my mind) that the "way" R seems to us when our brains have it is identical with the physical property R itself, but allows that when our brains have R we have a "first-person" way of identifying it that is not available to others for "third-person" identification of R, then we can reinstate our problem as the question why this physical property is regularly identified from the first-person position in the way that it is, rather than in the way that the appearance of yellow is.

In order to block the theistic argument from qualia by providing a materialistic explanation of phenomenal/physical correlations, one would have to adopt a very radical materialism indeed, rejecting not only the dualism of substances, but also the dualism of properties, and even the distinction of first- and third-person aspects or ways of identifying the sensible qualities, as well as the notion of a way in which conscious states seem to us when we are in them, as opposed to their place in the physical scheme of things. Thus one would have to *eliminate* phenomenal qualia, or reduce them in a most extreme way to physical qualities. It seems to me that this sort of eliminationism or reductionism can be refuted by seeing red and yellow and tasting onions.

Of course I know there are eminent philosophers who espouse it. How can they believe it? Thomas Nagel has written that "the only motive [he] can see for accepting [such extreme] kinds of reductionism [of mental to physical properties] is a desire to make the mind-body problem go away. None of them has any intrinsic plausibility."[22] I agree with Nagel's judgment, but I would add that the desire to make the mind/body problem go away is not laughable. It is a motive that is highly relevant to the present discussion. David Armstrong, following J. J. C. Smart, has argued for a reduction of phenomenal qualia (as well as other mental properties) to physical qualities at least partly on the ground that if they are not reduced, we will be left with a mental/physical correlation that physical science probably cannot explain.[23] Armstrong makes no mention of a possible theological explanation of the correlation, but I think it is fair to say that a main motive of his reductionism, indicated in his argument, is a desire to obtain an integrated naturalistic view of the world. He wants a view that neither appeals to a supernatural explanation nor leaves a central correlation unexplained. In order to obtain this integrated naturalistic world view, he is prepared to deny what I take to be obvious facts about phenomenal qualia.

Theism seems a less desperate expedient. Perhaps, since the demise of Aristotelianism, the problem of phenomenal qualia is at least as intractable for naturalism as the problem of evil is for theism. It is interesting to note that "eliminative" solutions have been proposed for both problems: denying that there really are any phenomenal qualia or that there really is any evil, as the case may be. Eliminative optimism and eliminative materialism seem about equally implausible to me.

Notes

1. John Locke, *An Essay Concerning Human Understanding,* ed. Peter H. Nidditch (Oxford: Clarendon Press, 1975), IV, x (bk. IV, chapter x).

2. Richard Swinburne, *The Existence of God* (Oxford: Clarendon Press, 1979), chapter 9. J. L. Mackie, *The Miracle of Theism: Arguments for and Against the Existence of God* (Oxford: Clarendon Press, 1982), chapter 7. I have criticized Mackie's reply to Swinburne in a review of *The Miracle of Theism,* in *The Philosophical Review,* 95 (1986), pp. 309–16.

3. It should be emphasized that I am speaking here about Aristotelianism as it was understood in the later medieval and early modern periods, and not about Aristotle himself. My presentation abstracts from many disagreements within Aristotelianism about details of the theory of sensation, and would not fit all Scholastics equally well. For a clear account of an important period of the history of

the Aristotelian theory, see Anneliese Maier, "Das Problem der 'species sensibiles in medio' und die neue Naturphilosophie des 14. Jahrhunderts," in her *Ausgehendes Mittelalter: Gesammelte Aufsätze zur Geistesgeschichte des 14. Jahrhunderts*, vol. 2 (Rome: Edizioni di Storia e Letteratura, 1967), pp. 419–51.

4. Galileo Galilei, *The Assayer* (1623), trans. Stillman Drake, excerpted in Richard H. Popkin, ed., *The Philosophy of the Sixteenth and Seventeenth Centuries* (New York: Free Press, 1966), p. 65. I do not mean to imply that mathematization was as important to *all* seventeenth-century anti-Aristotelian physicists as it was to Galileo.

5. M. R. Ayers, "Mechanism, Superaddition, and the Proof of God's Existence in Locke's Essay," *The Philosophical Review*, 90 (1981), p. 237. Ayers's statement applies specifically to Cudworth; what can be said about Locke, as Ayers points out, is somewhat more complicated.

6. Galileo, *The Assayer*, p. 65 in Popkin, ed., *The Philosophy of the Sixteenth and Seventeenth Centuries*.

7. Bracketed words added. Sixth *Meditation*, in René Descartes, *Oeuvres Philosophiques*, ed. F. Alquié, vol. 2 (Paris: Garnier, 1967), p. 234. The references to the old standard edition and English translation are AT VII, 88/HR I, 197.

8. Locke, *Essay*, IV, iii, 29.

9. Locke, *Essay*, IV, iii, 28; cf. IV, iii, 6.

10. Locke, *Essay*, IV, x, 10.

11. Locke, *Essay*, IV, x, 16. I am here accepting the traditional reading of this passage, in conscious opposition to that of M. R. Ayers, op. cit. (*Philosophical Review*, 90), p. 245, which seems to me (uncharacteristically) forced. Ayers thinks that Locke is holding open the possibility that some sort of motion and mechanical operation of a system of matter might *be* its thought, and that 'however put together' here must be understood to mean 'however put together *by chance*'.

12. J. L. Mackie, in *The Miracle of Theism*, chapter 4, recognizes that Berkeley's theism is crucial to the plausibility of his metaphysics at just this point, and sees that this is the basis of a serious Berkeleyan argument for theism. Mackie's defense against this theistic argument is also an attack on Berkeley's immaterialism.

13. Swinburne, *The Existence of God*, chapter 2. Swinburne also proposes an alternative analysis of scientific explanation in terms of the powers and liabilities of bodies, but argues that it will commonly support versions of the same explanations as the analysis in terms of laws. And to the extent that it is not equivalent, I cannot see that it is likely to help us beyond the point that we want explained, which is that bodies in certain physical states have the power, and liability, to give rise to certain phenomenal qualia.

14. Swinburne, *The Existence of God*, p. 171f.

15. See C. L. Hardin, "The Resemblances of Colors," *Philosophical Studies* 48 (1985), pp. 35–47.

16. Leibniz, "Meditations on Knowledge, Truth, and Ideas," G IV, 422f. [*Die*

philosophischen Schriften von Gottfried Wilhelm Leibniz, ed. C. I. Gerhard, vol. IV (Berlin, 1880), p. 422f. A standard English translation is in Leibniz, *Philosophical Papers and Letters,* trans. and ed. L. E. Loemker, 2d ed. (Dordrecht: D. Reidel, 1969), p. 291.]

17. Leibniz, *New Essays Concerning Human Understanding,* Preface (G V, 49).

18. J. L. Mackie seems to think that naturalism requires something like this. Acknowledging that "it is hard to see how there can be an intelligible law connecting material structures, however we describe them, with experiential content," he says that the materialist or naturalist "has to assume that there is a fundamental law of nature which says that such content will arise whenever there is a material structure of a certain complicated sort, and that that content will vary in a certain systematic way with the material basis—a fundamental law, because the basic fact of occurrent awareness seems not to be analyzable into any simpler components, so that the law of its emergence could not be derived from a combination of more basic laws" (*The Miracle of Theism,* p. 127).

19. See C. L. Hardin, "A New Look at Color," *American Philosophical Quarterly,* 21 (1984), pp. 125–33.

20. An alternative materialist approach would use a strong conception of metaphysical necessity rather than identity. It would claim that each phenomenal state supervenes on its physical correlate by metaphysical necessity. The short answer to this is that it is not easier to see how these correlations could be metaphysically necessary than to see how they could be scientifically explained. If they were metaphysically necessary, there would surely have to be a reason why. And while there may in principle be grounds of metaphysical necessity that escape our understanding (as I have argued in chapter 14 of this volume), it is rather implausible to postulate them in the present case, given the apparent arbitrariness of the correlations. Grounds could of course be manufactured by stipulation, by defining the identity of the phenomenal qualia as depending on the identity of the physical processes that cause them; but this would commit the fallacy of *ignoratio elenchi* ("ignoring the stated issue"). For the term 'phenomenal qualia' was introduced specifically to signify qualities whose identity is completely determined by subjective experience. To stipulate that the identity of phenomenal qualia depends on the identity of physical processes is to change the subject and, in effect, to deny that there are any phenomenal qualia in the original sense. I will respond, below, to a straightforward form of such denial.

21. Swinburne, *The Existence of God,* pp. 164–6.

22. Thomas Nagel, *Mortal Questions* (Cambridge: Cambridge University Press, 1979), p. 194.

23. D. M. Armstrong, *A Materialist Theory of the Mind* (London: Routledge & Kegan Paul, 1968), p. 50. Noting the mismatch, on which I have dwelt, between the complexity of physical processes and the apparent simplicity of phenomenal qualia, Armstrong states that the existence of "laws connecting these incredible physiological complexities with the relatively simple mental events . . . fits in very ill with the rest of the structure of science."

Index